DRIVE

DRIVE

What Makes a Leader
in Business and Beyond

John Viney

BLOOMSBURY

Copyright © 1999 by John Viney

All rights reserved. No part of this book may be used or
reproduced in any manner whatsoever without written
permission except in the case of brief quotations embodied
in critical articles or reviews, For information address
Bloomsbury Publishing, 175 Fifth Avenue, New York, N.Y. 10010.

Published by Bloomsbury Publishing, New York and London.
Distributed to the trade by St. Martin's Press

A CIP catalogue record for this book
is available from the Library of Congress

ISBN 1-58234-025-0

First published in Great Britain 1999 by Bloomsbury Publishing Plc.

First U.S. Edition 1999
10 9 8 7 6 5 4 3 2 1

Typeset by Hewer Text Ltd, Scotland
Printed in England by Clays Ltd, St Ives plc

CONTENTS

Preface

During the last fifteen years I have been required to reflect upon the nature of leadership. As a headhunter I am regularly asked for my view – or that of Heidrick & Struggles – on what leadership is, how it can be formed, recognized and cultivated. The invitation to give an opinion has come from many sources around the globe, from clients and candidates alike. It has long been the question that I most dread, knowing that it will always appear – like an unwanted friend – just at the wrong moment. If I do not have a clear answer to this question, what is my real value as a business consultant? This unspoken question seems to me the logical sequitur if I am unconvincing in my answer of the first.

For many of these fifteen years I have not had a convincing answer. I had examples, in increasing number as the years passed both of successful and failed leaders – but no single coherent view. I started reading numerous books on the subject – some worthy, others puzzling, most, frankly, dull. Those written by business leaders were particularly uninspiring. A few writers stand out, such as Manfred Kets de Vries, whose work from a psychoanalytic standpoint shines out like a monument to clarity amid a bewildering fog. John Kotter and Abraham Zalzenik have, equally, caught my attention. In general, however, I gained my greatest insight into leadership outside the business arena – reading a biography of Admiral Nelson, say, or the reflections of Sir Winston Churchill. Literature and history, which chronicle personalities, seem to offer more insight into leadership than business writings which try to find scientific measurements for something, ultimately, not reducible to a linear measure. In my own study of leadership I make substantial reference to leadership outside business, drawing on records of factual and sometimes fictional leaders to try to arrive at a sense of what leadership is.

Business leaders, aside from a few headline-hitting entrepreneurs, seldom enjoy the prestige of political or military leaders. They are perceived, perhaps, as having less power than those who command armies or nations. This is something of a misconception. The chief executive of a major global corporation has immense power – the power to generate wealth for shareholders and well-being for stakeholders. Indeed, with the decline of standing armies and navies in the West, business offers one of the major outlets for those ambitious to lead people and to leave their mark on an organization or entity. Political power will probably always hold greatest appeal for the ambitious would-be leader but, increasingly, political leaders are fettered by controls and checks such that their movements rarely show the mark of great leadership. A century of dictators has led to natural caution towards unrestrained leadership. We must look outside the political sphere if we are to see leadership in the raw. Business, to my mind, offers precisely that sphere and it is one, moreover, of which many readers will have direct experience.

This book tries to look at business leadership through the medium of leadership in other spheres. It draws from a number of disciplines, psychological, anthropological, historical and even physics – my early background. It tries to consider where leaders come from, the factors that drive them and those which, ultimately, bring them down. It is not a 'how to' book, but it might be useful for those who are interested in talent spotting. Its approach, rather than following one single methodology, is holistic. It tries, like its subject, to bring together diverse references to create a coherent understanding of the enigma that is business leadership.

I owe several debts of gratitude in writing this book. First I must thank my partners and colleagues at Heidrick & Struggles for giving me the time and support to complete it. The findings of the book, I should add, represent my own personal views, rather than those of Heidrick & Struggles. I should also like to thank Judith Osborne, whose editorial work has been a major contributory factor in the completion of the manuscript and who has provided many of the literary and historical references. Similarly, Joanna Russell has provided a mountain of information and checked (and re-checked) countless details. Finally, I should like to thank the numerous business leaders who, knowingly or not, have contributed to my better understanding of their craft.

John Viney
June 1999

Chapter 1

Introduction

'It is a strange desire to seek power and lose liberty.' – Sir
Francis Bacon

'My first day of peace will be my last one in power.' – Simon
Bolívar, the liberator and national hero of Venezuela, Colombia,
Ecuador, Peru and Bolivia.

Leadership, or a position of power, precludes peace either of mind
or body. Power can inhibit the spirit and trap the body. These
sentiments are shared by those who observe, and those who hold,
power, as in the examples above of the scholar and the general.
Bolívar's words may merely imply that he would not rest until his
vision of a united South America had been achieved. Equally they
might reflect the onerous burden that leadership represents. An
ambivalence by leaders towards their own power is an entirely sane
response. Power is dangerous, intoxicating, all-absorbing. It
removes people from the realm of the rational and the predictable
and places them on a pedestal vulnerable to others and to themselves; one false move and they can fall. Abraham Lincoln,
Mahatma Gandhi, John F. Kennedy and Martin Luther King,
Anwar Sadat and Itzak Rabin, Mrs Indira Gandhi and her son
Rajiv – the list is a long one – all fell to an assassin's bullet.
Napoleon and Bolívar were sent into exile. Others suffer ignominious deposition, as in the case of Margaret Thatcher and Mikhail
Gorbachev. These are all figures who have played on the world
stage. They have taken on governments, either assuming control of

them or setting themselves up in opposition to them, and have played in a game where the stakes are high. Peace and stability could scarcely be expected to be part of their portion.

People can attain positions of power without pursuing a political career, and the modern corporation provides many with the environment appropriate to exercise their ambition to lead. Here, perhaps, they might expect a little more peace than those who operate in the political arena. Less likely to encounter the assassin's gun, they nevertheless face a life which is an endless round of activity, little of it pleasing, all of it under the intense gaze of sceptical investors, sometimes only to end the victim of a board-room coup. The phrase 'blood on the carpet' may be metaphorical but there is nothing metaphorical about the pain of a deposed business leader.

The bulk of my career to date has been spent assessing people who to a greater or lesser degree seek a position of leadership in a corporation. A couple of years ago the London office of Heidrick & Struggles produced a study entitled, 'So you dream of being a Chief Executive'. We regularly produce studies on a range of boardroom related issues. None has been as popular as this one. Most candidates who come into our reception area leave bearing a copy. It is a dream that most people striving for success in business seem to cherish. Even immensely successful heads of functions, group finance directors of quoted companies who enjoy consider-able power, seem invariably to yearn for the opportunity to run their own corporate show. Heidrick & Struggles operates at the top end of the global executive search market. Those who make it into our reception area tend to be pretty senior individuals already. Their interest in the study is scarcely surprising. With my insight into the reality of leadership, however, I *do* find it surprising. Can they really know what they would be letting themselves in for? Most are destined never to find out. Many people observing our business make the rash assumption that it is easy to find people to fill vacant jobs. While it can be easy to find average people, ours is a quest for talent and talent is all too rare. The dearth of talent means that ours can be, at the very highest end of the market, a depress-ingly difficult task. No amount of work, problem-solving capabil-ity, inspiration and intuition can furnish a perfect and infallible business leader if they are not there to be found.

Business leaders, of course, are not perfect and infallible. One of my primary findings over the years has been that business leaders are very often very flawed. Their great strengths are frequently offset by very great weaknesses. Their more balanced peers tire along the way of the strenuous lifestyle required of the true seeker after power. They will reach a certain point in an organizational hierarchy and decide to remain on a comfortable plateau rather than start out again towards the peak. In this way they aim to restore a little balance to their lives. Meanwhile the power seeker disdains balance and with almost superhuman stamina presses onwards. By the time they reach the peak and drive their flag into the corporate outcrop such figures will have made immense sacrifices. They may have aged visibly in the process – the strain and effort having outward manifestations. They may well have left wives and families behind them, abandoned friends and hobbies and single-mindedly made themselves single-minded, narrow, driven only by the one requirement for power. Theirs is a dream to change an organization and to leave their own indelible mark upon its history.

Sometimes such people can achieve success as inspirational leaders. In a lecture to mark the 75th anniversary of the British Broadcasting Corporation, the present Director-General, John Birt, remarked of the founding Director-General, Lord Reith, that he was 'zealous, high-minded, deeply religious, authoritarian, driven, unclubbable, difficult, battle-scarred, lonely, self-absorbed, inwardly tormented but remarkable and visionary'. Reith himself was to remark to his diary: 'What a curse it is to have outstanding comprehensive ability and intelligence, combined with a desire to use them to maximum purpose.' Lord Reith was luckier than most: he found his moment and was able to channel his energies and his talents. Many people with abundant drive and equal talent fail to find their moment and any volume which seeks to deal with leadership must acknowledge the arbitrariness of fate.

The narrow and the power-crazed cannot lead businesses. If they are to be led – not managed, but led – they require whole people, big people, emotionally sound people. These people may not be perfect and, like everyone, they will have their frailties, but they will know their areas of imperfection and understand how to offset those frailties, usually by bringing people around them who are strong in the areas where they are weak. Corporate leadership is riddled with ironies. The biggest of all is that the people who are sufficiently well-balanced and broad-shouldered to take on a role leading a corporation are very often too well balanced to contemplate doing so. Happily for corporations there are always exceptions to the rule. Every generation throws up a few outstandingly competent chief executives and a handful of genuine business leaders (the distinction is a deliberate one).

It is my business to be fascinated by leadership. Companies often seek out the assistance of top search firms when they are in crisis; they have suddenly lost their chief executive with no one obvious to replace him or have been obliged to fire a chief executive and now need someone who can restore the fortunes of the business. Of these scenarios – and there are many more – the first is the easiest to handle. If the company is performing well then there will not be a shortage of people who express interest in managing it. There will be many fewer who meet the exacting standards of the nominating committee who will need maximum reassurance that the person they are recruiting from outside is genuinely and demonstrably superior in skills to any currently within the business. Such searches are taxing but usually soluble.

The troubled business where we are looking for someone who will be its saviour is of course the problematic and most challenging search. It is the search that really calls for a leader, someone who will change the entire course of the business. These are searches that can take long months and require sensitivity and a stealthy approach. Professionally speaking they are both the most difficult and the most satisfying. There is no greater professional satisfaction than watching the share price climb once the business is in the hands of your placement. Working with boards has given me numerous examples of good and bad management, too many examples of poor or absent leadership and occasional encounters with real inspirational leadership. It has become a professional requirement to understand what makes a chief executive or a chairman successful. In pursuit of this grail I have spent long hours considering leadership and leaders in all their facets. This book is the product of those hours of observation and experience of being alongside some of the best – and the worst – among business leaders.

The study of leaders and leadership and the attempt to quantify both has been a fascinating one and reflects what I perceive to be an almost universal fascination with the subject. What is the source of this fascination? In part, I think it is simple solipsism. Leadership is something we have all experienced; it is a subject on which, then, we can all be informed and hold opinions. From our earliest moments we experience a form of leadership. Our parents guide us, nurture us, teach us right from wrong, tease out our strengths and seek to diminish our weaknesses. To a child a parent is a God-like creature, all-powerful, all knowing. There is nothing a parent cannot do. Our lives and the most intimate part of ourselves, our personalities, are shaped by our relations with these parents and, of course, with our siblings who are themselves the products of these all-powerful parents. When we move on to school we find that we are led by teachers and as we assemble our groups of friends some among them will naturally become the pathfinders, the ones who dictate terms, choose games, and set the tone and express the character of the gang.

An adult perception of childhood is that it is a period of innocence, of an absence of responsibility and, as such, a blissful edenic state. The reality is very often the reverse of this. Some children, even those who are much loved, live in a state of fear (of school, of parents, of the arbitrariness of the rules and regulations which in a modern-mannered society must be inculcated in the young). Childhood can be not so much a blissful state as a totalitarian one and for many children the primary aim is to leave childhood behind. The desire to leave childhood behind may be driven by a desire to acquire the power exerted over them in the form of self-control and, indeed, control of others. Most little children, at least those in broadly functional families, will want to emulate their parents. Small children will play-act at being their parents and will take a morbid pleasure in inflicting maximum pain upon their dolls and soft toys. This is certainly an expression of frustration but also an expression of a barely suppressed desire to retaliate. As we grow older we acquire behavioural habits which are linked with leadership: the habit of following and the habit of aspiring to lead. As we reach maturity we grow aware of the macro-leadership that is exerted over us, of politics and cultural forces that differ with each generation but exert a roughly equivalent pull. Most of us, throughout our lives, find people to admire whom we wish to emulate but whom we settle for following.

One of the early issues with which I have grappled in writing this book has been disentangling leadership, fame and greatness. Clearly my central concern has been with leadership in business but I have wanted to understand what leadership is *per se* and, in considering leadership qualities, to assess them among that multifarious group generally called, in the UK, the great and good. While being aware that those who lead are not necessarily the same as those who are famous or great, I have often not troubled to make the distinction too clearly. I use, or refer to, the broad category of the famous and the great in the body of the text on the basis that they exert some kind of pull on us and are exemplary of certain respected characteristics.

Many teenagers wish to emulate a pop star or a sports star. We have recently lived through Girl Power. A few years ago Madonna provided the role model to teenage and, indeed, pre-pubescent girls alike. Is Madonna a leader? Could we consider Elvis Presley or John Lennon or Bob Dylan leaders? All have had massive influence on those who have followed them and Lennon even died at the hands of an assassin (or a deeply disturbed fan). It would be absurd to call them leaders. Rather, they are cultural icons. They are revered for their individualism – there is no other like them – but at the same time they are emblematic of a particular characteristic which moves their audience at a particular time. Presley, Lennon and Dylan are representative of youthful rebellion, in each case subtly different. Elvis, or 'the King', as he is known to his fans, represented rebellion against a middle-class, middle-aged, middle-American morality. Lennon and Dylan came to represent a different way of seeing the world, Lennon with his word-play and irony, Dylan with his reinvigoration of the protest song. Dylan, in particular, found words to define a generation. Madonna a few decades later became iconic of female sexuality, drive and ambition, coming to stand for a form of hard-nosed femininity.

Iconic figures are not merely those who emerge from youth culture; they are those who capture the essence of a mood or a body of people. Marilyn Monroe, with her vulnerability and voluptuous beauty was, in the words of the song, 'something more than sexual'. In her early, tragic death, over which there is still controversy, Monroe foreshadows Diana, Princess of Wales, whose funeral was marked by a rewriting of a song first written for Marilyn. Diana has come to embody the spirit of caring, has become somehow an exemplar of ethical conduct. Her appeal is all the greater because she was a flawed, deeply human person, neither perfect nor infallible. Diana, Princess of Wales, occupied centre stage while alive but in death came to represent something different, and profound, among the British people and indeed beyond the UK. That something appears to have been a need for ethical values, for a more humane and caring approach to those around us both in our immediate sphere and farther from home. The crowds that thronged the streets of London in September 1997 were much larger but perhaps similarly motivated to those which took to the streets earlier in the summer to welcome Tony Blair to Number 10 Downing Street. Britain wanted youth, vitality and compassion and felt it had found them in May in Blair only to lose them in August with Diana. Blair, to my mind, is a leader where Diana is an icon. We cannot measure the direct effect each has on the lives of those they touch and the comparison would be a facile one in any case. The difference between them is that the effect of an icon is symbolic, that of a leader is material. An icon is someone on whom we impose our dreams, a leader imposes his dreams on us.

There is an entire category of people who are famous and, in the eyes of many, 'great', those who occupy a pre-eminent position in their chosen field. The creative community of playwrights, authors, musicians can have tremendous impact not just on their immediate generation but on subsequent generations too. Bach, Mozart, Beethoven, Picasso, Leonardo da Vinci, Van Gogh, Shakespeare, Proust have in their different fields been immensely influential but again the effect is, if not symbolic, then emotional or intellectual. These 'great' artists are extraordinarily talented and often signal an entirely new approach to their art, but theirs is a material effect on the discipline within which they operate rather than on those who engage with that discipline. Unlike leaders, they do not have a direct dialogue with their followers and cannot control the change they effect. More problematic are the great scientists whose dis- coveries have had a most material effect on many thousands and millions. Newton, Einstein, Crick and Watson, Stephen Hawking, Murray Gell-Mann and Alexander Fleming have had an immense and material effect on our universe. Startlingly more original, inventive, innovative, intelligent than many that I would call leaders, the effects of their discoveries have been at some remove from the individuals concerned, achieved over long periods of time, with the intervention of numerous agencies. A leader is someone, then, who has direct and immediate measurable and material bearing on his, or her, environment.

The famous, the great and leaders (and people may be a mix or indeed all three of these) have one thing in common and that is a link with power. Leaders wield active power, the great and the famous exert a powerful hold on people. The famous often come to have power by dint of acquiring wealth. Much of the power these people have over others is sexual. It was Henry Kissinger who said 'power is the ultimate aphrodisiac', and certainly fame, greatness and leadership appear to bring out the libidinous in their followers. Consider the public relationships of Marilyn Monroe: she married Joe di Maggio, a great American sporting hero, then Arthur Miller, America's foremost living playwright (in one of the unlikeliest couplings of modern times), and had affairs first with John and then with Bobby Kennedy. The famous and heroic, the great and the leader – she bedded all three types. The great, the famous, leaders of men are very often highly sexed and much desired. Bill Clinton conforms to this, as did John F. Kennedy. The latter even shared a mistress with head of the Chicago mafia Sam Giamcana. We must marvel, of course, at the thirst for vicarious power on the part of the mistress whose lovers so strikingly combined the two most powerful forces in America, organized crime and institutional politics.

Business has had its own share of highly sexed leaders. Sir James Goldsmith was a strikingly attractive man, whom age and ill health could not rob of his vitality and charm, and accounts of him invariably focus on his appearance. He is described in terms of his extraordinary physicality in a *Times* profile published in 1996:

> Some 6ft 4in, with chilling blue eyes, a bald dome which looks as though it was designed for the laurel leaves of a Caesar, and the physique of a rangy mountain lion, he seems too eerily like the millionaire man of destiny from fiction to be true. His clothes, understated and international, convey the quiet

assurance of the first class departure lounge with only the slight
nod towards true plutocracy in the cashmere socks and
cufflinks. It is the voice that is truly singular. Dark chocolate
with occasional descents to the guttural and curious,
idiosyncratic pronunciation which renders Maastricht as
Mystrict and Forsyth as Vorsyte, it exercises a hypnotic
power . . .

That hypnotic power worked on many beautiful women. Apparently incapable of monogamy, he coined the phrase: 'When a man
marries his mistress he creates a vacancy' but pulled off the
extraordinary coup of keeping relations between all parties not
merely cordial but close, even in death.

Goldsmith was something more than a businessman. He was a
latter-day romantic hero, the type of figure who might have inspired
the creator of James Bond. At twenty he fell in love with a beautiful
young Bolivian girl whose father, a hugely wealthy tin magnate,
opposed the match. Goldsmith hired a plane and eloped with the girl
to Casablanca. There the bride was snatched from him, but, un-
deterred, Goldsmith confronted her father and eventually gained his
bride's hand. They married in a Scottish ceremony. Tragically his
bride was to die shortly after the birth of their first child. Good-
looking, urbane, a risk-taker with boundless energy and appetites to
match, it is hardly surprising that Goldsmith exerted a pull that was
partly one of sexual magnetism with those he met. In his exoticism
(he was the son of a Frenchwoman and a half-English, half-German
father) and fearlessness he conveyed a sense of limitlessness which
can only be seductive. Goldsmith's personal magnetism must have
contributed to his success and that success will have reinforced the
magnetism. It is by no means the case that only the sexually alluring
become successful, but it certainly helps. Research shows, for
instance, that the taller of two candidates for the American pre-
sidency is the more likely to be elected. Tall presidents have a far
greater likelihood of being re-elected for a second term, such is the
predilection by the American public for a sense of stature which is as
much a matter of physique as it is of personality. Alternatively,
energy and the presence of internal, rather than external, power can
do much to propel an individual, irrespective of their physical
stature. Jack Welch, the chief executive of General Electric who

is routinely voted America's most effective business leader, is no 6ft 4 inch giant, but a more compact 5 foot 8 inches. His extraordinary personal energy and power, however, lend him stature and presence well beyond the norm.

Once successful or powerful, the unsuspecting leader, whether good-looking or not, may suddenly be a focus of sexual attention that has more to do with the role occupied than with the person. Would Arthur Miller have appealed to Marilyn Monroe had he not been validated by the American public as a leading figure of his generation? Had he been Arthur Miller, sales executive, would his appeal have been as great? Similarly, Joe di Maggio. Their success gave both a cachet that was more compelling than their physical appearance. More importantly than this, their success was in part doubtless down to a drive and energy which has much in common with the sexual magnetism of a Goldsmith. Very often that drive and energy has been suppressed in the pursuit of success and has manifested itself as ambition. Once ambition has been satisfied, that energy becomes a quite different force.

The list of creative personalities throughout history who are known to have been homosexual is astonishing in its extent: Leonardo da Vinci and Michelangelo, arguably the two greatest figures of the Renaissance, Oscar Wilde, Tennessee Williams, Ludwig Wittgenstein, Benjamin Britten, Cole Porter and Noel Coward are just a handful of people whose sexual preferences were effectively outlawed in their lifetimes. Both Britten and Coward, however, lived to see the relaxation of the laws in the UK. Perhaps there is a link between nonconformity and creativity, between the alternative perspective on society gained from living at its margins. Perhaps, too, the act of repressing sexuality necessitates the expression of energy in other areas and hence the outpouring of creative energy. In Chapter 4 I shall look at the issue of marginalization and the extent to which it impacts on a leader.

Much later in this book I will be using an approach drawn from anthropology in studying the behaviour of small groups. One broadly anthropological insight for now is that societies have historically rewarded the strongest and most healthy and virile of a tribe or group with the right to take food and sex before the others. This most healthy, virile specimen is the alpha male. The alpha male reconfirms his right to dominance by his ability to impregnate women, a practice which in some power systems became institutionalized in the form of the harem. Women naturally gravitate towards the alpha male because he will afford protection for them and for any children they may bear. Indeed, the alpha male, in the process of impregnating his concubine, validates her existence as well as securing his own safety. Historical practices linger in our collective memory, becoming habit, so when a new chief executive is appointed and finds himself the object of sexual attention he may simply be experiencing the alpha male effect. Some of the world's most famous and infamous leaders have not, however, been particularly fine physical specimens. Julius Caesar, Napoleon, Nelson, and Hitler were all short even by the standards of their day, nor were they all immensely prepossessing, yet they led great forces and held sway over numerous people. Horatio Nelson was, apparently, no less attractive after the loss of an arm and an eye than he had been prior to these injuries! Drive and energy, as I shall explore in Chapters 2 and 3, can derive as much from perceived weakness as from perceived strength and it is that drive and energy which can convert into magnetism which is, in turn, sexual.

Part of the fascination with leaders, with the famous and the great, then, lies in the fact that they exert a sexual pull over us. Power is itself enticing because it is dangerous, thrilling. Its limits cannot be known. Some simply bask in reflected glory, in being of a sufficient calibre to appeal to someone who is held in the highest regard. Relationships with the famous and the powerful must often be conducted in secret. This adds to their piquancy. The taboo, if we believe in the lessons of the psychoanalysts, provides a sexual drive for us all, from the first moment we encounter and are diverted from a sexual relation to our mothers. This dicing with danger works on both sides; those in the public eye court discovery in compromising situations. In recent years there have been numerous scandals where public figures, politicians, pop stars and actors have been caught in liaisons which, for whatever reason, are regarded as illicit. Bill Clinton is the most obvious of these. It is a particularly Protestant, indeed puritanical, response to be shocked by a sexual scandal; Catholics seem to take a broader view.

A recurring theme of this book is the taste leaders have for danger and risk, a veritable thirst that most of us do not share.

Leaders or those who reach the pinnacle of success in their chosen field (and the two are not directly equivalent) act on a larger scale than most of us. Leaders also fascinate us because, however little we may wish to endure the hardships that seem a necessary part of attaining leadership status, we often wish for the end results. Not infrequently these are fabulous wealth (particularly on the part of business leaders) or extraordinary levels of public recognition. At the centre of our own worlds we all seek after recognition from others and strive to be the centre of others' worlds too. The allure of leaders, the fascination they hold for us and the emotional needs they fulfil, take up Chapter 6 in this book.

It is pat psychology, but nonetheless true for that, to say that leaders are proxy parents. We revere them because they will protect us and supply our most fundamental needs for nurture. One of the most obvious forms of social organization is the paternal structure which has found a relatively new form in the modern corporation. In my last book, *The Culture Wars*, I marvelled at a new experiment in political organization, the European Union. Underpinning this book is a fascination and respect for the most interesting new form of social organization to emerge in the last century: the corporation. A new form of hierarchy, it nevertheless borrows heavily from old-established models.

Most social groupings take the family as their operating model and point of departure – and in doing so posit, in general, an authoritative father figure. A patriarchy is a society where relationships are entirely defined in terms of lineage, such as those in the Old Testament. Coming up to date (although this is not a structure for which there is much tolerance in the modern world), cinemagoers will be familiar with Mario Puzo's/Francis Ford Coppola's patriarchal model in *The Godfather* ('never take sides against the family again') which is a clear patriarchy. In such examples the male is clearly the linchpin but there are some (though markedly fewer) matriarchal societies with a female linchpin (notably the largely mythical Amazonian tribes).

Paternalism can be seen at work in the burgeoning industries of the nineteenth century, both in Europe and in the United States, where those who assumed control took on aspects of paternity to justify their domination. Perhaps one of the most interesting examples of a paternalist business leader is George Pullman, who ran the Pullman Palace Car Company in nineteenth-century America and built a model town for his workers in Illinois which, characteristically, he called Pullman. The experiment broke down when Pullman failed to recognize that those in his charge were not mere children but individuals with needs and desires. When these needs and desires came into conflict with his own the relationship dissolved. Although, ultimately, his paternalist model failed, it is striking that it existed in that form at all.

All political systems acknowledge the seductive power of the father-led structure, hence the potency of *das Vaterland*, *la patrie* and the sinister appeal of Stalin's 'The state is a family, and I am your father.' Mere semantics, perhaps, but the persistence of these family-styled social structures is persuasive. They reinforce the essential conservatism of the human race. We prefer the familiar and hence prefer to take all our care, guidance and leadership from a form that apes the familiar parental one. We can also see some evidence, here, of the human instinct to aspire. As noted above, in maturity we become parents ourselves. The particular appeal of paternalist structures is that we can aspire to the role of head of family ourselves. It is no accident that paternalism reached its apotheosis in the nineteenth century when, through the medium of capitalism, it became possible for an individual to conceive of a material form of aspiration. (Hitherto for the bulk of the population the only form of aspiration to be encouraged was spiritual.) This was also a time when, as cities encroached on the countryside, populations deserted villages to find work in towns. The hardship of rural life was conveniently forgotten and a romantic vision of an organic society took its place – one where, as in the old craft traditions, the home was both the seat of the family and the place of work and the boss a benign father.

There is, as George Pullman found, a problem with paternalism: that paternalism is domination without a contract. With the erosion of poverty and the increase of sophistication comes the development of a more cynical, less reverential approach to those in control of our destinies, and the twentieth-century tendency has veered away from paternalism towards a far greater respect for those who exercise autonomy over themselves. This respect does not, however, represent an absolute rejection of authority, rather we like to feel that we have a degree of control over those to whom we give authority and a voice in judging their performance. We still like to have around us the comfort of a decision-making father figure.

And so, by way of a lengthy preamble, I come to a point which is highly topical and might have formed a subject for a chapter of this book but threatened, in so doing, to take over altogether: the role of women in business as leaders. Our first experience of parenting comes not from our father but from our mother, or from a proxy mother. In early childhood discipline is largely administered by the mother, and fathers – particularly twentieth-century fathers – are often quite absent figures. They appear at weekends for fun and games but the serious business of being moulded and developed falls to the lot, by and large, of women. Nonetheless it is a paternalist structure that is all-pervasive in the modern corporation and while some women do become leaders the pantheon of business leaders is overwhelmingly dominated by men.

At some point it would appear that the powerful mother figure of our early years becomes the nurturing, caring mother about whom we reminisce in adulthood, whose power we neutralize in the memory. There are numerous reasons why women have not been able to attain the level of their male counterparts and most have to do with social conditioning and norms of behaviour which are gender-specific. In his illuminating work *Trust*, economist Francis Fukuyama puts forward a fascinating argument for why some cultures have been better able than others to develop their economies away from small cottage industries towards major corporations. The crux of his argument is that the ability to hand over elements of the process of production and with them some power (necessary as a small family or entrepreneurial business grows in scale) depends on an ability to develop numerous relationships on a level of fluid, easy-going trust. Fukuyama calls this trait a tendency to associate, through religion, clubs, educational establishments.

With some adaptation the argument can be applied to the two genders. It is men in most societies who have been enabled to develop a life for themselves outside the home, whose social mode is one of many loose relationships and an easy-going camaraderie and trust. Women have spent much more of history in the home and have developed a more intimate focus on the world. Their relation to others takes the form not of a casual, easy-going association but of deep emotional bonds and intensely felt relationships. The corporation is adapted towards the easy-going and casual form of interaction, not the intense form, and so very often contrives to exclude women. The corporation is a highly masculine environment. It keeps hours that are convenient to men and it extends into environments – the bar, the golf course – which are congenial for men. Its uniform – the suit – has been adapted for women but has never become in the female version as simple and functional as in its male form. The female form is still sufficiently differently clad for appearance to continue to count. Despite much talk of the need for creativity, management disciplines which vaunt the linear and the predictable dominate business. Society's division of skills between the genders decrees that men are logical and linear, women much more likely to be creative and non-linear. At an unconscious level, many women do subscribe to these and see business as an inappropriate environment for their skills. Further, the notoriously cut-throat and competitive environment of a business may not appeal to women who have been conditioned to nurture and support. The subject is a very complicated one, to which a few stray observations cannot do justice. I shall consider elsewhere the factors that have contributed to male dominance in the upper echelons of business and how and why that dominance is being sustained. This book makes little pretence that business leadership is anything but a predominantly male terrain. Throughout the greater part of this book I use the male pronoun and refer to the chairman. This does not reflect (I hope) chauvinism on my part so much as the reality of business today. Tomorrow may be very different.

This book does not concern itself, either, with any guidance as to how a would-be leader might attain the coveted leadership position, although there are some signposts along the way. At the heart of my understanding of leadership is the notion that leadership is not rational and not predictable. One of the most important chapters of this book is that which draws the distinction between leadership and management and posits a third category of businessman, the entrepreneur. Entrepreneurs may be leaders or managers. Managers and leaders, however, are extremely different creatures. Most leaders will have experienced management on their course to a position of leadership but many make the mistake of thinking that being a successful manager will necessarily equip them to be a successful leader. There is no guarantee. On the contrary, an accomplished, even brilliant, manager achieves that status by dint of excellent logical skills, an ability to solve problems, to prioritize, to implement. It is a scientific cast of mind. A leader is an artist who creates, who starts something from scratch in the case of the entrepreneur or who takes something from one form to another, who recreates that thing (the corporation, the product). How can I reasonably offer a template for such a requirement?

Leaders will very often create themselves, work on their personalities, their abilities, their weaknesses. Some who aspire to leadership status will quite simply invent themselves, taking liberties with the truth. Perhaps the ultimate fantasist in the search for fame, greatness and now power is Lord Archer. If his biographer and investigative journalists are to be believed, Archer has invented himself first as a student of an American college, then as a member of Oxford University (he was, but of the Department of Education, which was only loosely connected to the university). He claimed he was the youngest councillor on the Greater London Council at the time, and then the youngest Member of Parliament of his day – neither of which claims was true (although he claims to have thought both were). He attributes to his father a past far more distinguished than the reality and similarly claimed family precedent for being a mayor by attributing to his grandfather the status of Lord Mayor of Bristol. Greater charges than these are levelled against Archer, but what interests me is not any possible illegality in his actions (that is a matter for others) but the imaginative rendering of his own past in order to secure a future dream.

Such people must cut themselves off from their past if they are to maintain the fiction. Years of invention can place an intolerable pressure on the inventor or, worse, can spill over into other aspects of their behaviour. The individual who is not honest about their personality is likely to play equally fast and loose with the truth in other areas. Nowhere has this truth been more clearly demonstrated than in the case of Robert Maxwell.

Successful leadership is about vision and the execution of a vision. It is about the confluence of a private dream and a public or corporate need. There are undoubtedly more people with leadership potential than there are leaders. Nowhere is this more true than in business. I stated above that leadership is not rational. No more are the markets within which businesses operate. To tolerate the unknowable, unpredictable circumstances within which a corporation operates, a century of management discipline has sought to apply logical and rational structures to the organization. These are well and good in many areas, in the development of sophisticated planning techniques, financial accounting methods and availability of information, but have had the unforeseen result of checking the source of some innovation. Many large corporations have lost the ability to spot the unusual, the maverick. To be more precise, they retain the ability to spot them but have lost the ability to tolerate them. A huge amount of talent goes into corporations but relatively little of it comes out as productive outputs.

Corporations, like the parents of wayward children, have a habit of breaking the will of their more unruly recruits. They deal best with obedient children and mould them into outstanding managers. This trait scarcely matters during the good times, when what is required of a chief executive is exemplary management. However, at times of crisis, when there is a need for a new vision, a new way of doing things, a corporation can come to regret its striving for conformity. Some of the world's most successful businesses are those which have given free rein to the mavericks, have backed them and had an inspirational resource on which to depend. Indeed, in Europe, a model is being developed which calls upon entrepreneurial rather than management skills at the business unit level, so allowing continuing innovation. I shall consider this in more detail in Chapter 7.

There is already a voluminous literature on leadership. Much of it seeks to measure and reduce to a process or formula something which I believe is not susceptible to either approach. Books by leaders themselves can be among the most disappointing. Such leaders do not have sufficient distance from themselves to judge what has genuinely set them apart from their peers. Curiously, it seems to be the consulting fraternity, who glimpse many leaders in contrast with one another, that has generated the more valuable insights. The literature seems to fall into either a trait approach or a process approach. Mine is inevitably closer to the former than to the latter but seeks to show that traits alone will not a leader make. In Chapter 9 I draw upon anthropological and psychoanalytic understanding to demonstrate the importance of context to a leader or, more particularly, the importance of a leader being able to read and adapt to different contexts. I depart from much of the literature in my rather narrow definition of a leader as someone who effects change on, in the case of business leaders, a corporation, usually (but not exclusively) one in crisis. Given my professional role as a chairman of an international search firm with a personal specialization in the boardroom appointing executive and non-executive directors to the boards of international corporations, this focus is scarcely surprising. Everyday there are numerous quite ordinary acts of leadership performed in the workplace and in the home. This book is concerned with the extraordinary acts of leadership, or rather (since I do not narrate particular events) with extraordinary, fully developed, leaders. It seems sometimes that the only thing these extraordinary leaders have in common is the fact that they have nothing in common. In fact, in Chapters 1 and 2 I establish that today, and indeed over time, exemplary leaders demonstrate a remarkable homogeneity of early experience. Early experience and the response to early experience provides an area of commonality across time. Leadership styles, however, are immensely historically specific. In Chapter 7 I look at a leadership style which reflects the current needs of a business environment which is increasingly international in scope. Had I written this book twenty years ago or were I to write it twenty years hence, the content of that chapter would differ substantially.

I began this introductory chapter with two negative reflections on power and leadership, suggesting that they are both restrictive and disturbing. Peppered throughout this text there are numerous examples of the negative aspects of leadership, culminating in Chapter 8, where I discuss leadership in its inevitable decline. One of the most disturbing elements I have seen in leaders is their capacity to self-destruct or to destroy the edifice they have constructed. The psychology behind this is complex. The Frankenstein effect is doubtless a contributory factory. The leader creates a beast that grows beyond his strength to contain it. Entrepreneurs who build a business and then cannot move it from its childhood to its adolescent and then adult state most often fall prey to this desire to dismantle what they have put together before it dismantles them. For some the act of creation is the high point of a career. Once the corporation has been created or, perhaps, re-created, the inventive leader cannot leave it alone. He must be forever tinkering and in time the need for stimuli and action leads him to disregard the best interests of the organization and to destroy step by step what he has put together. Sometimes the successful leader experiences a kind of self-disgust at his own obsession, which may have come to take a governing role in his life. Here, revolted by what he most desires, the leader must destroy in order to restore some remnant of self-respect.

Leadership is not an easy thing and being a leader can be an uneasy state. Philip Larkin, that most cynical of modern English poets, who confined his talents to the management of a university library and the writing of a relatively small number of exquisitely observed poems, expresses the sentiment well in a poem written for the birth of his friend Kingsley Amis's daughter. 'May you be ordinary,' he declares:

> In fact, may you be dull –
> If that is what a skilled,
> Vigilant, flexible,
> Unemphasized, enthralled
> Catching of happiness is called.

By and large the extraordinary individuals who become successful leaders will bypass the level-headed contentment for which most of us settle. Theirs is a different agenda. I hope that in the coming pages I capture the essence of that agenda.

Chapter 2

Leadership Begins in the Home:
Family Influences on Leaders

'They fuck you up, your mum and dad.' – Philip Larkin, *This Be the Verse*

'It is said that famous men are usually the product of an unhappy childhood. The stern compression of circumstances, the twinges of adversity, the spur of slights and taunts in early years, are needed to evoke that ruthless fixity of purpose and tenacious motherwit without which great actions are seldom accomplished.' – Sir Winston Churchill, in his biography of the Duke of Marlborough.

Leaders are nonconformists who dare to do what most of us disdain to consider. It is not simply the case that leaders *do* differ from the norm, but that they should do so. Conceiving, pursuing and successfully realizing a vision is not everyday fare. Most people prefer to keep within the boundaries of what is arbitrarily defined as normal, opting for the Prufrock principle. They see what it might take to achieve a moment of greatness and turn quietly away:

I have seen the moment of my greatness flicker,
And I have seen the eternal Footman hold my coat, and snicker,
And in short, I was afraid.

While humankind values its individuality it does so within the safety of generally recognized constraints. Entire industries have developed around our prevailing preference for homogeneity aided by our capability for mass production. Where would the fashion industry be without our herd mentality? Or the popular music industry? The very notion of fashion is based on trends, on patterns of behaviour which will be universally adopted. Leaders, on the other hand, may start fashions, but they seldom follow them (one thinks of Wellington boots and Gladstone bags – emblems of two great British leaders).

Where do leaders find the resources to cope with a high level of difference or otherness? From where do they draw the reserves of energy necessary to propel them to the top? One simple answer may be, in childhood. 'Childhood shows the man,' according to Milton, and another great poet, Wordsworth, echoes the sentiments: 'The child is father of the man.' In our own century the role of childhood trauma in personality formation has been the first plank in the huge edifice of psychoanalytic thought, and few would doubt that adult attitudes are built on the foundations of childhood experience. Childhood trauma and extreme experience can, much as Churchill suggests, provide the drive that fires a nascent leader. Circumstances can accustom these juvenile leaders to the fact of their difference such that otherness is almost integral to their personality and never becomes a frightening Prufrockian choice.

Certainly, through the ages, the leaders of our nations and armies and those who influence our opinions and lifestyle appear to have an above average experience of hardship or adversity in youth. When Prime Minister Tony Blair was ten years old his father suffered a stroke. It took him three years to regain his speech and, in the process, his own political ambitions disappointed, Blair Senior unconsciously transferred them to his son. The Prime Minister is on record as describing his father's illness as 'one of the formative events of my life'. The experience of family suffering gave rise to a certain view of the world: 'My father's illness impressed on me from an early age that life was going to be a struggle, that there were a lot of losers.' Tony Blair doubtless drew some of his drive and fortitude – both essential in a leader – from this period, but also some of his ability to empathize with others who suffer. Perhaps he also acquired the desire to lead from this experience, wanting to compensate his father for his early loss of experience and to allow him to experience success vicariously.

One of the commonest threads in the early lives of leaders is the actual loss of one or both parents. A survey of British prime minsters before 1940 is illustrative. From Wellington to Chamberlain some 63 per cent of prime ministers were orphans. This figure is well above the average for the period. The early loss of a parent throws on the child (especially where that child is the eldest in the family) a strong sense of responsibility towards the other members of the family. It forces on a boy child robbed of a father the necessity (in a patriarchal society) to take on the leadership role within the family. This early assumption of responsibility distances the child from his peers and sets up a different relation between him and his siblings which can set a precedent for later life.

This early loss of a parent is a feature of leadership in any sphere. Martin Taylor, former Chief Executive of Barclays Bank, lost his father when he was only eight years old. Sir Brian Pittman, Chairman of Lloyds Bank, never knew his father, who died when he was just nine weeks old. He has told an interviewer: 'It's not all downside. If you haven't got a father, you start to take responsibility at a terribly young age.'

The circumstances of a parent's death can also be significant. Perhaps one of the most macabre examples of a parent's death fashioning a child's life is that of the American crime writer James Ellroy. His mother was violently murdered when he was just eight years old. After a very troubled youth and numerous brushes with the law, Ellroy found release of a kind in fiction and his novel, *The Black Dahlia*, set in a different period from his mother's murder, seems nevertheless imbued with his horrific experience of loss. Recently he has written his account of an attempt to reopen and solve the case. Would he have been a crime writer without this experience? Would his fiction have been less shocking without the influence of that trauma?

James Elroy is scarcely a leader, merely a striking example of childhood trauma leaving a visible scar on the adult. The experience of parental loss, always traumatic, may, however, be accompanied by feelings other than horror. With two world wars this century causing massive loss of life, there has been ample opportunity for potential leaders to lose a parent in heroic circumstances. Vanni Treves, the senior partner of city law firm Macfarlanes and, among other non-executive roles, the Chairman of Channel Four, lost his father in 1944 when he died fighting with the allies in the battle to liberate Florence. The Chief Executive of Reuters, Peter Job, never knew his father, who was killed at Monte Cassino in 1944. Never having known his father, he had a certain freedom to build up a fantasy image of him. To what extent, I wonder, did these bereaved sons build an heroic image of their absent father which set a standard for performance they have subsequently striven to meet in their business careers? Has the lost father provided an imagined audience for them throughout their lives?

Ted Turner, media mogul and entrepreneur extraordinaire, unquestionably plays to the audience of his dead father: 'I had counted on him to make the judgment of whether or not I was a success.' After a difficult childhood, in which father Ed sought to unsettle his son on the basis that 'insecurity breeds greatness', aged just twenty-four Turner faced the suicide of his father. 'I was sad, pissed and determined,' he recalled. His determination to succeed for his absent father has encroached on all areas of his life. Not only is he vice-chairman of the world's biggest media conglomerate, he has also, in his time, been one of the world's best sailors – he won the America's Cup in 1977. Ed Turner's favourite sport was sailing.

Death need not necessarily be of a parent for it to affect the course of one's life. The loss of a sibling can have a profound effect on remaining children. The curious character of Peter Pan, the boy who never grows up, was the adult response to the early loss of an older sibling on the part of author J. M. Barrie. His brother David, their mother's favourite, fell through ice and drowned at the age of twelve. Barrie clearly thereafter invested the notion of a pre-pubescent boy with extraordinary importance and romance. His rather eerie fixation with the never never land and virtual adoption of a family of young boys who were to provide much of the copy for Peter Pan must be linked to his early loss of a brother (and the reverence for that truncated life by Barrie's mother). It seems to me no overstatement to claim that one of the great texts of children's literature derives directly from early sibling loss. As in the case of Ellroy, Barrie is no leader. His fiction, however, is a public demonstration of a private wound.

Leaders may display the wound less visibly than writers whose inner feelings and psyche are the raw materials on which they must draw. Nevertheless I know of leaders whose attitude to life has been influenced by sibling loss. The most obvious of these, in business, is Niall FitzGerald, Co-Chairman of Unilever, one of Europe's largest and most successful organizations. FitzGerald, while a child, lost a brother who was ten years his senior to cancer. We can imagine how much a younger child would look up to one so much his elder and revere him. Did this death prove the demon that drove FitzGerald – or one of them? Perhaps younger brothers of prematurely deceased siblings feel the need to achieve beyond the norm of human achievement, to live, as it were, their lost sibling's life as well as their own. Certainly, the inevitable sense of guilt felt by the child who survives may act as a spur to leave no second of the precious gift of life wasted. Little children, losing a close family member, sometimes feel that it is somehow their own fault that this calamity has befallen them, the consequence of their bad behaviour, perhaps. This assumption of fault can drive a child to strive for superhuman achievements by way of expiation.

The death of an older sibling turns the second-born into the eldest. In general, it is the eldest or first-born child who has the greatest chance of achieving greatness, or so, provocatively, statistics suggest. Indeed, numerous studies have suggested that oldest children have brains on their side too. In fact this is not so much genetic as environmental. First-born children enjoy the benefits of uninterrupted parental attention, learning directly from an adult model. Their younger siblings have decreasing claim on parental attention and learn from their older siblings. The absence of adult stimuli seems to affect second and subsequent children. In support of this theory it is interesting to note that younger children who enjoy significant success are often the youngest by a large number of years. Niall FitzGerald is a case in point here. His siblings were some ten years his elders. He was obliged to act like the only or oldest child, finding his own playmates but perhaps also striving to bridge the gap in years between himself and his siblings. Perhaps he pushed himself harder to make up those ten or so years than those who have a mere two- or three-year gap to bridge?

A further factor in the prominence of the first-born child may simply be the parental attitude. Any parent will know the extraordinary difference in the way they reacted to their second and subsequent children. First-time parents creep into the baby's bedroom at half-hourly intervals to check the child is still breathing, and chart every infantile movement to calculate development. They are both more relaxed and, simply, busier when the second and subsequent children arrive and are less inclined to give later children the sense of being unique and special, the centre of the parental world. Some of that first-time parental tension must also communicate itself to the child and in time it translates into a drive to achieve, to please or placate the ever-present parent. Second and later children are often more relaxed and laid back simply in response to the attitude of their parents. Children are, after all, primarily mimics. Later-born children watch first-borns and acquire a shorthand for learning. First-born children are pathfinders, they must find out for themselves. This pioneering aspect stays with the child into maturity. First-borns also usually have the advantage of superior size to use against their junior siblings. They become accustomed to being in front, to taking the lead.

Perhaps the cultural legacy of primogeniture also has its part to play in much of the west? The importance of the first-born son is generally, if subliminally, acknowledged. Certainly in the case of the Kennedy family it was explicitly acknowledged. The eldest-born son of the ill-fated children of Joseph and Rose Kennedy was not J.F.K. but Joe Junior. His father had written a script for the lives of his family which featured Joe in the starring role. With Joe's death in action in 1944 the father was obliged to transfer his extraordinary ambitions directly on to his second-born son, John Fitzgerald. Here the death of a sibling does not have just symbolic force for a younger child (and of course John was himself adult and a wounded war veteran at the time of his older brother's death), but actual, life-altering consequences. Indeed, sibling loss and its effects ricochet through the Kennedy family.

Birth order studies appears to be an academic discipline in its own right. A study of the birth order of British prime ministers up to 1992 shows intriguing results.

Birth order of British prime ministers 1721–1992

1st	2nd	3rd	4th	5th	6th or later
16	11	7	7	3	5

It would seem to be an open and shut case. Birth order counts, and being born first is best. However, precedence in terms of education and access to advantages has historically been given to the first-born son so we might have expected this weighting in favour of the first-born. Further, no fewer than fifteen prime ministers came to the role from the House of Lords, where the rule of primogeniture prevails. In short, the incidence of first-born children among British prime ministers seems to be predominantly socially conditioned, down to the power of primogeniture.

It is more interesting to conduct this exercise in the United States, where there is no second house where birth order plays a part. From George Washington to Bill Clinton 32 per cent of American presidents have been first-borns (counting presidents themselves rather than presidential terms). In some periods there is an extra-ordinarily high proportion of first-borns. Of the fourteen presidents serving after 1920 some 57.1 per cent have been the eldest of their families. This would seem to suggest that being first-born in the twentieth century confers distinct advantage. Three of the century's most influential presidents, Teddy Roosevelt, Woodrow Wilson and Dwight Eisenhower, were not first-borns at all but managed to run innovative and powerful administrations. To take another fairly arbitrary period, of the ten presidents who served between 1869 and 1921 only one was a first-born (the first of these, Ulysses S. Grant, who, interestingly enough, was a military leader before he was a political leader, as was Eisenhower). Birth order, it would seem is insufficient of itself to propel an individual towards greatness.

It would be interesting, were the data available, to assess the extent to which the later-born presidents were the younger brothers of older sisters and hence first-born boys. There can be little doubt that candidates for presidential selection were likely to have been well educated, and just as in the British system the rule of primogeniture seemed to prevail, in the US there were still advantages to being a first-born male. When funds were scarce it would be the first son who would take advantage of such opportunities (especially educational ones) as existed rather than the first child. Nevertheless, our findings are fairly inconclusive. Birth order may be a factor in preparing an individual to lead but it cannot be more than one small factor.

Older children, in general, are loath to acknowledge that they have any advantage over their younger siblings. On the contrary, older children commonly point to the injustice in the treatment meted out to them relative to their siblings. They focus on the greater leniency with which younger children appear to be treated: going to bed later, staying out later, dating the opposite sex younger – the familiar litany of intra-family complaints. Perhaps this is a part of a process observed by one-time disciple of Freud, Alfred Adler. He noted that the first-born child suffers usurpation when the next child arrives. Certainly, it is not without a twinge of guilt that the parent passes on to the new child items that have previously been solely for the use of the first-born. Adler's view was that the first-born and successive children (but, of course, not the youngest child) never fully recover from the shock of this act of usurpation. According to this theory these usurped children spend life in a constant quest to regain the full beam of parental approval, thus achieving to the limits of their abilities.

Adler's theory does not take account of the fact that first- and last-born children fare better in the success stakes than do middle children. Middle children must compete above and below them in the family pecking order for attention. Last-borns at least have the luxury of no one coming up from behind. These are, of course, all generalizations, borne out by statistics but not precluding middle children being highly successful individuals and leaders in their own right. Gerry Robinson, Chairman of Granada Plc and veteran of some of the fiercest take-over battles in recent British business history, is the ninth of ten children.

Sometimes it is not so much birth order that counts in the family as gender. Mary Robinson, much loved and respected former President of Ireland, was brought up as the only girl in a family with four brothers. The child of professional parents (both were doctors, although her mother gave up practising in order to raise the family), hers was an enlightened and comfortable upbringing in which she experienced the same benefits as her brothers, all being educated at Trinity College, Dublin. It does not seem unreasonable to infer that as the only girl among four boys she would enjoy a certain degree of special status. This special status may not always act to the advantage of the child, especially where the gender of the lone figure is male rather than female. The rather pathetic figure of

Bramwell Brontë comes to mind. An artist and the only brother of nineteenth-century England's most illustrious family of authors, Charlotte, Emily and Anne, his self-image appears to have suffered under the gaze of his talented sisters. His most famous act seems to have been his removal of his own image from his portrait of himself and his sisters.

The familial position into which one is born may dictate the environment in which success will be achieved. Political and military leadership, for example, is more likely to come to the older rather than to the younger child. Younger children fare relatively better in cultural spheres. Attitudes to authority are, in this way, clearly linked to birth order. The older child who takes on a leadership role in relation to younger children will, typically, mimic the conduct of his or her parents. Instead of questioning authority they subscribe to its values and ape it. Younger children who are freed from the shackles of their parents' permanent attention develop alongside their chronological peers and are more likely, therefore, to be governed by peer than parental pressure and thus more prone to rebellion.

Creativity is more often than not derived from an iconoclastic world-view. The younger child is relatively more free than his or her oldest siblings to look at the world from a new perspective, to speak his or her own mind, rather than simply to voice the view that the parent, or authority figure, might wish to hear. While Regan and Goneril, the two eldest daughters of Shakespeare's King Lear, tell the foolish old man precisely what he wants to hear, irrespective of its truth, it is the youngest child, Cordelia, who has the independence of mind to utter a most unpalatable truth. Joseph, in the Old Testament, provides a biblical example of a younger child who sees the world differently. Joseph rises to political influence (if not perhaps greatness) based on his ability to give an imaginative rendering of Pharaoh's dreams. Both Cordelia and Joseph are the favourites of their parents and resented by their siblings accordingly. The youngest child gains the confidence to be imaginative and independent when their status as the youngest combines with that of the favoured child.

The list of younger children who have disturbed the status quo makes interesting reading. It includes Simon Bolívar, the national hero of Venezuela, Colombia, Ecuador, Peru and Bolivia. His ambitions in Latin America rivalled those of his near contemporary and fellow younger child Napoleon Bonaparte in Europe. Oliver Cromwell, who led the Parliamentarians to victory in the English Civil War, was a revolutionary younger child who achieved that most iconoclastic act of presiding over the execution of a king. Lenin, a later revolutionary and architect of Russian communism, was another younger child who authorized regicide. The effects of Lenin's revolution roused counter-revolutionary Lech Walesa, a trade unionist who led the Polish trade union Solidarity before becoming Poland's first post-Soviet president. He too is a younger child. Curiously some younger children have gone on to found religious movements, reinforcing the notion that younger children can develop an alternative way of seeing the world. John Calvin, father of austere Protestantism, John Wesley, founder of the Methodists, and Brigham Young, who took over the leadership of the Mormons from Joseph Smith and led the settlement of Salt Lake City, were all younger children. Freed from the convention of conforming, which seems to be the lot of the older child, younger children can attain positions of leadership as easily as their elder siblings. Their style of leadership is, however, likely to differ.

The business environment is perhaps one in which the first-born is more likely to succeed than his or her younger siblings. That is not to say that there are not some hugely successful business leaders who are younger children. Two who immediately spring to mind are Sir Richard Sykes, Chief Executive of Glaxo Wellcome, and his counterpart at SmithKline Beecham, Jan Leschley. Large organizations have an inbuilt need to respect authority, and the organizational structure of a big corporation apes those of the Army and the Church which, to the rebellious mind, at least, represent the very embodiment of authority both secular and spiritual. Indeed, Freud, in considering group psychology, identifies two artificial groups: the Church and the Army. Writing a century later he would, doubtless, have placed the corporation within the same category. As the Church has Christ (Freud took the *Catholic* Church as his model) and the Army has a commander-in-chief, so the corporation has a chief executive. This, from the outside at least, inflexible model is one with which older children might be expected to feel more comfort than, at the other extreme, a youngest child.

Older and younger children alike enter business, but perhaps position in the family will dictate the type of business in which an individual will feel at ease. So older children might be drawn to large companies, younger children to small ventures. Older siblings might favour a hierarchical structure with defined roles and clear lines of command. Younger children might be more comfortable in entrepreneurial ventures where they can develop a new structure or be involved in the management of their own destiny. Bill Gates and the late Jimmy Goldsmith, two very different figures (although both the scions of wealthy professional families), and both younger children, developed structures within which to manage their own destinies.

The global corporation is a new construct requiring individuals to provide leadership across diverse cultural boundaries. The chief executive at the helm of a business which encompasses managers and workers of numerous nationalities cannot be too authoritarian in style, for the massed ranks of those he or she must motivate will not stand for it. Those who lead pan-European businesses need some of the iconoclasm of the younger child mixed with the penchant for leadership of the oldest child. Niall FitzGerald, whom we have already encountered and who as Chief Executive of Anglo-Dutch business Unilever is the head of one of Europe's most respected, truly cross-border companies, offers an interesting mix in his own background. Born a youngest child by a very long margin, he benefited from a more relaxed parental attitude while also gaining that eldest-child benefit of substantial access to knowledge – and hence power – of the adult world through greater exposure to parents with fewer distractions. Since his siblings were much older they will not have been playmates. He will have devised his own games and method of play rather than, as most younger children do, participated in those devised by pathfinding elders. This combination perhaps gives FitzGerald (and we have also noted the tragedy of his elder brother's death) some of the mixture which enables him to lead so diverse a business as Unilever. Ultimately, as a former boss has gone on the record as saying, it is the trait of the youngest child which is most apparent in FitzGerald: 'Niall is a genuine iconoclast. Nothing is sacred. Nothing is unthinkable.'

A leader has a vision which he or she realizes and which changes the lives or opinions of those around them. Perhaps, then, it is the younger child, the iconoclast, who has the greater likelihood of this ground-breaking vision? Perhaps the oldest child is more likely to run and maintain a huge established edifice? What of only children? The only child occupies a different position again, since they clearly do not ever lose parental attention or feel usurpation by a younger sibling. In the absence of effective contraception, only children are a relative rarity in the annals of history, although maternal death in childbirth led to a number of only children with complex step-relations by dint of multiple marriages. One notable only child is Indira Gandhi, another Queen Victoria – both women born with a mandate to lead. Only children have no other children over whom to exercise their embryonic leadership skills and grow up in a climate where the authority of the parent goes largely unchallenged, since, as the sole object for parental attention, the only child is not induced to rebel.

Only children can come to have an uncomfortable relation to their peers. One of Britain's largest businesses is currently being run by an only child in the shape of Sir John Browne, Chief Executive of British Petroleum. His is an interesting case. His respect for authority is implicit in his decision to follow his father into BP and in his comfort, in mid-life, with living with his elderly mother. He is, as with many only children, deeply introverted and a recent article in the *Times* notes of him: 'Browne is a bit of a mystery and even those who work close to him describe him as intensely private.' BP is a culture which particularly likes its chief executives to shun the limelight and so, in the light of Browne's many talents, it is not surprising that he has come, at a young age (for he is still only fifty) to such prominence.

Browne's excellent intellect (he has a first in physics from Cambridge and a second degree from Stanford) and his capacity for hard work have been important factors in his success. There are other elements in his upbringing which mark him out as a little different from his peers and which may have enabled his success. He is the child of a Romanian mother and a British father, so he has a mixed cultural inheritance. As the child of a BP executive he led a typically peripatetic childhood, moving from country to country before being settled into a boarding school. Indeed, with his international credentials from birth, through childhood, education and then his career in a multinational company, Browne meets very

closely the archetype of the international leader that I outline in
The Culture Wars. These various factors – and we might add what
commentators refer to as 'his diminutive stature' – have doubtless
contributed as much to Browne's success as the accident of being
an only child.

One of my professional concerns is with the question of motivation. Why should someone be interested in the particular assign-
ment on which I am working? The motivation behind leadership is
multi-faceted and highly individualized. One recurrent theme
among leaders would seem to be a desire to overcome or make
up for early adversity. The desire to overcome poverty can drive
many to succeed. The tale of rags to riches has been an important
one throughout the ages, and Dick Whittington, who achieves that
about-turn, is a folk hero, though one with a real-life foundation.
In *Gone with the Wind*, as her family suffers the torment of the
Civil War, Scarlett O'Hara, in one of the film's most memorable
and melodramatic moments, standing on the ruins of her family
plantation, addresses God and declaims: 'As God is my witness, I
shall never be hungry again.' And she is resolute, bucking any
convention necessary to ensure that she can provide for the family
(for the record, Katie Scarlett is the youngest but favourite daughter).

Oprah Winfrey, another woman from America's deep South,
and the world's most successful business woman, has overcome
numerous disadvantages in her rise to become the world's highest-
paid entertainer. Recently featured on the cover of *Vogue* magazine
and asked if she had ever dreamed of such an event, she declared:
'Dreamed of being in *Vogue*. I'm a black woman from Mississippi'.

Winfrey's start in life featured multiple disadvantages. The result
of a teenage fling, she was brought up by her grandmother in
extreme poverty before moving to Wisconsin in her pre-teen years
to live with her mother. There she was sexually abused by her male
relatives and at the age of fourteen gave birth to a premature baby
who died shortly afterwards. When she moved to live with her
businessman father her life acquired discipline and shape and she
gained from him her commitment to education. Her teenage years
gave her the strength and some of the skills to become successful,
but the demons that drive her undoubtedly derive from the first
fourteen years of her life.

Oprah Winfrey is an extreme case of rags to riches, but the self-made man who has risen from humble origins remains a reasonably frequent occurrence in business and politics. The last prime minister of Britain, John Major, came from a humble home. Indeed the tumbling fortunes of his family may have been a spur to Major to succeed. Major had the sobering experience of seeing his father, trapeze artist and music-hall performer turned garden gnome manufacturer, fail in business. The family then moved from a leafy suburb to one of the poorer regions of London. A loss in status in early life can serve as a primary spur in later life when the adult seeks to regain the paradise lost of comfort, wealth and status. Lord Sterling, who is the Chairman of P&O, is one of the most obvious corporate businessmen who qualifies as a self-made man, while Alan Sugar, who built up Amstrad, and Michael Green, who runs Carlton Communications, both came from working-class Jewish origins in London's East End.

Few modern British business leaders have known the degree of hardship experienced in early life by C. K. Chow, the Chief Executive of GKN. Chow was born in Kowloon, where three families were crammed into one flat, and he walked for forty-five minutes to get to school every day. His father was a teacher who had fled his native China at the time of the revolution having been a member of Chiang Kai-shek's Nationalist Army. His Chinese qualifications were not recognized in Hong Kong and in the 1950s when Chow was growing up Hong Kong had not yet reached its boom period. Chow is straightforward about what has driven him in his adult life: 'My childhood created a certain sense of what I have to call insecurity. I was cautious in preparing for the future. Ensuring financial security has driven me over the years as well.'

C. K. Chow's father was an influential and heroic figure in his life whose decision to flee the country of his birth was based, according to the son, on 'integrity and principle'. The role of a living parent in terms of the influence that parent brings to bear on the child is a critical factor in the development of leaders, or great figures. Indira Gandhi's status as an only child has a bearing on her subsequent leadership only in so far as we might speculate that had she had a brother then he, rather than she, might have taken up the baton of leadership from Pandit Nehru. More interesting than this speculation is the role of a dominant parent in the life of a leader. Nehru occupies an extraordinary part in the history of India as the first prime minister after independence and a charismatic figure, one who must have exerted a considerable authority over his daughter. In much the same way Benazir Bhutto (not an only child but the favoured child of four) took on the mantle of leadership when her imprisoned father, Prime Minister of Pakistan Zulfikar Bhutto, asked his daughter to continue his work. She followed in his footsteps in the acquisition of power as she had in the acquisition of knowledge, for she had followed him to Oxford and, like him, had been elected President of the Union.

Formidable, or simply influential, parents feature prominently in the lives of leaders. Margaret Thatcher was greatly influenced by her father, as was Martin Luther King, whose father, a Baptist minister of some standing in his local community, changed his own and his son's names to Martin Luther King. As an aside, it is interesting to note that two great orators of the twentieth century, British Prime Minister David Lloyd George and Martin Luther King, were raised by ministers of the Church. Lloyd George was brought up by his uncle, who was a Methodist lay preacher. It may be that the gift of oratory is genetic and that ministry refined innate skills in the father figures which the sons applied in a political context. Equally, the religious conviction on the part of King's father and Lloyd George's uncle may have bred a sense of possibility and a confidence in God's favour which enabled the children to strive and succeed.

In the business world influential parent figures feature as much as in other fields of endeavour. Jan Leschley, Chief Executive of SmithKline Beecham, has described how his mother provided the steel in the family, while his father, something of a dreamer, seemed an absent figure. 'There is a Danish saying about people who can put their finger in the earth and smell where they are. My mother was like that.' Leschley, the youngest of two brothers, was also particularly fortunate in his sibling relationship. Peter, the elder by three years, was an important role model who taught Leschley to play the game of tennis which was to provide him with a career until his early thirties. 'My brother understood discipline and became a sort of father.' In a strange echo of Tony Blair's experience, Peter Leschley, this surrogate father figure, was struck down in 1971 by a mysterious fever which left him paralysed. The tragedy led Leschley to abandon the tennis circuit and start a career in the pharmaceutical industry.

Another business beneficiary of a strong mother was Sir Brian Pitman (Chairman of Lloyds Bank), who, as we have seen, lost his father shortly after he was born and was raised by his mother. He is fulsome in his praise of her role: 'She was the single biggest influence in my life without a doubt . . . Mothers set values, and if you are lucky enough to have a mother who sets the right values, you are blessed indeed.' This is an almost uncanny echo of Sigmund Freud's words: '. . . if a man has been his mother's undisputed darling he retains throughout life the triumphant feeling, the confidence in success, which not seldom brings actual success along with it.'

It took, of course, a mother's favourite child to make the imaginative leap to the Oedipus theory which underpinned much of Freud's thought: 'A single idea of general value dawned on me. I have found, in my own case too, the phenomenon of being in love with my mother and jealous of my father, and I now consider it a universal event in early childhood.' It took a supreme self-confidence or, in his own words, egotism to move from the particular to the universal with such consummate ease. That favourite child, Benazir Bhutto, cites the same quality of confidence coming from her father. '. . . I suppose the single most important factor in my upbringing was a sense of security and a sense of confidence which my father gave to all his children, and even if I said something foolish, he gave it as much weight as though it were the most wonderful insight. I think this gives a child confidence and enables a child then to develop a thinking process.'

A strong parent is not an unqualified blessing. Bill Clinton's bold, brash and rather brassy mother has, in true Freudian style, proven the model for some of his peccadilloes. Both Gennifer Flowers and Monica Lewinsky bear a closer resemblance to his mother than to his wife. A strong parent can overwhelm some children. In Jane Austen's *Pride and Prejudice*, Lady Catherine de Burgh so dominates her hapless daughter that she knocks the spirit from her. As a consequence, Mr Darcy's aunt is woefully ill-prepared for the highly spirited conduct of the novel's heroine, Elizabeth Bennet. Coming up to date, the emotionally immature and weak older sons of Don Corleone in Mario Puzo's *The Godfather* are overwhelmed by their powerful parent. It is Michael, the third-born son, who has the strength to emulate the father. It takes character to maximize the benefits of a strong parent. One of America's strongest and most dynamic presidents, Theodore Rosevelt, both adored and feared the father of whom he wrote: 'I realize more and more every day that I am as much inferior to Father morally and mentally as physically.' Clearly Roosevelt proved a match for his parent, but strong and successful parents can inhibit their children every bit as much as they can enable them to succeed.

Perhaps a sense of self-confidence, or self-belief, is one of the most important aspects in a leader's make-up, the single biggest gift a parent can bestow on a child. Attitudes to self, the extent of self-esteem, can make the difference between a benevolent and successful leader and a tyrannical despot. Sir Winston Churchill offers an interesting example of an individual who appears to combine considerable self-belief on the one hand with an essentially poor self-image on the other. Certainly his extraordinary drive was suggestive of a need to prove himself. Evidence for Churchill's self-belief lies in his conviction that he was destined for greatness. When at sixty-five he took over the wartime premiership he remarked: 'This cannot be accident, it must be design. I was kept for this job.' Dr Anthony Storr, in his essay entitled 'Churchill's Black Dog', depicts a man who at sixty-five had retained an extraordinary sense of himself as hero. It was this inflated sense of self which was to be Britain's salvation: 'Only a man convinced that he had a heroic mission, who believed that, in spite of all evidence to the contrary, he could yet triumph, and who could identify himself with a nation's destiny, could have conveyed his inspiration to others.' Dr Storr's Churchill could as easily be a deluded fantasist or someone with quite extraordinary belief in themselves, instilled at a young age.

The thrust of Dr Storr's essay is that Churchill experienced neglect in childhood due to the political ambitions of his father, which kept him from the home and the youth and social distractions of his mother. This much is true, but Storr underplays the role of Mrs Everest, Churchill's devoted nanny, whom Churchill himself acknowledged at the time of her death as 'my dearest and most intimate friend during the whole of my twenty years I had lived'. While certainly Churchill developed an idealized notion of his little-known parents, his day-to-day life was rooted in the absolute security of one woman's complete love and devotion, that woman being his nanny. For the first eight years of his life Churchill slept in Mrs Everest's room, was washed, changed and dressed by her, and for five of those eight years he was the only child, the sole beneficiary of unstinting love. His sense of possibility, of deep self-confidence, must have emanated from that source.

In 1947 Churchill wrote a moving and revealing essay entitled 'The Dream'. In this he is in his studio at his home in Chartwell and is copying a portrait of his father when his father appears before him and elicits from his son a description of the state of the world some fifty years after his death. At the end of Winston's description of mass slaughter in the Boer War and the two world wars, Randolph says: 'Winston, you have told me a terrible tale. I would never have believed that such things could happen. I am glad I did not live to see them. As I listened to you unfolding these fearful facts you seemed to know a great deal about them. I never expected that you would develop so far or so fully. Of course you are too old now to think about such things, but when I hear you talk I really wonder you didn't go into politics. You might have done a lot to help. You might have made a name for yourself.' At no point has the son taken the opportunity to apprise the parent of his position in life. He allows his father to labour under a misapprehension and enjoys the position of superior knowledge, for this is the conceit on which the piece turns. The essay reveals a fundamental resentment towards a figure who undermined Winston's own implicit self-belief. The essay is an extended version of 'I told you so'. It testifies to the paradox at the heart of his nature, self-belief and self-doubt in equal measure, the same tension which led him to say, famously, of himself to Violet Bonham-Carter: 'We are all worms. But I do believe that I am a glow-worm.'

The example of Churchill points to the vital importance of our early experiences of life and love. Perhaps the single biggest influence on a child is the quality of care received in early childhood. It is in the very first days of life that the origin of self-esteem is fixed which can determine the shape of our lives. We start life in a paradoxical situation as the centre of our own universe, utterly solipsistic but also totally dependent on one omnipotent carer. We begin to enter the social realm through a complex interaction with our mothers, which begins quite literally by the response we read in her face to our intact selves. Through a complex process called mirroring, we perceive through the medium of our mothers and their responses to us the boundaries of possibility in relation to our selves and learn what is and is not acceptable in us, finding either approval or disapproval and modifying our conduct accordingly. This mirroring process is the start of our interaction with others, which will continue throughout our lives. It is the process from which we draw our sense of ourselves and whence comes our self-esteem. Our experiences from early childhood can colour the remainder of our lives and come back in the form of neurotic behaviour, or particular responses to situations which reflect those of our first experience.

The case of the nineteenth-century British statesman, Lord Curzon, offers a sad footnote to the vital role that our main carers can have on us in our early lives. Curzon had the misfortune to come under the control of a harsh and sadistic nanny, Miss Paraman, who beat him savagely and disciplined him into taking on a massive burden of work. She forced him to acquire her own parsimony and attention to each and every detail and perpetually set her will against his. Throughout his adult life Curzon behaved as if Nanny Paraman were watching over him. Even when Viceroy of India he continued to do all his own filing, packed all his own trunks, posted all his own letters and worked regularly an eighteen- or nineteen-hour day both on official duties and the minutiae of daily existence. He lost sight of all sense of priority and with it lost all hope of power. His frustration throughout life was that he always seemed close to power but ultimately there was a more powerful force than he. As Viceroy of India he could be overruled by the Secretary of State and as Foreign Secretary he was frustrated first by Lloyd George and later by Stanley Baldwin. The more desperate he became for power, the less able he became to grasp it and, in the end, he was passed over to lead his party when, against Baldwin, he would have been the obvious choice. Curzon was a man driven by a need to get even with Miss Paraman, to right the wrong of her injustice to him in his childhood and to gain the power over himself, over his environment and over those in authority that had eluded him in his infancy. His tragedy was that he had no mode of behaviour beyond that which had been instilled in him in early childhood and so he remained perpetually in sway to his nanny, endlessly repeating the dynamic of their relationship with all those who held authority over him. She was the demon who both drove and destroyed him and no amount of adult effort could overcome that influence from infancy.

The legacy of one's parents or primary carers is, then, a vital contributory factor in the making of a personality and of course critical in the development of a leader. The absence or the withholding of love on the part of a parent can drive a child. Former Chancellor Helmut Kohl seems to have been driven by just such a demon. His elder brother, Walter, died in Normandy in 1944. He had been their father's favourite and the father was devastated by his loss. Kohl's sister has told of Helmut's uneasy position in the family, since he was unplanned and born to an already financially strapped family at a time of economic crisis. Kohl has been an enormously driven man whose drive may derive in part from a need to ensure the approval of a disapproving parent. Perhaps he has striven for the love and appeal of the German people, the fatherland, as some kind of proxy for that of his father.

For some leaders the motivation is more positive. They have sought to live up to the ideals of a much loved and greatly loving parent, like Margaret Thatcher and Benazir Bhutto, who strove to achieve in the very fields of endeavour held in highest esteem by their parents. Whether the motivation is positive or negative, at the heart of a driven personality there will often be an intensity of emotion in relation to a parent or parent figure. Jack Welch, Chairman of General Electric (an only child and son of a railroad conductor), credits his mother with playing the most powerful part in his life: 'Don't get me started on my mother, she is my whole game.'

While early childhood is a time when the personality is forged and when responses are learned such that they become irrevocable habit, it is not simply experiences in early childhood, or even in teenage years, that can provide a spur and drive. George Shaheen has built Andersen Consulting from scratch in 1989 to $6.1 billion in 1997, one of the most respected consulting firms, or indeed service businesses, in the world. The watershed in his life came in

1978 with the death of his first wife, which gave him a need for security that drove him to succeed and, interestingly, to succeed within the context of a partnership. Perhaps a partnership structure with its overtones of trust and sharing holds particular appeal to a twin, for Shaheen is one of the relatively rare businessmen who is one half of twins.

Modern psychoanalytic thought gives more credence to the experience of adulthood. Erik Erikson, for instance, writing in 1950, identifies eight ages of man of which three are in adulthood. This means that five are in childhood, and one period of immense importance to any leader is that of their education. The school or educational establishment is a relatively modern construction. For generations people received their education at the hand of tutors in the home. Some great leaders have had great tutors, notably Alexander the Great whose tutor was the philosopher Aristotle, but for more modern leaders for whom we have more reliable biographical information education has taken place in the schoolroom.

School can sometimes provide a surrogate parent, and a good teacher will take a bright child and encourage and build self-esteem. Educational attainments, however, are not necessarily a prerequisite for leadership. Both Sir Winston Churchill and Albert Einstein were famously poor scholars, and some of the greatest authors writing in the English language were self-taught. British public figures from the eighteenth until the middle of the twentieth century were largely the product of the public school system. Indeed, families such as William Gladstone's, with aspirations to better themselves, sent their sons to Eton precisely to allow them to develop a useful network of contacts. In the twentieth century our prime ministers have been free to have more humble educational antecedents and our last, John Major, went to a state school and no university at all.

Business, of course, is concerned with expertise and competence which is generally susceptible to measurement. It comes as no surprise that education is an important factor. A survey undertaken by the *Sunday Times* and Hemington Scott in 1997, featuring some 15,000 company directors of whom some 5,000 provided substantial information, found that almost half of all Britain's company directors share a traditional public school background. Eton's numerous alumni include Dominic Cadbury and Martin Taylor. What the survey fails to identify is that Taylor, for instance, was a scholarship boy, present at the school not because of the wealth of his family but because of the range of his abilities. At the top of British businesses, however, it tends to be the grammar schools rather than the public schools which are best represented.

British business has become increasingly meritocratic, as has the education system. Certainly it is the case that Oxbridge features prominently on the CVs of many successful people, but entry has been fiercely competitive for some years and so it comes as little surprise that its graduates have entered and succeeded in the competitive environment of business. At the top of British businesses, however, there remain a number of people with relatively modest educational attainments. Some, notably the entrepreneurs and founders of businesses, have shied away from conventional education altogether. British Telecom is headed by Sir Peter Bonfield, whose educational attainments are more than adequate if not in the first league. After a grammar school career he took a degree in mechanical engineering at Loughborough University. It was his primary education, however, which seems to have had a lasting effect on his attitudes. He was sent to convent school between the ages of four and eleven and records: 'I still have a complete phobia about being late for meetings – I can see the sisters' rulers hovering over me.' He may speak in jest, but some of his flair for organization and hard work comes from this early period in his education.

Other business leaders have turned their back on education. Larry Ellison, who founded Oracle and is regarded as one of America's most successful entrepreneurs, has a classic rags-to-riches background. Abandoned by both parents, he was brought up by relatives and successfully secured a place at university. This, however, was the late sixties and, finding better things to do, Ellison dropped out. One of his great, often repeated, adages is 'It's better to be lucky than smart', and in his case the absence of a formal education has not been a check on his career.

Good or bad scholastic achievement is no particular guarantor of success or failure in life, and the attitude of one's peers does not seem to offer much indication of whether an individual will be able to lead them later. Unlike his older brother, Tony Blair was not even a prefect at Fettes College (one of Scotland's best schools, to which, incidentally, he won a scholarship). The Duke of Wellington, similarly, would not have been marked out as anything particularly special at Eton, where he was largely a solitary child, and he was similarly unremarkable in the French schools he attended. That period assimilating French culture may, however, have paid off on the battlefield at Waterloo. Greatness, nonetheless, does not seem given to showing itself in the schoolroom.

Were we to try to perform a Pygmalion-style experiment and cultivate a leader for the next century, what would we need to do? From the above the most obvious answer would be to provide two parents, ensure that one is extremely loving and then, quite early in life, remove the other. Again and again as I consider the backgrounds of top people in my own sphere of business I find the early loss of a parent as a recurrent theme. Lord David Simon, ex-Chairman of British Petroleum, was eleven years old before he met his real father. Sir William Purves, former Chairman of Hong Kong Shanghai Banking Corporation, lost his father at the age of thirteen. His father, incidentally, had been injured in the First World War and never fully recovered from the injury. But it is not just in business that the loss of a parent is a recurrent motif. Nelson Mandela, one of the century's most charismatic figures, lost his father at thirteen.

Failing that, we should ensure that some other extraordinary misfortune comes the way of our poor guinea-pig, perhaps an accident that sets the child at a disadvantage such that they drive themselves to overcome it. One high-achieving executive of my acquaintance was deaf until he was six or seven, but pushed himself thereafter to ensure that he achieved high honours at school and subsequently in his career. Similarly, a highly regarded chief executive of a Top 100 company has battled against dyslexia. Having ensured some form of disadvantage or handicap for our embryonic leader, we would need to provide encouragement and perhaps apply a certain degree of pressure to create some tension, some impetus to action. But were we to do all these things, could we guarantee that at the end of it we had produced a leader? Unfortunately, we would be just as likely to produce deeply confused individuals, unable to find their way in life, whose drive turns inwards and becomes self-destructive. There quite simply is no recipe that will produce leaders, just as there is no knowing whether those who have leadership potential will have the opportunity to demonstrate that potential. As Anthony Storr points out, had Churchill died at the age of sixty-four he would have been said to have failed in his life's endeavour.

Most of the business leaders we have considered in this chapter were born within the last sixty years. Over the next sixty very different social conditions will prevail. We have not had world wars in which father figures can meet heroic deaths, mothers stay at home with children much less often than in the first two-thirds of the century, and the professional and working classes alike are having increasing recourse to child care outside the home. Will these factors affect the development of a future generation of leaders? They may well. However, it is now increasingly the choice of women to have children outside the confines of a conventional relationship and the one-parent family is a fact of modern living, whether by design or not. Huge investments will continue to be made by parents in their children and children will continue to lose, through divorce and remarriage perhaps, rather than death, one parent. Forms of social organization will change, but in changing they will simply recreate different scenarios from which a different set of leaders to meet a different set of situations will emerge.

Is leadership a matter of nature or nurture? From the examples in this chapter we must conclude that environmental factors are extremely important in providing the spur to act. Churchill is right: easy living and comfort do not seem conducive to greatness. But not every first-born, orphaned child, brought up in poverty with a deep sense that the world owes them something, is destined to succeed. It takes a particular cast of mind and type of character to turn extraordinary misfortune to the good. If there is a trait which does characterize leaders it is opportunism. Successful people are very often those who steadfastly refuse to be daunted by disadvantage and have the ability to turn disadvantage to good effect. They are people who seize opportunity and take risks. Leadership then seems to be a matter of personality and character. By this token a leader must be born. Sadly, numerous leaders may be born with sufficient character to succeed but only a handful will find the moment to exercise their leadership skills and put that character to the test. While leaders may be born, it is through circumstance and happenstance that they are made.

Chapter 3

The Will to Lead:
The Influence of Personality on Leaders

'What the great conductors of the past had in common was an unshakeable belief in their view of music, and an ability to summon tremendous energy at the moment of performance. This surge of energy is not something that even-tempered people can experience. It indicates a person with manic-depressive tendencies – someone whose natural inclination is to hold back, an introvert who becomes extrovert only through the medium of an orchestra and the sound it creates.' – *Financial Times* article

If leadership is as much about personality and character as about early influence it follows that there might be a clear leadership profile. There are certainly facets of personality which seem to recur from one individual to another irrespective of the environment in which they lead. These are nicely encapsulated in the above description of the great conductors in the past: unshakeable belief; tremendous energy, verging on mania and introversion.

Some of these characteristics are more marked in leaders in one sphere than in another. The tortured artist is something of a stereotype – Virginia Woolf, Vincent Van Gogh, and Robert Schumann are but three figures from the worlds of letters, art and music respectively who suffered acute mental illness. Woolf and Van Gogh both committed suicide and Schumann died insane in an asylum, having suffered throughout his life from manic depression. Churchill's black dog, the pall of depression that enveloped him for long periods of his life and, in his latter years, all but consumed him, Newton's paranoia – these are well-chronicled instances of mental problems which did not actively impede the extraordinary achievements of either man.

Performers too, particularly and paradoxically comedians, seem to suffer a high incidence of depression. Tony Hancock committed suicide, Spike Milligan suffers from depression and John Cleese has undergone many years of therapy. The stock market, however, would take a dim view of a chief executive whose demons took the form of mental instability, so while some business leaders may suffer depression it is not a matter of public record. Most, however, are introverted. Even the most public facing of business personalities, Richard Branson and Bill Gates, are shy and introverted by nature, no matter how much their media image might suggest otherwise.

There seems no question that leaders must have an unshakeable belief in the cause, or body, they represent. If they do not have faith, why should those who follow them have faith? Conviction alone does not a leader make, however, for a follower may be every bit as convinced of the justice of the cause as their leader. The distinguishing feature by which we may know a leader is courage. Two modern leaders on the world stage, Vaclav Havel, the first President of the Czech Republic, and Nelson Mandela, South Africa's first post-Apartheid President, have both put themselves at great personal risk and endured imprisonment in the cause of their powerful beliefs. They could not have done so without conviction and courage in equal measure. Mandela and Havel are leaders on a grand scale. Most leaders are not required to put their lives at risk or to endure, as in Mandela's case, twenty-seven years of imprisonment. Nevertheless, endurance is a key trait in the personality of any leader. Recent historians of warfare have pointed to the relentless boredom of, in particular, trench warfare. The experience of that relentlessness needed particular fortitude to match the courage and conviction which took the soldier over the top and into no man's land. In positions of modern leadership there is a similar quality of boredom, from the relentless meeting schedules which afflict leaders in any walk of life and the relentlessness of knowing one's time is seldom one's own. The intensity of the public gaze and the burden of public expectations further require a particular brand of endurance on the part of our leaders.

Business leaders are scarcely in the same league as those who hold the fortunes of states in their hands. Nevertheless, a corporation can be a sprawling entity which will touch the lives of numerous people, giving the leader of that corporation senatorial-style power. It is mistaken to underestimate the scale of a business leader's influence. They may seem far removed from the image of the great conductor with which I began this chapter but the analogy holds. Conductors lead a group of highly trained experts in the interpretation of a piece which is received by a diverse audience to whom the conductor is immediately accountable (they may walk out or switch off if they do not approve). The company chief executive similarly leads a group of highly trained experts in the interpretation of a market situation and is answerable to a broad audience of stakeholders. The chief executive (or chairman) does not undergo the same intensity of performance (unless we count the AGM or board meetings) but they experience precisely the surge of energy we have seen in the con-ductor at the moment when they are most challenged. In short, leaders enjoy the fight.

It is curious looking at the pantheon of business leaders to find that several have gone on from early sporting successes to achieve-ment in the boardroom. Perhaps the most obvious of such figures is Tony O'Reilly, who went from being a renowned rugby player to heading up the Heinz corporation (from which he has now retired) along with managing a host of investments in his native Ireland, including Waterford Wedgwood and a daily newspaper. O'Reilly brought to business what he had taken into sport – a preparedness to be prepared and to endure gruelling training. No sportsmen – excepting some football players, it would seem – can afford to lead lives of excessive indulgence but must be capable of a certain asceticism if they are to maintain peak levels of fitness and performance. This quality of self-denial in pursuit of a longer-term goal and, indeed, the willpower to maintain the denial, is excellent training for the boardroom. Of course, O'Reilly was part of a team where each member has a clearly defined role, just as in the corporate hierarchy.

It is not just in team sports that business figures have achieved earlier success. Jan Leschley, the Chief Executive of SmithKline Beecham, played competitive tennis in his youth and ranked, at one time, tenth in the world. Tennis players participate in team events (the Davis Cup for example) and, of course, play in doubles but it is primarily a sport where individual prowess is very much on show. Leschley's habit of taking sole responsibility for success or failure on court must have been a good apprenticeship for his second career in one of the world's largest pharmaceutical companies.

Some businessmen who have been able to transfer their skills from the sports arena to the boardroom have been able to move with ease from one sport to another. Lord McLaurin, the man who turned Tesco Plc into the leading British retailer, was fêted more at school for his sporting than for his scholastic achievements. He made Kent's second XI cricket team, then moved on to Herts and the Minor Counties; he was also a serious footballer and remains a fine golfer.

It is not difficult to conceive that these top sportsmen turned top businessmen have abundant qualities of endurance and, indeed, determination. But conviction and courage – surely not? Certainly a business leader does not necessarily stake his life on a decision, but he will stake his reputation. Lord McLaurin undoubtedly had the courage of his convictions when he dared to challenge one of the sacred cows of the Tesco business.

In 1977 Tesco's share price was low and its image suffering against the other retailers. McLaurin took on the might of Sir Jack Cohen, the store's founder and his mentor, and convinced Cohen and the board to abandon the Green Shield stamps which had been central to the store's retailing policy. This might seem a trivial occurrence, but the stamps were an important part of the company's culture and legacy for the future. McLaurin was obliged to work hard to convince the board of his own empirically tested belief that customers did not want the stamps (he made it his practice to stand in checkout queues and observe at first hand the buying practices of his customers). At the end of the meeting in which McLaurin emerged victorious, his boss, Jack Cohen, is said to have grabbed him by the lapels and shaken him, warning of the consequences if he was wrong. McLaurin had, quite simply, staked his career on the issue. Happily, this proved to be the first step in the movement away from the pile 'em high, sell it cheap philosophy towards Tesco's current status as a top-quality retailer. McLaurin won; but he would not have done so without both courage and conviction.

It would seem that only by taking a significant risk can a

significant shift in a company's fortunes be achieved. Sir Barrie Stephens, the power behind the growth of Siebe plc (which has now merged with British engineering business BTR), staked all on the acquisition of Foxboro'. This was the third in a series of acquisitions, and while for Stephens the business was a potential world-beater the financial community took a different view. Stephens geared up in order to buy the business and the share price halved virtually overnight. Nonetheless, it was Stephens who was proven right, not the analyst community, who had to bow to the justice of his conviction when he licked Foxboro' into shape. An analyst notes: 'He is a slightly odd fish, but a brave man. He was clearly determined to build a leading controls company come hell or high water and prepared to suffer the City's reaction.'

A man of less courage or less conviction might have faltered in the face of scepticism from investors. Stephens, however, had that faintly prosaic vision of wanting to build 'a leading controls company' and defied advice. He is on record as referring to Siebe as 'my beloved Siebe' and is virtually its founder, or parent. The business serves as an extension of himself, like a favourite child whose motives and responses are intimately understood. When Stephens took risks with Siebe he took risks with his own flesh and blood.

Most of the big turnaround successes of recent years have taken courage and a high level of risk. Archie Norman's background would appear to be one of conservatism and lack of risk, incorporating an education at Charterhouse, Cambridge and Harvard and a career with Citibank, McKinsey and then retailer Kingfisher. However, he risked his reputation as the wonder child of British business by taking on the embattled retailer Asda plc. Those who may have doubted whether the retailer could come back from the brink of financial collapse have watched Norman turn in a staggering performance, with the business outperforming the stock market by 100 per cent since 1992. From a headhunting perspective Norman might have managed a comeback had he failed in the endeavour at Asda, but few chairmen would have entrusted him with a FTSE 100 company and few headhunters would have dared to suggest it. Norman's steadfast ability to fly in the face of most advisers and commentators is the more remarkable since he was, originally, an adviser and commentator himself. Norman simply had the courage and the self-belief to trust his own counsel above that of his counsellors.

We could be forgiven for assuming that the unshakeable belief that some leaders display is no more than an unshakeable belief in themselves. Certainly there is a need for leaders to have self-respect. Joan Didion, one of America's leading essayists and commentators on modern life, writes compellingly on the subject:

> To have that sense of one's intrinsic worth which constitutes self-respect is potentially to have everything: the ability to discriminate, to love and to remain indifferent. To lack it is to be locked within oneself, paradoxically incapable of either love or indifference. If we do not respect ourselves, we are upon the one hand forced to despise those who have so few resources as to consort with us, so little perception as to remain blind to our fatal weaknesses. On the other we are peculiarly in thrall to everyone we see, curiously determined to live out – since our self-image is untenable – their false notions of us.

The absence of self-respect can certainly inhibit greatness. Richard Burton was one of the nineteenth century's many characters who was larger than life. Fluent in two dozen languages, a master swordsman and a brilliant translator of works such as *The Arabian Nights*, he was also an anthropologist, poet, scholar, soldier and archaeologist. Indeed, he was Renaissance Man. As an explorer he discovered Lake Tanganyika and took part in the search for the source of the Nile. Unquestionably one of the most gifted men of his generation, Burton achieved eminence but never fully lived up to his potential. He was not as great an explorer as Stanley or Livingstone or even his great rival Speke. There were better anthropologists, and even if there were few linguists of his skill there were people who put inferior skills to better use. His most recent biographer, Frank McLynn, puts this down to a personality defect and depressive tendency: '. . . the very nature of his huge gifts – the talent for disguise, the linguistic genius, the scholarly abilities as a translator . . . denotes a lack of firm identity at the centre, almost as though no single human personality could marshal and control so much.'

Burton was an extraordinary fantasist, someone who tried out other personalities in the absence of one central personality of his own which he could respect and develop. His personal inadequacy makes for a highly complex character but also for great personal disappointment.

With other figures neurosis has been less of a handicap, rather it has acted as a spur. A figure not wholly unlike Burton in terms of his interest in Arab society, his sexuality and his penchant for fantasy is T. E. Lawrence, Lawrence of Arabia. Christopher Isherwood characterized Lawrence as an adolescent who never fully matured, who "suffered in his own person, the neurotic ills of a generation", and that thirties generation of which Isherwood was a part saw Lawrence as the neurotic hero. Indeed, monarchs, statesmen and intellectuals alike were fulsome in their praise of him when he died. But while the neurotic hero suited an age which was, in the aftermath of the First World War, sated with heroism of a more macho variety, for most leaders a degree of self-respect is a prerequisite. Or, to put it another way, a degree of self-respect is a prerequisite if a leader is to be successful.

One of the century's least successful British prime ministers must be Neville Chamberlain. The younger son of a famous father, Neville Chamberlain grew up in the shadow of a personality that was larger than his own, that of his father Joseph. He knew himself to be second in his father's affections to his elder brother Austen, who was hand-picked to succeed their illustrious parent in politics. The family were notoriously self-contained: Neville's upbringing was provincial and closeted and both brothers were pathologically shy. Overshadowed in childhood by his father and in young adulthood by his brother, Neville, marrying late in life, then became subject to the strong personality of his wife. He was judged a cold and aloof man, as Harold Macmillan wrote of him: 'In his earlier days his undoubted intellectual arrogance was partly concealed. After he became prime minister, and especially after Munich, it developed almost to a form of mania.' Yet Chamberlain did not so much suffer from arrogance as shield his intellectual insecurity with the mask of arrogance. Historian David Cannadine sums up Chamberlain with ruthless insight as:

> . . . a man of limited talents and ruthlessly subdued emotions, who was powerfully driven, sometimes by the need to

emancipate himself from the domination of others, sometimes by the need to prove himself to himself in the light of past failures, and sometimes by the need to show that being a non-university provincial didn't matter. His aloofness was thus born more of insecurity than of arrogance, and the ease with which he criticized others was but a way of protecting himself.[1]

Chamberlain may have been an ineffectual leader and a rather distant, slightly disagreeable figure, but he came to power by accident rather than design and he was misguided rather than malevolent. He has had the misfortune to be cast for ever more as the dupe of Hitler who believed in 'peace in our time'.

The modern political institutions of most of the West guard against despotism. Iraq has not been so fortunate in its institutions, and one of the most alarming examples of a leader who is driven, in part, by a need to gain universal respect to compensate for its fundamental absence in himself is Saddam Hussein. Hussein's psyche no doubt merits an entire volume to itself and I can only be hopelessly reductive, but he provides an outstanding illustration of the 'Monte Cristo complex'. This phrase was coined by Manfred Kets de Vries, a practising psychoanalyst and a Professor of Organizational Behaviour at the European Business School INSEAD. The Monte Cristo complex describes a need by an individual to get even with the world for crimes committed in the past, or (and this is an important distinction) crimes *perceived* to have been committed. Events which, to an observer, might seem trivial can acquire immense importance in the mind of those that they affect.

A man of great brutality, who became involved in his first murder at the age of twelve, Saddam Hussein was born a landless peasant. His father died before his birth and he suffered cruelty at the hands of his stepfather. Deprived of any form of education until he was ten years old, he went in his teens to live with an uncle who came to wield considerable local political power and huge influence over the young Saddam. Coming late to education, Saddam did not excel and failed to gain the grades to allow him entry to the prestigious military academy and he seems to have conferred most of his honours, military and academic, upon himself. Indeed, Saddam Hussein has constructed an entire mythology about himself, tracing his dynasty back, via Iraq's Hashemite ruling dynasty, to Mohammed. Furthermore, he sees himself as a descendant of the ancient Akadian and Chaldean rulers of Mesopotamia – Hammurabi and Nebuchadnezzar. He sets himself up as an icon to be worshipped: his image adorns every street in Baghdad and his aides in a bizarre act of homage ape his moustachioed appearance. *The Godfather* is Saddam Hussein's favourite film, and perhaps we can see why by reference to the book which gave rise to the film. Mario Puzo writes: 'in this world there comes a time when the most humble of men, if he keeps his eyes open, can take revenge on the most powerful'. This has been Saddam Hussein's creed, and he is living proof of the danger of someone whose self-image is attacked in early childhood. In an unspeakable fashion he is using the full paraphernalia of his power to do to others as he was done by in childhood.

It takes dramatic failure or fraud for a businessman's psyche to be paraded before the public. Few have been more publicly scrutinized than that of hero turned villain Robert Maxwell. His was an extraordinary personality. He combined the capability for extraordinary charm with an equal ability to be extremely crude. A man of voracious appetite, he ate and drank excessively and had a constant need not just to feed his flesh but to feed his ego with flattery. He was fiercely possessive and experienced frenzied jealousy if the attention of a favourite wandered from him. With an obsessive need to control, he kept his children yoked to him and bugged the phones of his employees. Apparently a devoted family man, he was a compulsive womanizer and a bully to wife and children alike. An egomaniac, Maxwell was a law unto himself. Nothing was beyond his reach, nothing beyond the pale, hence he plundered the newspaper business Mirror Group's pension fund when he needed to finance his empire. It was fitting that Maxwell was a media baron since the media is the medium by which our modern grasp of reality is manufactured. Maxwell's own reality was entirely manufactured. He built a myth about himself and, when that myth could no longer be sustained, he brought the story to its close by, we can only assume, bringing about his enigmatic death.

Maxwell has been described as psychopathic, and certainly his complicated personality can not be easily explained. His early childhood was one of abject poverty in a small village in the

Carpathian mountains on the Czech–Romanian borders. In 1940, at seventeen, he escaped the Nazi persecution which claimed the rest of his family and came to Britain, where he joined the Army and launched himself on a life of apparent heroism, hedonism and power. There are elements in Maxwell's background that are reminiscent of Saddam Hussein's: the poverty, the absence of education and the shared need to overcome that poverty and amass great, very conspicuous wealth. The cruelty and oppression Maxwell experienced was that of being Jewish at the worst possible point in history.

In Maxwell, the Monte Cristo complex, the need to get even, sat alongside a need to perpetuate the early adoration he had encountered. Unlike Saddam Hussein, Robert Maxwell had love and attention lavished on him in early childhood by a woman who, despite considerable strength of character and personality, indulged her son in every whim, even in the renouncing of his Jewish Orthodox faith. His mother, Hannah Sclomovitch, was apparently intelligent, strong-minded and a very dominating parent who focused all ambition on Robert (born Labji Hoch, later Jan), for many years her only son. Maxwell, during his early years, was at the centre of an adoring ring of womenfolk, his mother and sisters, in whose eyes he was all powerful and always right.

Far from suffering a dearth of self-esteem, Maxwell suffered its opposite, a glut. He was every inch a narcissist, and this self-love coupled with a strong sense of grievance made him into a textbook case of what Manfred Ket de Vries terms a reactive narcissist. De Vries's description could be directly attributed to Maxwell himself, for it is a description of his personality:

> True reactive narcissists tend to have a grandiose sense of self importance. They habitually take advantage of others in order to achieve their own ends . . . there is a sense of entitlement, the feeling that they deserve especially favourable treatment and that the rules set for others do not apply to them. Furthermore, they are addicted to compliments – they can never get enough. They lack empathy, being unable to experience how others feel. Last, but certainly not least, their envy of others and their rage when prevented from getting their own way, can be formidable.[2]

The other side of the coin, according to de Vries, is the constructive narcissist who can become an excellent leader: 'constructive narcissists have the capacity for introspection; they radiate a sense of positive vitality and are capable of empathetic feelings'. Business leaders not infrequently conform to this model.

A figure who has always been rather larger than life is Lord King, Life President of British Airways and its former Chairman and Chief Executive. His early life was modest. He was the second child of four born to a rather withdrawn and stern soldier and his much younger, artistic Irish Catholic wife. It was King's mother who was the driving force in the family: according to her son 'she was a powerhouse'. Her artistic side has been passed on to her son, who is a romantic and who, fired by such novels as *The Forsyte Saga*, determined to make something of himself. The energetic, driven King certainly made something of himself and of several organizations along the way. He met the Pope, various American presidents and has been a close friend of Margaret Thatcher. A working-class lad, he became the Master of the Belvoir Hunt, beating the upper classes at their own game. He married, through his second bride, into the titled classes, before eventually being granted a title of his own. A fantasist ('The only reason you do anything in the first place is because you have a Walter Mitty person inside you'), he has propagated a myth of extraordinary toughness which friends claim is false, noting instead a sharp brain, extraordinary intuition and courage.

As much as Robert Maxwell embodied the reactive narcissist, King would appear to be a prototype for the constructive counterpart. 'Life is a romance. You are either attracted to the power of doing something or you are not. If you want to be someone then you must do something properly, create something . . . I am now what I always was in my own mind.' Sir Barrie Stephens of Siebe is another such as Lord King.

There is, of course, a fine dividing line between having a healthy degree of self-respect and a disproportionate sense of self-belief. Some would say that the dirty tricks campaign against Virgin for which Lord King took considerable flak was evidence of a belief in one's own invincibility. Were he to have been in any way culpable then the charge that he was a reactive, rather than a constructive, narcissist might have some validity, since reactive narcissists expect favourable treatment and believe themselves subject to a different set of rules from those which apply to others. On the whole, however, Lord King's legacy to British business has been one of highly successful and enduring organizations. Seldom can a true reactive narcissist make such a claim.

Arguably, the most striking recent example of an excess of self-belief and an absence of self-awareness from modern times is Lord King's friend, Margaret Thatcher. Geoffrey Howe summed up her unshakeable belief in herself thus: 'The insistence on the undivided sovereignty of her opinion, dressed up as the nation's sovereignty, was her undoing.' In his essay on 'Self-Reliance' he declares: 'To believe your own thought, to believe that what is true for you in your private heart is true for all men – that is genius'. Anthony Storr, commenting on this view in his study of gurus, notes that this is not genius but narcissism, 'self-absorption hovering on the brink of madness'.[3] Baroness Thatcher's narcissism was, ultimately, both the single greatest cause of her success and of her downfall – a poisoned chalice.

The constructive narcissist is not too far distant from the charismatic leader and the charismatic leader can just as easily be a fiend as a friend, can be inspired or deluded. The notion of charisma derives from the work of Max Weber, a German-born political scientist who developed his theory of charisma in *Wirtschaft und Gesellschaft* (*Economy and Society*) in the first half of this century. Weber uses the term 'charisma' to refer to the impact of a new belief system on social life. The concept, which derives from the notion of the 'gift of grace', has its origin in major cultural shifts such as the development away from polytheism to monotheism, or Judaism to Christianity, but is equally applicable to less seismic cultural changes. In the strictest sense Jesus Christ would qualify as a charismatic leader, as would, to cite one of Weber's own examples, Bismarck. Put in simplest terms, a charismatic leader is one who by virtue of his or her new ideas can bring about a significant cultural change. Weber is at pains to stress that the term must be used in a value-free sense. Charisma exists where it is proven in the eyes of adherents. Thus Weber concedes that the Mormons and the ecstatic shamans must be held to be charismatic, because of the effect on their followers. In this way charisma can work as easily to the bad as to the good; hence Hitler qualifies as a charismatic leader.

A charismatic leader, in order to be so constituted, must have a band of followers who, by adherence to the leader, are elevated from the mass of mankind to become an élite central group (rather like Jesus's disciples or Hitler's inner sanctum of Goering, Goebbels, Heydrick, Himmler and Bormann). The charismatic leader has unshakeable belief in his own ability to take decisions which are right, and he communicates that belief to others who accept its justice. Norbert Elias takes up Weber's theme and likens the charismatic leader to a figure riding on thin ice:

> If he reaches the other side, there are many historians who, showing the common inclination to equate success with personal greatness, will credit him with an extraordinary gift of doing the right thing in difficult situations. If the ice breaks, drowning him and his followers, he is likely to pass into history as an unsuccessful adventurer. The ability of such people to transmit to others their unshakeable belief in their own gift of taking correct decisions, is one of the means by which the central group is cemented together despite all the rivalries and conflicts of interest.[4]

The charismatic leader's conviction or self-belief is merely an intuition and the charismatic leader is someone who takes repeated incalculable risks. Strictly speaking, a truly charismatic business leader is not one who takes the helm of a large going concern and maintains it in its original form. A charismatic business leader is a chief executive who assumes his position at a time when the organization needs to undergo extraordinary change and, quite simply, transforms the business. Weber notes: 'In its genuine form charismatic rule has a specifically extraordinary character.' Bureaucracies and corporate structures are intolerant of too much diversity and so relatively few charismatic leaders emerge from this source. Entrepreneurs are more likely to qualify as charismatic since they create the new from nothing but their personal vision, often from nothing much beyond their personality. Robert Maxwell was as much a charismatic leader – given that it is a value-free term – as is Richard Branson.

In the political sphere Nelson Mandela is undoubtedly a charismatic leader. Neal Ascherson wrote of him: 'Nelson Mandela is where a man and a slogan meet. While he was kept on Robben Island his name travelled all over the world as a hieroglyph meaning freedom. He was a street and a square in a dozen cities, a song in many languages, a bronze head on embankments, a block of flats, a T-Shirt.' And in the same way, Margaret Thatcher must be accorded due status as a charismatic leader for, however much we doubt the longevity of her political achievements, she did bring about a sea change in the attitude of the British people. Indeed, as American student of leadership Howard Gardner observes: 'Thatcher changed the terms of the debate in her own country.'[5] Deeply flawed perhaps, narcissistic certainly, but in fairness we must accord Margaret Thatcher the judgment that she is charismatic.

The hubris implicit in Margaret Thatcher's career is very much in line with Nietzsche's conception of the heroic personality (and Nietzsche was a significant influence on Max Weber). This nineteenth-century German philosopher conceived the Uebermensch, literally the Overman, as the heroic model for a secular age. The Overman is an ideal, never reached but always striven for, and Napoleon, one of Nietzsche's heroes, wins the philosopher's regard because he strove to improve himself, created himself in a heroic mould, despite the fact that ultimately he became corrupted by his own desire for power. The quest for heroism inevitably involves self-destruction through over-reaching, over-ambition. The struggle, however, is more important than the outcome.

Nietzsche saw the construction of a persona of power as an artistic act:

> To give style to one's character – a great and rare art! He exercises it who surveys all that his nature presents in strength and weakness and then moulds to an artistic plan until everything appears as art and reason, and even the weaknesses delight the eye . . . It will be the strong, imperious natures which experience their subtlest joy in exercising such control, in such constraint.

Some leaders, as in the case of Saddam Hussein, create a mythology for themselves which bears little or no relation to their actual antecedents and personal history, the way Jimmy Gatz turns himself into the splendid and enigmatic Jay Gatsby in Fitzgerald's novel. Most leaders construct a style for themselves which is less flamboyant but which noticeably sets them at a distance from the mass of mankind. They perform, play a part and keep protected the most private parts of themselves. One of the most noticeable things about the business leaders I have encountered is their extraordinary capacity for self-control. Most are highly self-contained, the very antithesis of flamboyant. Indeed, business leaders frequently appear cold and remote.

Clive Thompson, the Chairman of Rentokil and of the Confederation of British Industry, is formal in manner. His interests focus largely on business. He keeps himself very much to himself, resisting an entry in *Who's Who*. He is not a man after celebrity, so much as success. Lord McLaurin is smooth and polished and there are few cracks in the persona. Indeed, his degree of control can seem artificial and one unkind journalist was moved to describe him as 'like one of those perfectly designed Thunderbird characters'. McLaurin's career has been spent in what for some long period was the family business (now a quoted company). It was not the family business into which he was born but into which he married. Founders of businesses are notoriously protective of their baby and too much pushiness or overt ambition on the part of the aspiring heir can lead to loss of favour. Similarly, in a business where several peers are jockeying for position it is easy to spot and neutralize the boisterous and the loud. The discreet, more withdrawn candidates are left to prosper quietly.

Lord Marshall, Chairman of British Airways, has been described as 'bionic' but Lord King, who recruited him into BA, says that 'he's a quiet man, but most powerful'. The two who built British Airways into one of Britain's pre-eminent businesses have been described as polar opposites: 'Where Lord King was rumbustious, self-opinionated and very much a personality-orientated businessman, Marshall was straightforward, efficient and a very hard worker.' Others, less charitably, have described Marshall as a man who could make an iceberg seem radiant. Together King and Marshall became a rounded personality with the appropriate blend of management and leadership skills. Marshall's apparent deficit of personality compensated for King's superabundance.

Niall FitzGerald, Joint Chairman of Unilever, has described his former colleague, now the chairman of ICI, Charles Miller-Smith, as: 'a modest self-contained man who speaks his mind when he has to and keeps quiet the rest of the time'. McLaurin, Marshall and Miller-Smith have an air of the non-committal about them. They leave themselves open to change but ensure that they are not in a position to be hostage to fortune. They are watchful and alert. There is a certain tension about them, as if a large amount of energy is being restrained like a coiled spring.

Energy is undoubtedly a characteristic that business leaders seem to share. Most put in long hours (eighty or ninety hour weeks are far from unusual) in the service of the company and rise at dawn in order to do so. The early rising on the part of business leaders is part of a more generalized disciplining of the body. Sir John Egan, jogs two miles around Regent's Park each morning prior to going to the Victoria offices of BAA (British Airports Authority, formerly), an organization which he has made into, arguably, the most successful of Britain's privatized businesses. Lord Marshall, in his sixties, still plays tennis and skis. A life of international meetings, punitive travel schedules and the requirement for considerable after-hours socializing – the lot of the average chief executive of a premier business – is not for the weak-willed, the faint-hearted or the less than fit.

It is not, however, simply a matter of keeping the body in trim for the lifestyle. These chief executives have a compulsion or fanaticism about them. They must be the best. Larry Ellison of Oracle is driven more than most. A few years ago he suffered a bicycling accident that left his elbow and arm shattered. It was thought unlikely that he would ever regain use of the limb. Ellison put himself through a gruelling weight-training campaign which, according to his doctor, would 'break anyone but an élite athlete'. Self-belief can, also, slip into self-regard and vanity. These driven, highly successful men will not let themselves fall short of the highest standards. Indeed, Ellison finds it irksome to come second to Bill Gates at Microsoft and has an almost obsessive rivalry with him. Perhaps it is this rivalry which motivates his interest in Apple, which has developed the only rival to Microsoft's Windows package?

Prodigious energy combined with remorseless self-discipline is not, of course, confined to business leaders. Twenty-seven years in prison accustomed Nelson Mandela to a spartan regime. He used to wake at 4.30 a.m. Now he allows himself a lie in until 5.00 a.m. He used to enjoy a morning jog but, in the interests of security, has had to compromise on an exercise bike – this in a man in his eighties. Mandela also shares the trait of extraordinary self-containment. Ahmed Kathrada, who shared a prison cell with him for seven years, reports that he and Walter Sisulu had sometimes to force Mandela to stop reading and talk to them.

These highly self-contained individuals share a common temperament in that they are introverts. Introversion and extraversion, despite being words in common parlance, are concepts of very modern derivation, arising from Carl Jung's interpretation of the conflicting work of Freud and Adler. The extravert is someone who is in search of others, the introvert someone needing to establish autonomy and independence and so more likely, left to themselves, to shy away from people. Most people incline towards one or other of the two temperamental types, although by far the majority are extraverted, or energized by others. A mere 25 per cent of the population are introverted. Perhaps this explains why we place so much focus on the importance of interpersonal relationships, on sharing and empathizing with others?

Leaders can rarely afford to be too close to those they command. Leadership is based on one individual having authority over others and that authority, while it must involve mutual respect, is not at all about equality. Leadership is about superiority. One person stands above the rest. To maintain that superiority the leader cannot be known too closely. His humanity and fallibility should not be a matter of public knowledge. For the extravert leader who craves the presence of others the maintenance of a proper guard cannot be easy. Leaders are faced with difficult choices, are obliged to make decisions which will not be universally popular. The best leaders are often those who stand apart.

Two American presidents famous for their singular distance from others are Woodrow Wilson and Abraham Lincoln. Wilson, in a moving address about Lincoln, perhaps showed more about his own introversion than that of the man he describes. Either way it is a fascinating insight into introversion, solitude and leadership:

> I nowhere get the impression in any narrative or reminiscence [of Lincoln] that the writer had in fact penetrated to the heart of his mystery, or that any man could penetrate to the heart of it. That brooding spirit has no real familiars. I get the impression that it never spoke out in complete self-revelation, and that it could not reveal itself completely to anyone. It was a very lonely spirit that looked out from underneath those shaggy brows and comprehended men without fully communing with them, as if, in spite of all its genial efforts at comradeship, it dwelt apart, saw its visions of duty where no man looked on. There is a very holy and very terrible isolation for the conscience of every man who seeks to read the destiny in affairs for others as well as for himself, for a nation as well as for individuals. That privacy no man can intrude upon. That lonely search of the spirit for the right perhaps no man can assist.

Wilson saw, as Lincoln before him undoubtedly had seen also, the extraordinary weight of responsibility that comes with presidential office and must set the bearer apart. Leaders who make judgements that will affect hundreds of thousands, as did Wilson's neutral stance on the First World War, cannot do so in the midst of the mêlée. They require distance, perspective and space. Architects of a nation's destiny, they must brood upon it much as an artist on his canvas.

Many cultures have accorded the head of state a divine right to rule. Certainly the British Civil War was fought, in part, over this issue. The head of state has a certain divinity by dint of the God-like power and authority which automatically sets them apart and it is useful – perhaps necessary – that their characters be so constructed as to enable them to tolerate their distance and solitude. Indeed, instinctively we cast those who sit in judgment over us in similarly quasi-divine positions. Popular culture, usually an excellent barometer of popular attitudes, routinely casts its detectives as somewhat difficult personalities who stand apart from the greater part of humanity, dealing in truth and rejecting false-hood, rewarding good and punishing bad. From Sherlock Holmes to Inspector Morse, our detectives are almost invariably unmarried, irascible, introverted, emotionally troubled but ineffably right.

A position of judgment must preclude personal involvement. It is acceptable for a leader to make 'genial efforts at comradeship', but to be a true comrade while also a leader, to be equal while also superior, is impossible. Leaders are obliged to dispense with the services of close allies or associates, as John Major famously dispensed with the services of his Chancellor Norman Lamont (now Lord Lamont). Lord Marshall in his role as chairman of Inchcape was obliged to oust the chief executive, Charles Mackay, who had brought him on to the board in the first place. These cannot have been easy decisions, but neither a prime minister nor a chairman can afford sentiment. It is the chairman's duty, along with the non-executive or outside directors, to ensure that the chief executive is doing a good job and, if he is not, to remove him. Lord Marshall would have failed in his role as chairman to pursue any other course. It cannot have been an easy decision, but would have been infinitely harder for an extravert, who takes succour from relations with others.

An introvert is not someone who is unable to perform. On the contrary, an introvert can sometimes perform unusually well – but it will sap the introvert's energies to play to a public. Tom Peters, management guru, is just such an introvert who delivers an outstanding lecture but having done so, needs to sleep for a substantial period to recover. Peters, like other introverts, is energized by the act of demonstrating his particular expertise, not by the act of performance *per se*. At the head of this chapter I have used a reference to great conductors. I take issue with the notion that the introverted conductor becomes extravert through the medium of the music. Once an introvert always an introvert; the conductor is energized, fulfilled and realized by the demonstration of that expertise.

Introverts are in the minority in terms of the overall population. Extreme introverts are rarer still and, as with most extremes, liable to be seen as odd, abnormal, even mad. Two cases of scientific introverts, separated by several centuries, but in other ways not unlike are Sir Isaac Newton and Bill Gates. Isaac Newton was an unpopular child, given to solitary pursuits: 'he was always a sober, silent, thinking lad, and was never known scarce to play with the boys abroad, at their silly amusements'. Bill Gates, similarly, was a rather solitary child given to acquiring extraordinary expertise, which gave him the reputation for being a know-all, and a former school fellow described him as 'very easy to sort of dislike'.

At one point in his childhood, the precociously bright Gates was sent to a child psychiatrist. This led to him being sent to a special school which, ahead of its time, had introduced computer studies. His computer teacher said he taught Gates all he knew and that it took about a week. Gates then learned his computer skills for himself. By the time he left school he had written a computer programme to produce the school's timetables (which is still in use); set up his own software firm to process traffic statistics; been employed by a defence contractor in Vancouver to sort out bugs in their computer; and, in the process, made a significant sum of money. At nineteen he founded Microsoft.

Isaac Newton went to a school where his genius was recognized but where scant mathematics was taught. Newton taught himself mathematics and reached the frontier of the subject, developing within four years both the differential and the integral calculus. Had he been a young man in the twentieth century he would doubtless, rather like Gates, have been something of a computer nerd. Certainly, in his absorption in his work, Newton gave little care to his person: 'So intent, so serious upon his studies that he ate very sparingly, nay, ofttimes he has forgot to eat at all, so that, going into his chamber, I have found his mess untouched, of which, when I have reminded him, he would reply – 'Have I!' and then, making to the table, would eat a bit or two standing, for I cannot say I ever saw him sit at table by himself . . . He very rarely went to bed till two or three of the clock, sometimes not until five or six.'

In the past most profiles we read of Bill Gates have focused on the man's lack of attention to his person – he is routinely described as grubby and untidy and accused of paying limited attention to personal hygiene. He has cleaned his act up somewhat, perhaps under the influence of his wife ('being single takes up a lot of time'). The more malicious have described him as verging on the autistic, and certainly he finds eye contact difficult and is given, while talking, to rocking or tapping his foot on the floor frenziedly. Newton in his middle years experienced a period of psychosis and paranoia and throughout life was very reluctant to concede any intellectual debt to others. He needed to feel in absolute control over his environment.

Control is important to Gates. Observes note that it would make sense for him to break up Microsoft into business units and conclude that he does not do this because he does not want to lose control. And Gates certainly has control, not just of Microsoft but of its sector, over which his company has a virtual stranglehold. Newton was one of the greatest thinkers the world has ever known. Gates does not rival Newton intellectually but in his own sphere of business he is a giant, currently one of the richest men in the world, and certainly the richest in America. Both men are classic, extreme introverts, whose satisfaction in life derives not from others but from their own expertise.

There are various methods by which psychological types can be identified which, broadly speaking, correlate closely with Jung's distinction between introvert and extrovert. In his fascinating study *Solitude*, Anthony Storr[6] offers a gloss of what these are. The notion of divergers and convergers derives from a study of clever schoolchildren which determined genuine differences between the scientist and the artist. To paraphrase, convergers favour the hard sciences or, curiously, classics. They are comfortable with questions to which there is a clear and unambiguous answer. Convergers' hobbies are likely to be mechanical or technical. They tend to be very little interested in other people, to have quite conventional attitudes to authority, and can be emotionally inhibited. Divergers, on the other hand, will choose arts subjects or, perhaps, biology, prefer open-ended questions to which they can apply their imagination, and tend, in their spare time, to engage with people rather than things. The converger/introvert and diverger/extravert parallels do not, apparently, hold up to extensive testing but convergers and introverts alike are 'more at ease with inanimate objects or with abstract concepts than they are with people'.

Perhaps business particularly lends itself to the converger/introvert type? We have established that business might lend itself to older children because it is, essentially, conservative and follows a fairly traditional hierarchical structure. Perhaps, for similar reasons, it appeals to the introvert. And yet surely running a business has a great deal to do with motivating people? Doesn't that suggest that extraverts, those who empathize with people, are the more likely to make good business leaders? Interestingly, some of the introverts we have considered above seem to have no problem with motivating a mass of people. The culture that Bill Gates has developed at Microsoft is very open, very 'touchy-feely', with a campus feel to it. Gates is known as Bill by all, and there is little formality about the place, the dress code is famously relaxed and, even, nerdy (short sleeves, open-toed sandals), a far cry from the buttoned-up corporate style of many hugely successful organizations.

Lord Marshall, he of the iceberg chilliness, was the brains and the heart behind 'Putting people first', the campaign that was integral to the extraordinary change of culture at British Airways. His staff have always regarded Marshall as a very human business leader. Human, but none the less a little distant for all that. Motivating a team is not, after all, about developing excellent relationships with each and every member of that team. On the contrary, motivating a team relies upon the leader of that team maintaining distance. The novelist, E. M. Forster, wrote of T. E. Lawrence's extraordinary ability to invite the confidences of others without any need or expectation of reciprocity: 'Though I was frank with him, he was never frank in return, nor did I resent his refusal to be so. This explains in part why he was a great leader of men: he was able to reject intimacy without impairing affection.'

Leadership is about mystique: we want to be known by our leaders but we do not necessarily want to know them in return. The distance implicit in their personality and approach to us confirms their distance from us as individuals and the justice of their position of judgement over us.

Inspiring people is, ironically, a much more abstract skill than would appear probable. According to the converger/diverger dichotomy it is the converger/introvert who is at ease with the abstract and with the technical or mechanical. Put crudely, the workforce is an integral part of the organizational machine. Motivating that workforce is, then, a technical skill. Even looking at the human aspects of business leadership it emerges that business suits the introvert. Seen in this light business becomes much more of a science than an art and the likeness between Gates and

Newton, exemplars of business and science respectively, seems more explicable.

A point not yet mentioned is the apparent predisposition of leaders to periods of manic depression, intense mood swings, and here I feel I must see a distinction between the greatness of a conductor referred to at the start of the chapter and that of a business leader. Anthony Storr gives us an excellent description of someone suffering mania or depression:

> 'A person in the throes of mania or deep depression is usually unable to produce work of any value. Restlessness, inability to concentrate, the rapid 'flight of ideas' in mania make sustained work impossible. Retardation of thought processes, feelings of hopelessness and helplessness, the belief that nothing is worthwhile undertaking, the conviction that anything which is produced will be valueless all serve to prevent the severely depressed person from being creative.'[7]

Dr Storr goes on to point out that, paradoxically, very many highly creative people are prone to precisely these symptoms.

There is, however, a marked distinction that can be drawn between creative people and those who are in a position of leadership at the head of a company. Quite simply, a chief executive must be in a position where sustained work is entirely possible. A writer or an artist does not cease being either of those things because, for a period, they experience a creative block brought about by depression. A chief executive who cannot work ceases to be a chief executive. The parallel I see between the great conductor and the chief executive must then be a little more fluid.

There is, of course, an exception to every rule. Ted Turner has been treated with lithium for a mild case of manic depression. The periods of frenetic activity which characterize the condition from which he suffers have coincided with his more ambitious deal-doing. In Turner's case, mental illness does not appear to have impeded his success. Alternatively, modern medicine has kept it in check. As a young man and in the wake of his father's suicide, Turner often used to talk about suicide and behaved with utter recklessness. Without lithium, it is possible that his mood swings would have governed and destroyed him.

Business leaders divert from the norm, often simply to the extent that whatever they feel or do they do on a grand scale. Some, given power, seem driven to abuse it. One highly charismatic leader I have come across is a strong and intuitive judge of people but not one to confront an issue directly. Instead, where he has an issue with an individual he will tackle it obliquely and, in the process, substantially undermine the confidence and capability of the person who has caused him to doubt, leading him to conclude that his suspicions were correct. This mental cruelty, for such it was, was brought about by the chairman's need to test his intuition. (He used to interrogate the direct reports of the chief executive, whom he did not entirely trust, to such an extent that the mistrust was shared. The chief executive found himself under attack from above and below and saw the connivance between the two levels and, understandably, buckled under the strain.) This particular chairman is not the only business leader I have come across who sets out to create tension and discomfiture. I have sat in a meeting on more than one occasion with another chairman whose meeting room had no fewer than five doors opening into it. Invariably during the course of a meeting someone would issue through one of the doors, but rarely would someone come through the same door twice. It made for an unsettling atmosphere and I had the feeling that I was sitting in the middle of a French farce for which no one had given me the script.

At their worst business leaders enjoy their ability to manipulate a situation or an individual. I have observed a situation where the lover of a chief executive prevailed upon him to give her cuckolded husband a seat on the board. He did so and derived, I think, a rather dubious satisfaction from this corporate *ménage à trois*. Of course, power is a heady aphrodisiac and I have known deeply unprepossessing business leaders whose power and unshakeable self-belief makes them of devastating appeal to women and enables them to engage in a thoroughly promiscuous lifestyle. Perhaps there is nothing so very odd in any of these behavioural traits. Perhaps it is normal to want to behave in this way, merely relatively abnormal to have the opportunity. Power of course brings with it abundant possibility. Leaders may be many things but they need not be particularly honourable or moral. The sexual profligacy of John F. Kennedy has not, ultimately, greatly reduced his stature in the eyes of most Americans. Opinion divides about Bill Clinton but, if the polls are any measure at all, his personal conduct has not shaken his popularity.

Modern leadership is not something that the majority of people would wish for. In this media age even comparatively minor leaders, business leaders, for instance, exist entirely in the public domain. It takes extraordinary courage to withstand this scrutiny, and uncommon strength of personality. It also takes extraordinary desire to undertake a leadership role. Political leaders may well aspire to lead their country from a motive of national pride or duty just as religious leaders are driven by deep beliefs and missionary fervour. Mixed in with these virtuous sentiments are more mercenary ones. Many leaders seek status and authority over others. Some simply enjoy the exercise of power for its own sake. Others have a vain, if fairly innocent, desire to be remembered by posterity. Business leaders are, not infrequently, mercenary in the true sense of the word: they crave money. In the final analysis, business is about money. It is about generating wealth and gaining a good return on investment. One thing that *must* drive businessmen and women is the simple profit principle. Sir James Goldsmith balked at those who made any alternative claim regarding their motives in business. Speaking of corporate raiders, he said they 'shouldn't put on a halo. They are doing it for personal gain'. Some business leaders are uncompromising in their pursuit of personal wealth. All leaders are uncompromising in pursuit of their personal vision. Modern leadership requires a degree of oddity, even zealotry. We may not altogether like the personalities of those who lead us, even while we follow them. The price we have to pay in order to have leaders among us is a certain indulgence, a degree of compromise towards these extremes of personality.

NOTES

1 David Cannadine, *The Pleasures of the Past*, Penguin Books, 1997.
2 Manfred F. R. Kets de Vries, *The Leadership Mystique*, essay in *Leadership: Classical, Contemporary and Critical Approaches*, edited by Keith Grint, Oxford University Press, 1997.
3 Anthony Storr, *Feet of Clay*, Harper Collins, 1997.
4 Norbert Elias, *The Court Society*, translated by Edmund Jephcott, Basil Blackwell, 1983.

5 *Leading Minds: An Anatomy of Leadership* by Howard Gardner in collaboration with Emma Laskin, Harper Collins, 1997.

6 In both *Solitude*, published 1997 by Harper Collins, and *Churchill's Black Dog*, published 1997 by Harper Collins, Anthony Storr writes extensively about the psyche of Sir Isaac Newton and my information on Newton derives from these sources.

7 Anthony Storr, *Solitude*, p. 143.

Chapter 4

The Leader Who Came in From the Cold: The Leader as Outsider

'All men dream: but not equally. Those who dream by night in the dusty recesses of their minds wake in the day to find that it was vanity: but the dreamers of the day are dangerous men, for they may act their dream with open eyes to make it possible.' – T. E. Lawrence, *Seven Pillars of Wisdom*

Leaders may seem remote from us by dint of their personality. Equally, they seem remote because their experience is entirely unlike our own, or that of the prevailing group. They are frequently outsiders who stand apart, looking on. All communities have their outsiders. These are people who by temperament or training are at a remove and have, at best, an ambivalent attitude to the group. They value their difference which in part defines their identity but want, also, to be valued by the group. Often, it is not enough to be valued equally. Outsiders frequently want to be the most valued member of the group. This inner tension or desire to be both on the inside and the outside is often at the heart of a leader's psyche. The dream of ultimate approval by the group is often the dream that a leader will dream with his eyes open.

One of the precepts that underpins Western philosophic thought is that man's fundamental need for recognition provides the animus for action. This need separates man from beast. Indeed, it is implicit in one of the three parts of the soul defined by Plato in the *Republic* by the term *thymos*. This translates, rather unsatisfactorily, as 'spiritedness' but is taken by commentators to refer to the sense of value man demands both in the sense of self-esteem and of recognition by others. A desire to lead, in Platonic terms, at least, is a natural, admirable quality. The other two parts of the soul in Plato's famous tripartite division are *reason* and *desire*. The need for recognition is something distinct, then, from reason. It is irrational, an emotional requirement, perhaps, rather than an intellectual choice. This need also extends beyond the individual to those institutions with which the individual is connected, so in the *Republic* the class of the guardians who will defend the city are imbued with a sense of public-spiritedness, a pride in what is theirs and in themselves. Religion and nationalism are both passions rooted in man's *thymos*, his sense of pride in himself and in what he holds dear.

For much of history this sense of pride was seen as something of an aristocratic virtue, and the thirst for glory sat with princes and kings. Louis XIV explicitly expresses the sentiment: 'The love of gloire surpasses all others in my soul . . . The ardour of my age and the violent desire I had to increase my reputation gave me a strong desire for action . . .' A need for recognition, writ large as a desire for glory, is historically the stuff of which leaders are made. Kings like Louis XIV were, of course, absolute monarchs and they ruled without recourse to elected representatives. They saw themselves as superior beings and needed to be recognized as such. Modern thought disdains such élitism. Rousseau saw a need for glory or recognition as mere vanity or *amour-propre*.

The philosophers whose theories lie behind the development of liberal democracies, Hobbes and Locke, took exception to the notion of a need for recognition, focusing instead on the importance of desire and reason to the exclusion of the need for glory. Hobbes put forward the view that governments' legitimacy derives not from any divine right of kings, or the natural superiority of those in power, but from the rights of those people who are subject to the government. One of the principal natural rights of man was the right to material comfort. This rational desire was to take over from the irrational desire to gain recognition and be seen to be a superior being. So societies' values turned away from great acts by great men and towards a series of smaller acts by smaller men leading to the greater good of many.

Francis Fukuyama, an American economist and commentator on modern society, identifies two types of *thymos*. The first, isothymia, is the desire to be recognized as the equal of other people, the form of *thymos* that Hobbes and Locke, presumably, would have found most acceptable. The second, megalothymia, is the desire to be recognized as superior to other people. In a century which has been dominated by tyrants enslaved to megalothymia it is small wonder that Western society, at least, now celebrates the isothymic to the exclusion of the megalothymic notion. Indeed Western governments are tightly constrained by institutions designed to protect the populace against any megalothymia on the part of the powerful.

The punk rock era gave us the refrain 'No more heroes any more', and the assertion would appear to have some validity. We are living in the post-modern era which eschews the big idea, rejects all attempts to universalize and calls into question the notion of a single reality. It is concerned instead with pluralism and pastiche, with proliferation and the populist. Post-modernism's fundamental distrust of totalizing concepts in favour of an insistence on fragmentation and a multiplicity of perspectives militates against heroes. In the post-war period we have, of course, seen political heroes. Mahatma Gandhi, Nelson Mandela, Martin Luther King have all been heroes who unite behind the banner of freedom, fighting for those two great tenets of liberal democracy – liberty and equality. Their heroic status derives, too, from the fact that they have stood up against the big, bad ideas of this and the previous centuries: colonialism, nationalism and racism (all instances of instutionalized, cultural megalothymia).

By and large, however, heroism is out of fashion. The super hero who espouses any form of moral certitude, who embodies universalizing or totalizing values, is banished from the post-modern epoch. Now is the age of the little man. Superman is an ordinary figure who occasionally does superhuman things. In the period immediately before the First World War English society valorized Captain Scott, whose ill-fated expedition to the South Pole caught the public imagination. He embodied courage, endurance and humanity. Perhaps because the carnage of the First World War gave first-hand experience of courage and endurance to millions and proved that the experience was neither beautiful nor ennobling, these exemplary figures lost their allure. We are more likely, today, to revere the peak of fitness maintained by a mountaineer than the heroic courage he or she demonstrates in scaling a particular peak. Indeed, we expect our manufactured heroes to embody quite shallow values. Hence a record company can take a group of girls and dub them Scary, Sporty, Baby, Posh and Ginger Spice, bedeck them in ordinariness and enrich them beyond their wildest dreams. We connive, in short, in a dumbing down of our heroes. We even rob them of their given names in favour of names which are emblematic of not very much.

The Spice Girls have probably had their fifteen minutes of fame. Our age has, however, created more enduring icons (icons, note, not heroes). Madonna, for instance, is a self-manufactured truly post-modern heroine for our times. Defined by her name, she has constructed a reality for herself as a sexual icon which makes her name as a description of her identity neatly oxymoronic and paradoxical. Perpetually reinventing herself, she is redolent of change, uncertainty, statement and counter-statement. Like other stars of our age she embodies a kind of ironic inversion and as a heroine she is an insubstantial, immaterial girl of our times.

For all the ironic inversion, Madonna is one of the few superstars who is fairly unashamedly megalothymic. She may be iconic of every woman but she is nevertheless concerned with being the best. Perhaps for this reason we delight in debunking her, as, routinely, the modern press seems to debunk anyone who appears to assert a form of authority. In these modern times leadership is a more frightening prospect than ever before. The modern media waits to prey on the most minor celebrity and leaders must risk the style and substance of their leadership being under continual scrutiny and discussion. In an age when a fall from grace can be broadcast across the information superhighway it would scarcely be surprising if future leaders *manqué* chose to remain in the byways of history. As Thomas Carlyle said: 'happy the people whose annals are blank in history books'.

The prevailing attitudes of our society towards those who set themselves up as superior to others (a mixture of awe, envy and resentment) might militate against the emergence of more leaders. In reality, these conditions simply require people with an even greater megalothymic urge than previously. In short, the second half of the twentieth century has provided a forum in which the person with little to lose and much to gain, the individual with a need to get on to get even, is more likely to prosper in the leadership stakes than the scion of the establishment. This has been the age of the outsider, like none other.

In 1956 Colin Wilson wrote *The Outsider*, a stimulating study in which, in essence, he reviews the outsider as he has appeared in literature and as he is embodied in a handful of notable people. Wilson defines the outsider as one who stands outside the normal run of people because he does not accept the given, he is forever interested in forging the new. He is like Nietzsche's Uebermensch, intent upon pushing himself forward, extending and over-extending himself. The self is his laboratory and he must explore its limits – both positive and negative. He has the capability to be a prophet or a saint but might, just as easily, be damned. In his summary of Hesse's *Steppenwolf* Wilson writes:

> . . . the Outsider is the mainstay of the bourgeois. Without him the bourgeois could not exist. The vitality of the ordinary members of society is dependent on its Outsiders. Many Outsiders unify themselves, realize themselves as poets or saints. Others remain tragically divided and unproductive, but even they supply soul-energy to society; it is their strenuousness that purifies thought and prevents the bourgeois world from foundering under its own dead-weight; they are society's spiritual dynamos.

The outsider is a particularly fitting construct for the post-modern age, for outsiders, by Wilson's definition, construct themselves, they work on themselves either individually or collectively. Madonna is, without question, an outsider by Wilson's terms. The eldest daughter of a large Catholic family who lost their mother young (Madonna was just five), it was she who took over mothering the others. The parental role did not sit easily on an adolescent who was by nature a rebel, and she set out to remove herself from a life of drudgery and take on a life of stardom. Her life has been ruthlessly planned and her persona as meticulously constructed.

Wilson deals with individuals but there are entire groups which identify themselves in opposition to prevailing norms and play with fixed assumptions about reality. The gay community in particular has proven excellent at inverting the norms of society and playing back to the mainstream its assumptions, subtly rewritten, about those whose sexuality sets them apart. Heterosexual responses to the gay community have often assumed that gay men are effeminate. In the period of Village People and Frankie Goes to Hollywood the gay community developed an image for itself which took a stock image of machismo and inverted it. Hence for a while there was a recognizable gay uniform of a small moustache, cropped hair and leathers known, colloquially, as a 'clone'.

The gay community offers an interesting paradigm of a group which has been set on the margins of society but which seems to have generated many of society's great figures. Homosexuality has not been outlawed in all cultures. The ancient Greeks regarded same-gender sex as another norm, coexisting easily with heterosexuality. It has, however, been very recently that homosexuality has become acceptable in most Western cultures. Even where homosexuality is legal, it remains troublesome for some people. The extraordinary attempt to identify AIDS as a gay plague shows the extent to which homosexuality remains beyond the pale – or threatening – to many. Today there is a recognizable gay community with a clear voice. For much of history homosexual men have been without a public voice. Very often gay men (and women) have been called upon to disguise their sexual preferences and frequently marry and bear children. They have been required to pretend and to dissemble and to become excellent mimics.

The sphere in which homosexuality seems most common is the artistic. Art usually observes life and offers some form of commentary upon it. Those already on the outside because of their sexual preferences have, perhaps, certain advantages as observers. If they must conform to the prevailing social mores of their cultures gay persons must observe the habits and gestures of the people they will be obliged to emulate with minute attention. The pay-off may be a capacity to render that observation in some artefact. Perhaps one of the world's most sustained pieces of observation is Marcel Proust's À La Récherche du Temps Perdu – penned by a gay man from his sick bed at a remove from the world. It is not just the repressed gay who has access to this vision. One of America's greatest living writers and commentators, indeed the chronicler of modern America, Gore Vidal, who is out, brings a clarity of vision that may derive from that distance which is a consequence of being in a sexual minority.

Being on the sexual margins may lend gay people acute observation skills, and the ability to emphasize and to understand suffering which can be important skills for an artist. That so many gay people in history have been engaged in the arts may say as much about the tolerance of the art world – in its broadest sense – as it does about individual artists. Those who engage in art, music, literature, the visual arts, are concerned with pushing boundaries, with exploration and with the new. They are, as a result, tolerant, broad-minded and open and receptive to difference. Hence artists have found it easier to acknowledge their homosexuality.

It may be the case that gay people have been drawn towards the arts. Equally, however, there can be little doubt that gay people occupy positions of power and influence in other spheres of life. They must, however, be much harder to identify. In British politics there have recently been a couple of notable and highly controversial 'outings'. No doubt this is not the first time in history that the Cabinet has included several gay ministers, although it must be the first time that revelations about the homosexuality of a minister not noted for his popularity have led to widespread public support for that minister.

Corporations are not places that are naturally responsive to different lifestyles. Gay people – and of course there are gay people operating extremely successfully in a number of corporations – do not broadcast their sexual identity but suppress it. They find elaborate excuses as to why they never bring their partner to the Christmas party and avoid close discussions of what they did at the weekend. Gay people who lead double lives – out during their leisure time but firmly in the closet during working hours – have some of the watchfulness which I have described in artists. They also have some of the fierce drive that comes as a natural by-product of being outside for an entirely arbitrary reason. The injustice of prejudice against homosexuality must be a driver to some who respond by a determination to get even and, perhaps, ahead of heterosexual peers. Sometimes, being gay can facilitate success. Heterosexual couples have the diversion of children and family life to consider and cannot be as flexible in the hours they devote or their freedom to travel. I would hazard a guess that gay people are more likely to be advisers to corporates than corporate animals themselves. In this way they can maintain a certain distance and maximize the benefits of being, already, on the outside.

The value of an outside view, an external perspective, is of course broadly acknowledged in society and in business. The role of a broker is one that many cultures know, the marriage broker or matchmaker being a figure who has had tremendous influence at a social level in the past. Any institution can benefit from external advice, from the view of an impartial adviser, particularly at times of crisis. Management consultancy, for instance, has enjoyed its ascendancy in part because of the recognition that it is not always possible to be objective from within an institution and that people from outside might be better placed to understand a complicated dynamic within which so-called insiders may be implicated. Of course management consultancies are also important because of their ability to harness some of the best brains of each generation and train them in sophisticated problem-solving techniques, but this does not diminish the importance of their objectivity. Counselling and therapy have become an accepted part of modern stressful living in which individuals turn to strangers for support in crisis. This is true in marriage, an institution which would not be thought likely to withstand intrusion by a third party. If that third party is an impartial counsellor, then a marriage that is on the rocks can be salvaged, given the benefit of an independent adviser and arbitrator.

Nowhere in business is the benefit of an external perspective acknowledged more overtly than in the hiring of non-executive directors to the boards of public companies. In the United States the non-executive director is actually known as an outside director, and the corporate governance debate that wages on both sides of the Atlantic and is gaining force in continental Europe places emphasis on the value of an outside view precisely for its independence. These part-time directors who will, in the UK, typically attend some eight to ten board meetings a year, are mandated to represent the interests of the shareholders but should not be allowed to be mere watchdogs or whistleblowers. Instead, they can be highly creative, contributing to debates about strategy, performance measurement and operational decisions. They bring to bear the benefits of a different set of experiences from their status as, in a literal sense, outsiders.

Some outside or non-executive directors might well be 'outsiders' in the sense that I understand the term, but many will be very like the rest of the team on the board. Much time is given in the course of the governance debate to the fact that the non-executive team resembles very closely the executive team on the basis that people do tend to recruit in their own image. Certainly in the UK women are a minority (indeed a rarity) on boards. There is increasing evidence that companies are looking more imaginatively for their non-executives and, notably, more internationally. Nevertheless, the bulk of non-executives are business*men* of mature years (likely to be over fifty) and are mostly, although not exclusively, British.

An outsider to my mind is someone who *feels* their difference from the prevailing culture. That difference may not be the most obvious. Take the case of Margaret Thatcher. She was Britain's first female prime minister and, while much can easily be made of her gender difference, this was not the only or indeed the most important way in which she differed from her peers in the Conservative Party. The prevailing culture of the party in the 1960s and 1970s was aristocratic. Characters such as Sir Alec Douglas-Home and Harold, later Lord, Macmillan, true establishment figures, represented the typical Conservative MP. Indeed, with the single exception of Margaret Thatcher's predecessor, Edward Heath, the party had always been led by representatives of the upper (or upper-middle) landowning classes.

Margaret Thatcher's sex certainly marginalized her to some extent, but so too did her relatively humble origins. Educated at a state grammar school, she was the first member of her family to go to university, where she studied a trade rather than a classical discipline. Middle-class she certainly was – but her heritage was that of respectable, nonconformist tradespeople, not the landed gentry. How did this palpable class difference operate to Thatcher's advantage? Did it supply the drive that took her to the pinnacle of British politics? I would dispute this. That drive had more to do with her relationship with her father and her need to come up to his very high expectations of her and hers of herself. What her difference from her fellows in the Conservative Party gave her was opportunity. In 1975 she stood for election to head her party at a time when stalwart party members who might easily have beaten her were prevented from so doing by a sense of class

solidarity, or loyalty, or fear of rocking the boat. Thatcher, the
outsider, had no such loyalties, and, having nothing to lose,
everything to gain, took the risk of exposing her ambitions. It
paid off.

Did Margaret Thatcher *feel* that she was different? From her
conduct, I think it can be inferred that she did. In the 1960s and
1970s she bided her time, took the counsel of senior politicians (she
was mentored by Keith Joseph and Alec Douglas-Home) and
behaved impeccably as a cabinet minister. She gave no undue
cause for alarm, hid her colours and quietly built a reputation for
herself as competent. We know from her own writing that she had
a strong sense of her destiny and an extraordinarily robust sense of
self-confidence but she did not proclaim this aloud. She allowed no
one the opportunity to stand in her way and, once opportunity
presented itself to her, grasped it with typical courage. Certainly I
think that Margaret Thatcher knew she was an outsider and felt
her difference, but I would very much doubt that it was on the basis
of gender that she felt herself to be an outsider, however much that
may have compounded her fundamental difference in caste.

Some outsiders are destined to remain forever on the outside,
since opportunity is everything. Margaret Thatcher was fortunate
that she brought her particular vision to a party and a nation at a
time when both appeared to have lost their way. Edward Heath
had been widely seen as an ineffectual leader and during a period of
recession the Labour government was felt to have made too many
concessions to a militant labour force. Thatcher's resolute refusal
to compromise, passionate advocacy of the rights of the individual
and antipathy to nationalized industry and worker representatives
found favour with a disillusioned public. Nobody but an outsider
could have transformed the party as Thatcher did, and only as head
of the party could she do it. Her difference from other party
members gave her the strength to fight the status quo. She stood
outside the prevailing value system and owed nothing to anyone
within it.

Tony Blair, to my mind, is something of an outsider and one who
has risen to prominence because he dared to take a risk at a time
when opportunity suddenly and unexpectedly presented itself. A
rebel at school, Blair has long been a quiet rebel in the Labour
Party. He entered parliament in 1983, when the party's fortunes

were at their nadir. He consistently saw the need for change but, rather like Margaret Thatcher, never rocked the boat to the extent that his likely ascendancy would be cut short. Blair has been accused of ruthlessly pushing aside his friend Gordon Brown and betraying a pact the two had made that Brown, not Blair, would be the leader of the party. In fact, even before the untimely death of the previous leader, John Smith, it had become obvious that it was Blair, not Brown, who had the winning way with the public. Indeed, in the Shadow Cabinet Blair, as Shadow Home Secretary, out-performed the Shadow Chancellor (in part because the role of a Shadow Home Secretary is the easier of the two in which to win accolades). Whether or not Blair betrayed a friendship is irrelevant; for the good of the party, it was right and proper that he should seize the opportunity to stand for leader as soon as it was presented. Blair is a less obvious outsider than Thatcher, but he is an outsider nonetheless. His vision for the Labour Party and for Britain is distinct and different from that which had gone before. Blair was not part of the strong group of Scottish Labour MPs (of which, of course, Gordon Brown is a very prominent member). Nor was he part of the group who believed that Labour was about believing in looking after people rather than people looking after themselves. Blair, coming from neither of these two strong camps, has imposed a different view and has made it acceptable for people to have a concern for social justice while also maintaining an interest in self-improvement. Blair has modernized the party and has been able to do so from without. The public, indeed, voted for him on that basis. Outsiders can drive through change. They can do difficult things that are forbidden to those on the inside who often suffer a conflict of loyalties. They can stamp their entire personality on a style or system – so we had Thatcherism and now we have Blairites.

But what of outsiders who knew themselves to be outsiders and were driven by that fact? History is littered with them. Few are as grand as Alexander the Great. The son of a king, he might not appear an obvious outsider, but his father was a Macedonian and, as such, on the margins of the classical Greek world. On his accession, Philip II of Macedon inherited a kingdom that was subject to the powerful Greek states of Athens, Sparta and Thebes. The kingdom was also prone to attack from the north. By his death

Philip had removed the threat from the north, taken control of Thrace, and at the battle of Chaeronea beaten the Greek city states into submission. Not only had Philip established Macedonian imperial ambitions, he had also developed a professional army and established a meritocratic ethic within it. Alexander was not his first son, nor the son of Philip's first or favourite wife. He was, however, the son of a Greek mother and a son very much in the father's image. One of the primary legends about Alexander is his boyhood taming of a wayward stallion. His strength and valour were established from a very young age.

How could Alexander, with this legacy, be an outsider? The answer is that he represented a region that, whatever its military might, was regarded as an upstart, its people uneducated and uncouth, by their Greek neighbours. These neighbours were the arbiters of culture. Indeed, the Greeks rather sneered at the Macedonians:

> Not that the Greeks regarded the Macedonians as truly ethnic
> brothers. Greek they spoke, but in a rustic, uncultivated style;
> the Greeks of the southern cities affected not to understand it at
> all. Their traditions, moreover, were entirely unGreek. The
> citizens of the city states held their political culture – of equality
> between free men and democratic self-government – an essential
> element in the quality of Greekness. No such culture obtained in
> the Kingdom of Macedon . . .

Alexander's tutor was Aristotle, Plato's most brilliant pupil and the founding father of empiricism. With him Alexander studied Homer and from him he received a special copy of the *Iliad* which he is said to have kept under his pillow thereafter. Alexander can hardly have been insensitive to the extraordinary cultural capital of the Greek world and his virtual exclusion from this. No matter that Macedon had become the premier state of the Greek world, it was profoundly un-Greek and its leaders no less so. Can this have been part of the drive that motivated Alexander's extraordinary campaigns and made him into the most successful conqueror in history, an inspiration to all future conquerors, not one of whom has matched his achievement? It does not seem unreasonable to suppose that Alexander's bid to spread Greek culture throughout the known world stemmed from his own sense of being on the outside.

There is a parallel to be drawn between Alexander, Napoleon and Adolf Hitler. All nursed extraordinary ambitions, all were highly driven and captured and retained the loyalty of their followers. Before over-reaching themselves both Napoleon and Hitler made very significant territorial gains; they did not rival Alexander's, but were unrivalled in their respective centuries. Just as Alexander came from Macedonia and so was on the fringes, at best, of Greek civilization, so Napoleon was not French but was born on the island of Corsica as Napoleon Buonaparte. He changed his name to Bonaparte in 1796 to rid it of its Italianate connotations. Hitler was also an outsider in the context of the German state since he was born in Braunau in Upper Austria. Hitler was an outsider in more than one sense, of course, his social class and the pedigree of his family being issues of pathological concern to him, but he shares with Alexander that sense of being on the outside both culturally and geographically.

Alexander had at his disposal a different way of doing things from that which prevailed in the Greek city states. He lived within Macedonian conventions but was schooled in those of the Greeks and so could borrow selectively from either source and combine the different approaches in novel ways. Somebody who is an outsider by dint of geography or ethnicity has the advantage of having more than one way of looking at the world.

Migration has given rise to extraordinary success. Indeed, the world's most migrant population, the Jews, have been successful wherever they have settled. Accounting for between 1 and 3 per cent of the population of Europe and the United States, Jewish people are represented in the lists of the eminent to a degree far above statistical expectation (some ten times more often than would be statistically expected).[1] Doubtless there are many possible explanations for the extraordinary success rate of Jewish people, and many different factors are, inevitably, at play, but one must be the benefit of differing viewpoints. Orthodox Jews who sustain their religious beliefs within a tight-knit community but otherwise in their professional lives integrate with the community into which they have settled definitely mix perspectives, which can only enrich their decision-making capability, insight and creativity.

The United States, the world's only remaining superpower, has been made great by the interplay of different perspectives. Its population has brought together people from around the globe, and continues to receive fresh injections nowadays from the Pacific Rim rather than from Europe. It comes as little surprise that a population founded on emigration has been so successful, since it is generally the young and able-bodied who feel free to emigrate and it is also often those with a vision for self-improvement. During the eighteenth, nineteenth and early twentieth centuries émigrés took from their homeland the accumulated wisdom of generations and grafted it on to that of their fellow émigrés, joining together to exploit the abundant opportunity of the United States. Hollywood, the best-known symbol of American greatness, enjoyed its golden age in the 1930s and 1940s, when much of its talent both in front of and behind the screen came from émigré Europeans. Interestingly, two of the most senior corporate figures in Silicon Valley are also both émigré Europeans. Andy Grove of Intel and Eckhard Pfeiffer both hail from Eastern Europe.

It is perhaps in the creative arena that the benefit of an outsider's vision is most obvious. The Irish, for example, who see themselves as very much separate from the prevailing and imposed English culture, have given the canon some of its greatest figures: W. B. Yeats, James Joyce, Samuel Beckett and, more recently, Seamus Heaney.

Late nineteenth- and early twentieth-century English literature was influenced to a considerable extent by Americans who had settled in the UK. Henry James is the archetypal observer of difference. Virtually his entire prodigious output of novels chronicles the experience of the American middle and upper classes unleashed on the English. A man who spent his life touring the stately homes of England (as an unpaying guest) and settled ultimately in the quaint Sussex town of Rye, James never lost his essential distance from the English. T. S. Eliot similarly made his home in Britain and even worked in one of London's financial institutions before he joined the publisher Faber & Faber, but he was an outsider, with an outsider's vision. His New England roots, his Catholicism, are important parts of his work. Perhaps, too, his experience as the husband of someone on the fringes of social acceptance because of her fragile mental state contributed to his overall sense of alienation and marginalization. Another American, Sylvia Plath, was an outsider in England (and how she suffered in the dismal dank Devonshire countryside) but also on the margins because of her own repeated breakdowns. Ezra Pound shares the same dual sense of distance.

Some of the greatest writers of literature in the English language chronicle black experience, notably Derek Walcott and Toni Morrison – both Nobel prize winners. The outsider stands between places, occupying an odd middle ground of heightened sensitivity, able to observe and record what most insiders barely acknowledge. Some of England's greatest novelists have felt themselves distanced from the prevailing culture on grounds of social class. Charles Dickens, Thomas Hardy and D. H. Lawrence all experienced that degree of marginalization and analysed it in their writings. English music, too, has its outsiders: Edward Elgar was born poor, provincial and Catholic – marginalized in three different ways. Historian David Cannadine writes perceptively of Elgar:

> There is a famous photograph of Elgar taken at the moment he had completed the orchestral scoring of *The Dream of Gerontius*. He wears a buttoned-up jacket and a wing collar, and sports a walrus moustache of formidable proportions. In dress and demeanour, he looks stiff, starched and stuffed: Colonel Blimp before his time. And yet the eyes suggest a very different personality: dreamy, passionate, visionary, a man of poetic imagination with his sights set surely on the sublime. Which of these is the real Elgar? Both? Either? Neither? It is difficult to be sure. For the picture is not only contradictory, it is also deceptive: a carefully contrived self-image masquerading as a spontaneous and unselfconscious record.[2]

In this piece of staged personal myth-making Elgar is typical of outsiders. Outsiders are often first-rate actors, brilliant dissemblers who can move with relative ease between the different worlds that they inhabit. An ability to project a persona is a critically important skill to any would-be leader. Throughout history great orators, those who have been able to convey their message from a public platform, have been some of the most successful leaders – although not necessarily the most benign (Hitler, after all, was a renowned orator). William Gladstone and Abraham Lincoln were among the best orators of their respective periods and Churchill's speeches were a vital factor in his hugely successful wartime leadership.

Alexander the Great was also a fabled orator at a time when oratory was a highly revered skill, and when appearing before his men he took great care to do so in costume. He wore an iron helmet that was so highly polished it shone like silver. The helmet was adorned with long, snowy plumes. He wore an iron throat piece that was studded with gems and carried a sword. He also wore a magnificent cloak on top. Without the benefit of modern media, Alexander had to create an immediate impression on the men that he led. Modern leaders owe less to the moment but nevertheless have to develop an image that is acceptable and consistent. Think of Nelson Mandela, whose sartorial elegance combines the traditional colour of native costume with the cut and style of classical Western clothes. With an unfailing instinct Mandela plays to his mixed audience.

The link between leadership and acting has long been established but in the United States it has become explicit. When B movie actor Ronald Reagan became President it was seen by some as symptomatic of the US presidential election system with its penchant for razzamatazz. In reality, it is highly logical for someone with committed political interest and a flair for playing a part to aspire to political position. Reagan has set something of a precedent, for Arnold Schwarzenegger harbours political ambitions and, as celebrity causes have become commonplace, it is likely that celebrity senators and congressmen will follow suit. And is this so very different from the British system, where political leaders regularly come from a legal background (Tony Blair being no exception)? A barrister, after all, is no less skilful an actor than a film star.

The artifice necessary to leadership is second nature to the outsider, who moves between worlds, heightening some aspects of personality in one environment, others in another. Richard Branson's beard and pullover are as much a part of his success as the ubiquitous Virgin logo. Branson is unquestionably an outsider by temperament. Educated at the British public school Stowe, he was at pains not to fit in there, just as he has managed not to fit in with any institution subsequently. He could not even fit in with the financial institutions, and having taken his beloved Virgin public spared nothing to regain its private status once more. Branson's persona is that he is one of us. He is the lad next door. He likes bands, planes and trains, loud music and balloons. Even his inarticulacy fits with the image; no spin-doctoring for him. He assuredly is not one of us, however. He is his own man. A rather introverted man and one who understands his market, but not so much from empathy as from observation.

Being on the outside can give an individual almost superhuman drive: it can also endow almost limitless freedom. Bringing about change from within an existing structure is fraught with difficulty. We automatically expect our peers within a given situation or culture to behave in a fairly predictable fashion. We know them, we know the conditions which have given rise to their predicament and the possible choices they face. Consider the board of a company. The chief executive and key executive directors have worked together for a number of years. The chief executive has won the race for succession as the most able and the best equipped to deal with the ups and downs and the perennial vicissitudes of business. What if sudden unforeseen crisis were to hit the organization? Would he still be best placed to lead the organization or would he find himself constrained by the very persona that has served him so well up to now? It is very hard to step out of one's skin and to do things differently.

I can think of few people who have successfully altered the course of a company from within at times of crisis. Vernon Sankey, Chief Executive of Reckitt & Colman, who had spent a couple of decades in the business before taking on the top job, might have been one. He showed extraordinary courage in turning what had been a typically British, Imperial-style business into a global streamlined one, even selling off the eponymous mustards to Unilever along the way in an attempt to stave off crisis. Perhaps his recent departure from the business, however, makes the point that the insider's scope to manage change is curtailed? The company now needs an outside vision to effect dramatic and positive change. Generally, at a time of crisis, the newcomer finds it immeasurably easier to effect change than the insider. In a new environment a chief executive can slough off elements of an old persona and can adapt and amend that persona, almost stage-managing the effect he creates. In contrast, the insider may know too much and may not be able to choose to disregard certain facts.

Charles Miller-Smith typifies the successful outsider at the helm of a major corporation. After a long career at Unilever in which he and Niall FitzGerald were head-on-head competitors, Miller-Smith left when it became obvious that FitzGerald was the likely successor to the top slot, moving on to be the first outsider to head ICI. He has effected a remarkable corporate transformation. He does not sit in his office and wait to be brought intelligence. He walks the building, gathering evidence with his own eyes and ears and assembling his own truth. The outsider carries no baggage and owes no favours. He may have much to prove, but he can set the terms within which he proves himself. So Miller-Smith has been able to buy and sell reassemble the ICI business in ways that would have been politically sensitive for an ICI insider and has brought to the business that very critical thing: an alternative perspective. One of the most important purchases he has made on ICI's behalf is that of the specialty chemicals business in Unilever which he had himself built up.

Is Charles Miller-Smith a natural outsider? Indeed, is anyone in business a natural outsider? Business after all is a fundamentally conservative enterprise. True radicals and iconoclasts, if they have commercial aspirations at all, are most likely to pursue them, as Branson has done, in an entrepreneurial venture. Business is, in large organizations, at least about joining, about working as part of a team and identifying with a large corporate entity. Even those who want to make serious money would often be better advised to embark on their own business than to join a corporate hierarchy. But business is not all about money, it is also about power, and outside the political arena there are few environments where power is to be had on such a scale as the international corporation. For those outsiders who want to be on the inside, who have a strong megalothymic urge to be recognized as superior to others, then there are few better options today than running a multinational.

Nor is the corporate apprenticeship particularly difficult for the outsider. The corporation is an environment where the individual can remain as introverted and as private as he chooses. Competence is not a matter of personality. The extrovert who is widely liked as a young manager may, moving higher up the corporate ladder, find it hard to sustain friendships and increasing power simultaneously. The introvert, on the other hand, who does not depend for energy on the good will of others will not face the same dilemma. The outsider may not be entirely at ease with all aspects of a corporate career but will be capable of acting the part, of dissembling in the interests of the long-term achievement. The outsider may give the appearance of belonging however much, emotionally, they are detached. In a multinational the ambitious outsider will find that overseas placements give early exposure to responsibility and power. The outsider is, of course, more likely to translate easily from one environment to another, being more self-sufficient, less in need of the cultural paraphernalia which comes with life on the inside. Business, in many ways, is more hospitable to the outsider than to the insider. Or rather business leadership selects people from the outside with a keen interest on gaining access to the inside.

Many chief executives that I have met are outsiders on the inside. It may not be immediately apparent that they are distinct in some way from those alongside whom they have developed their careers. Sir John Browne at BP Amoco, for example, has enjoyed a career path which is, aside from the degree of success, unremarkable for a chief executive. He has spent the entirety of his working life with BP. He does, however, bring an alternative perspective to bear on life. His parentage (English and Romanian) and peripatetic lifestyle in childhood gave him international awareness and sensitivity, a sympathy for difference and first-hand experience of being the person on the outside. He does not see the world in a typically British way. He also has an uncommonly sharp brain and sees things with extraordinary clarity. A classic introvert, Browne's personal reserve distances him from those over whom he must exercise his authority. In these characteristics he is not untypical of the person who, on the surface very much an insider, is actually someone who has maintained their distance within the safe confines of a corporate structure.

There are *groups* of outsiders in business as in life. Business, after all, is dominated by the male, the white, the grey-haired. Women are the most obvious group of people whom business seems to close ranks to keep firmly on the outside. Much is said in corporate boardrooms about wanting to bring women on to the board but little is achieved. There are any number of reasons why this is so, and the subject forms a book in its own right. Perhaps men consciously exclude women out of an innate desire for women to be subservient. More possibly, men exclude women because they do not particularly understand the different type of contribution a woman can make in the boardroom. Two senior female colleagues of mine are themselves board directors and bring a tremendous ability to spot and defuse tension that their male counterparts ignore at their peril. They have a sensitivity to others and an ability to repress their own egos which makes them immensely effective in a group situation. Over and above this they are of course both highly able, articulate women with highly successful corporate careers behind them. That highly successful corporate careers elude many able women may be down to a multiplicity of factors. Business is not, for instance, geared to the needs – emotional and physical – of women who are also mothers. It is also not an environment that particularly celebrates the caring aspect of humanity. Business is not as ruthlessly uncaring as is sometimes depicted, but many more women choose and are successful in the caring or socially motivated professions – doctors, nurses, education, civil service – than in business. I have noticed that women who do succeed are often outsiders by dint of some reason unconnected to their gender. Marjorie Scardino hit the headlines in the UK when she was appointed as the first – and so far, the only – woman to be the chief executive of a top PLC. She is not British but American. Perhaps one of the most interesting women business leaders – and there is no doubt of her leadership status – is Orit Gadeish, who seems to be an outsider from whichever perspective one chooses to glimpse her.

Gadeish is the Chairman of Bain & Company, one of the leading firms of strategic management consultants worldwide. Her profession then is that of an outsider. Management consultancy is not an environment where people are encouraged to be too overtly different from their peers. Indeed, some consulting cultures are accused of cloning, so standard is the appearance of their employees. No one could accuse Gadeish of cloning anyone: '. . . you first

notice her skirt; it starts about eight inches above her knee. Then
her hair; viewed from the side and back it's magenta. Then her long
red finger-nails. She is complex, intense, driven, painfully direct,
sometimes ribald, and a lot of fun . . .'

Gadeish is not American. She was raised in Israel, the daughter
of an army commander, and spent a couple of years in army
intelligence before going to the United States. She is, like many
top management consultants, an alumna of the Harvard Business
School. Unlike most, however, she joined speaking little English
and still managed to graduate in the top 5 per cent of her class.
Fiercely able and ambitious in equal measure, Gadeish was
ranked the twenty-sixth most powerful woman in American
business and her personality and talents enabled the turnaround
of Bain in the early 1990s. Interestingly, her skills are also ones
that can be seen as highly feminine: in particular, an ability to
read people. She is a trained psychologist and an avid reader of
literature, from which she claims to bring much of her insight
into motivation; apparently that British exercise in sustained
observation of a swathe of society, *A Dance to the Music of
Time*, is a favourite text. A non-American in a highly American
firm (Bain has, rightly or wrongly, been seen to be a bit 'preppy'
in style), a woman in the boardroom and a consultant who
derives her living from being on the outside – Gadeish is an
outsider from all angles.

Gadeish unites the observer's powers of observation and empathy to an extraordinary degree. One of her clients said of her:
'Orit has that talent for making you feel you're the most important
person in the room. She bleeds your blood.' It is unfair, but
tempting, to take a statement intended to compliment Gadeish
and see in it a faint semantic suggestion of a vampiric woman
bleeding the blood of her clients, taking over their personality.
Nevertheless societies have often had an extremely ambivalent
attitude to powerful women which makes it extremely difficult
for women to succeed on their own terms. Inevitably, women must
be seen as seductive sirens or neutral mothers. It is interesting to
note that (in the same article) a competitor describes her in more
homely terms: 'She's like a Jewish mother figure . . .' Gadeish
would probably disdain any reductive tag, including that of 'an
outsider'. The terms independent and unorthodox, original and

intuitive may have more appeal. In according an individual the status of an outsider we contrive to degrade them. An outsider is not like us; he or she plays the game by different rules, for a different purpose. They cannot, therefore, be judged by the same terms. We may resent our close neighbour's success if they have the same value system as our own and yet go beyond us. To quote Gore Vidal: 'Every time a friend succeeds I die a little.' We are less likely to begrudge the success of someone who is entirely unlike us. The very difference and distinction of the outsider neutralizes their threat. It is as if the outsider does not quite count. It there is any truth in this psychology then it is hardly surprising that influential women have been allowed to succeed where they are visible outsiders. They are allowed to be successful women in part because they are not quite women. They are something other.

The outsider crops up in the unlikeliest contexts. 'How did the daughter of an Italian builder come to be the most powerful woman in India?' This not unreasonable question was posed by a recent newspaper of Sonia Gandhi. Born in a small town just outside Turin to a Roman Catholic couple, this naturalized Indian is the figure on whom the hopes of the Congress Party of India rested at the last election. Refusing to fight a parliamentary seat, she threw her weight behind the party which was led in turn by her children's great-grandfather, their grandmother and their father. There can be little question that the party wants Sonia Gandhi for her relationship to her husband and mother-in-law. But there must be more to it than that. If the party merely wanted to continue its association with the Nehru/Gandhi family then it would have been more logical to have gone to one of Sonia and Rajiv's still young, but nonetheless adult, children. Instead the focus of attention rests entirely on Sonia. Why should this be if not because of the power of Sonia as an outsider? She is something quite other than the representative of any other party and in her otherness there is, again, something of neutrality.

The outsider is a powerful force for it represents otherness. Modern psychoanalytic theory makes much of the power of the other: '. . . man's desire finds its meaning in the desire of the other, not so much because the other holds the key to the object desired, as because the first object of desire is to be recognized by the other . . .'[3] and difference has an undeniable potency or exoticism.

Sonia Gandhi strikes an important note for Congress. On the one hand she is a link to its past and on the other she is a note on its future, its forward-looking, international, non-parochial stance. She is a metaphor, a living embodiment of how the party can achieve metamorphosis.

While a European woman has acquired symbolic status in India, Indians are gradually acquiring increased status at the helm of Western businesses. Not surprisingly it is the professional outsiders – the professional services businesses – which have given scope to these most visible outsiders. Arthur Andersen, the audit and consulting firm, and McKinsey, the world's best known management consultancy, have appointed Jamshed 'Jim' Wadia and Rajat Gupta as Managing Partner and Managing Director respectively. In the UK in 1998 an Indian for the first time became chief executive of a major financial services firm and a leading PLC to boot when he took the top job in that once most imperial of businesses, Standard Chartered. Rana Talwar is the second Asian chief executive, following in the footsteps of C. K. Chow who is the Chief Executive of GKN Plc. The small select group of Indian chief executives have the useful experience of being raised in India, a country without infrastructure, where people rise or fall on their own merits and where there is abundant experience of diversity and ambiguity. Consultants are frequently judged on their 'tolerance to ambiguity'; Indians perhaps have a head start. Professional services businesses are fiercely meritocratic. Service to the client is the primary yardstick and irrelevancies like race, creed and colour do not intervene in the career of an able executive.

Rana Talwar is an outsider in a very literal sense. In other ways he is a typical product of his background and career in the international bank Citibank. The son of a former Chief Secretary of Punjab, Talwar was a firmly middle-class Indian who was educated at St Stephen's College in New Delhi. He and his family have relocated from Chicago to Holland Park, one of London's most attractive residential areas. Talwar's son is at Wharton and his daughter is just starting university. His leisure interests are golf, tennis, bridge and travel. Talwar's is the profile of a fairly typical executive. It is not typical of a British Asian, where there is greater emphasis on running the family firm. Britain's richest Asian,

Lakshmi Mittal, runs the family Ispat Steel Group and the Hinduja brothers similarly control a family business worth a reputed £2 billion. But then Talwar is a British Asian. Talwar is visibly different and this makes him an outsider within the British establishment. On the other hand, as far as Standard Chartered is concerned Talwar is important precisely because he has an *inside* track on a market which is critical to the bank. Standard Chartered, after all, has a major presence in Asia and the Indian subcontinent.

The United States is poised to have an African–American in control of Fortune 500 company for the first time in its history. Kenneth Chenault, currently president and Chief Operating officer, is tipped to take over as Chairman of American Express when current Chairman Harvey Golub retires. Chenault has a classic insider's – for which read, establishment – background. He is the son of a dentist who practised in a white middle-class town on Long Island. At school – the prestigious Waldorf School on Long Island – he was both an honour student and a star athlete, and was elected class president and captain of the soccer, basketball and track teams. After Harvard Law School, Chenault practised corporate law for a couple of years before joining Bain & Co as a management consultant. Lou Gerstner, then American Express President and now the Chairman of IBM, spotted Chenault and hired him into AmEx in 1981 as Strategic Planning Director. From then on Chenault had a meteoric rise through the ranks of the business, surviving the reorganization that followed the firing of James Robinson, the then chairman, and becoming close to Golub who is said to like Chenault's ability to get things done without hogging the limelight.

But for the matter of his colour – and it is a very big but – Chenault would appear to be the classic insider. He is reported by friends to have said, while at university: 'I've got to get into the system to help my people.' From this we can infer that Chenault's ethnicity has been a matter of fierce pride and a certain defiance. He has gained the power he now has for three reasons. First, he has undoubted and outstanding abilities. Second, he is driven by a passion to succeed – 'As a kid I knew I wanted to be a leader in something, but I just didn't know of what' and third, he has constructed an extremely effective persona. He is immensely popular, with a low level of ego and a high level of ability. Chenault's appearance of being an insider is part of the necessary strategy of an outsider who requires – and deserves – recognition.

An outsider is someone who has a different grasp on reality from the common one. A leader is frequently someone who can impose that alternative reality on others. T. E. Lawrence, with whose words I opened this chapter was the archetypal leader from the outside. An intellectual, a thinker and an observer, a homosexual, and a shy, solitary academic, he had a romantic vision of Arabia which led him to be its most courageous defender and one of the greatest heroes of the age. Lawrence invented himself and turned himself from a man of dreams into a man of action. Eschewing most honours, Lawrence's distance from the world was remarked upon by Churchill as he unveiled a memorial to Lawrence at Oxford High School for Boys:

> The world naturally looks with some awe upon a man who appears unconcernedly indifferent to home, money, comfort, rank, or even power and fame. The world feels not without a certain apprehension, that here is someone outside its jurisdiction; someone before whom its allurements may be spread in vain; someone strangely enfranchised, untamed, untrammelled by convention, moving independently of the ordinary currents of action; a being readily capable of violent revolt or supreme sacrifice . . .

Some outsiders are very far from indifferent to home, comfort and the trappings of ordinary life which Lawrence so distinctively disdained. All outsiders, like Lawrence, are governed by their own internal laws. Their identity may derive from their relation to certain norms, but outsiders will play with those norms and will realign them such that they continually surprise. Outsiders, those who invent and reinvent themselves and push the very limits of their identities, are truly megalothymic. Their identity depends on being seen to have any existence. Outsiders play on a public stage and in their very quest for recognition they betray their lust to be on the inside. Success for the outsider is ambivalent. Being, finally, on the inside can seem a betrayal of self. The outsider, having spent a lifetime of alienation, ends in being alienated even from himself. Thomas Hardy, who unquestionably felt himself to be an outsider, wrote movingly of this final let-down in 'Wessex Heights':

> Down there I seem to be false to myself, my simple self that
>   was,
> And is not now, and I see him watching, wondering what
>   crass cause
> Can have merged him into such a strange continuator as this,
> Who yet has something in common with himself, my chrysalis.

Some outsiders will be satisfied but few will ever be entirely at ease with themselves. How is it possible, after all, to be at ease with a self which necessarily shifts and seldom settles? It is this lack of ease that renders the outsider vulnerable. The ideal state for the outsider is to be continually aspiring and never arriving, for the dream once realized can turn to nightmare.

Businesses need outsiders. They do not want those who are frustrated by their status as outsiders. They need those whose dream is to create or transform something. The outsider who can make a lasting and positive impact on a business is one who takes advantage of their alternative perspective, or different experience of life, to invent – or reinvent – an organization. The story of Roberto Goizueta should convince sceptics of the virtues of giving opportunity to maverick outsiders. The son of a sugar magnate in Cuba, Goizueta joined Coca Cola in Havana in 1954. Six years later he fled Castro's revolution, taking with him his wife, $40 and 100 Coca Cola shares. By 1981 he had climbed to the top at Coca Cola and he set about creating the greatest increase in shareholder value in business history. At the time of his death in October 1998 the business had been transformed from a sleepy, parochial one into the paradigm of a successful operation, its value having gone from $4 billion to $145 billion. A visionary outsider has the freedom, both social and emotional, to bring about extraordinary change that an insider can barely dream of. We close ranks against the outsider at our peril.

NOTES

1 Dean Keith Simonton, *Greatness: Who makes history and why*, Guildford Press, 1994.
2 David Cannadine, *Sir Edward Elgar. The Pleasures of the Past*, Penguin Books, 1997.
3 Jacques Lacan, *Ecrits*, taken from Malcolm Bowie, *Lacan*, Fontana, 1991.

Chapter 5

What's in a Name?
On Leaders, Managers and Entrepreneurs

'It seems to me that business leaders have much more in
common with artists, scientists, and other creative thinkers than
they do with managers.' – Abraham Zaleznik, Konosuke
Matsushita Professor of Leadership Emeritus, Harvard Business
School, in *Managers and Leaders: Are They Different?*

Those in positions of power and authority would probably resist
being called outsiders, the more so, ironically, if they are genuinely
outsiders. Few, however, would resist the term 'leader'. Western
societies revere leaders as much as they fear them. The twentieth
century has seen leaders, in equal measure, destroy and repair
civilizations. We know that leaders can embody menace as well as
romance, that they can challenge us, inspire us and free us or
destroy, unsettle and abuse us. Any institution, be it a state, a
political party or a corporation, needs leadership at some point in
its evolution. No institution needs leadership all the time, unless it
is in a state of continuous change. Instead, institutions need a blend
of leadership and management in different proportions at different
times.

Large institutions need fewer leaders than they need managers.
An organization entirely comprised of leaders would be one
without a cohesive structure. This is fortunate since organizations
have become expert in the development of managers but remain
amateurish in their development of leaders. Leadership and
management are very different from one another. The value
we place on leadership is such that the term 'management' seems

to have acquired a pejorative sense in contrast. Certainly, there are many outstandingly able individuals at the helm of major corporations who would balk at the term 'manager', even when their skills are palpably those of management. We are right to value leadership, but not at the expense of management. Almost certainly, given a choice, the majority of chief executives today would prefer to be called leaders. Just as certainly, many more are managers than leaders. Another term that seems widely misapplied is 'entrepreneur'. Some who blithely use the term of themselves would doubtless think again if forced to go and start something from scratch, to finance the project with their own (or borrowed) cash and to risk themselves and their livelihood in the venture. Such people may be entrepreneurial – they may have the skills, for instance, to build something within an existing organization – but they are not true entrepreneurs. Leadership, management, entrepreneurship – these are recurring terms in the business lexicon, used too frequently with too little precision or understanding.

The most common misconception, that the act of running an organization, irrespective of its scale, automatically confers leadership status, may have been reinforced by the changing patterns in job titles. The title 'chief executive' has become the norm in most Anglo-Saxon organizations. A few decades ago this was not the case. The person with primary executive responsibility for the organization was known, in Britain, as the managing director. The title remains common in smaller organizations and at divisional level, and some chief executives are officially styled group managing director, especially where there is an executive chairman in place. It is a useful title in so far as it conveys the fact that management is at the heart of the task. In highly successful companies the task required of the chief executive may be that of *maintaining* success. This will doubtless require a complex set of skills but it does not require the development of a new vision for the business. That requires a leader. If a manager maintains, then a leader transforms. Management is a rational task, leadership something far more intuitive. Management then is a learned skill; leadership, while it can be developed and refined, is innate. Leadership is generally the product of early experience and personality. Leadership and management appear to be quite independent, perhaps even opposite, while entrepreneurship is something else again.

Unquestionably the individual who bears the title chief executive (or its equivalent) has ultimate executive power and authority within an organization. So long as there have been institutions which legislate or hold power over people there have been organizational structures which, more often than not, focus on one clear individual at the centre and an administrative staff immediately below that figure. The hierarchy within the Christian church or the army reflects precisely this structure. Authority can, in the first instance, manifest itself in various ways. The theory of charisma developed by German sociologist Max Weber can be useful in understanding the different manifestations of authority. He identifies three clear types. The first of these, which he terms legal authority, is based on 'rational grounds – resting on a belief in the legality of enacted rules and the right of those elevated to authority under such rules to issue commands'. The second, which is of less relevance to us, Weber terms traditional authority 'resting on an established belief in the sanctity of immemorial traditions and the legitimacy of those exercising authority under them'. The third is charismatic authority 'resting on an established belief in the sanctity, heroism or exemplary character of an individual person, and of the normative patterns of order revealed or ordained by him'. The first and the third of these fit respectively management and leadership. The distinction seems to be that the first places more importance on the office than on the individual, while the third focuses on the personality. The second of Weber's categories is a model that would work where authority is a legacy passed by heredity through the familial line. It applies to a family-run firm where power passes from one generation to the next.

Weber offers a schema for the way authority manifests itself and changes in accordance with need, time and circumstances, which holds true across the boundaries of time and space. He reveals a process whereby charismatic authority must, inevitably, become routinized if it is to be prolonged. In the case of a religion, say Christianity, this is easy to chart. The charismatic leader is Jesus Christ himself. The disciples are his administrative staff, those who believe in the leader and so by virtue of their belief confirm his status as leader. From the disciples comes the structure of the

Church of Rome with the Pope at its head and, eventually, an entire hierarchy of clerics. From the original charismatic leader there comes, over time, an entire bureaucracy. This bureaucracy is essential if the mission of the original leader is to be achieved. In the case of Christ's mission it is imperative that his message be broadcast far and wide. Over time, however, something which had initially been revolutionary and transformational becomes traditional and routine. In short, unless we are to have a situation of endless revolution or anarchy then change must become fixed, and the new become the norm if the purpose of that change is to be satisfied. Charismatic authority, which is rooted in the irrational terrain of the personality of an individual, gives way to legal authority and to bureaucratic administration, the root of which is not the power of personality but the power of knowledge.

There is a cycle in business of origination, routinization, re-inspiration and then routinization. Most new ventures are the brain-child of a founder or entrepreneur who has a vision and the drive to pursue it. In time, assuming the business is successful, the founder must either develop his or her own management skills or import them from outside. Those businesses which cannot make the transition to being managed will remain small. When a mature business stagnates – perhaps it is over-managed or perhaps the operating environment has shifted away from the organization's key strengths – then is the moment for a leader. A leader will come with a new vision, will energize the workforce to pursue that vision and will relentlessly evangelize until the vision has come to pass. In the wake of a leader a manager again becomes essential to sustain the vision. Indeed a business may be run very well by a succession of managers, needing leaders very rarely. Perpetual change is as damaging to a business as perpetual stasis, hence leaders and managers are of equal importance.

The American automobile industry provides a useful model for trying to understand the differences between an entrepreneur, a leader and a manager. The car industry was set up by inventors and designers who gave their name to the cars they developed. In a rapidly developing industry (500 cars were sold in 1900 in America, 65,000 in 1907 and by 1915 the one million milestone had been passed) the entrepreneurs had to develop an efficient administration as quickly as possible or they would not survive. There is a parallel here with the numerous small businesses that have grown up in Silicon Valley, developed by technological wizards, of which only a handful will be able to grow into great companies.

General Motors (GM) was the brainchild of William Durant, who had the vision to see how fast the industry would expand and how ill-equipped to cope with demand were the small businesses which then featured on the landscape. He set about developing a conglomerate – which was to be the major competitor to Henry Ford's operation – by a series of company creations and combinations which brought together the likes of Buick (his starting point), Cadillac, Oldsmobile and Oakland. Durant was a man of vision and a man of action. He was not, however, a manager. The man who was to succeed him, Alfred P. Sloan, said of him: 'I admired his automotive genius . . . But I thought he was too casual in his ways for an administrator and he overloaded himself . . . I was particularly concerned that he had expanded GM between 1918 and 1920 without an explicit policy of management with which to control the various parts of the organization.' Durant's unfettered vision gave rise to organizational anarchy, and if the business were to survive he needed to be removed from it and professional management put in place. This founder-led business had outgrown the founder's capabilities.

Durant had the founder's knack, however, of attracting key figures in the early days of the business to back it. Pierre DuPont, head of the DuPont business, was on the Board of GM. DuPont had excellent credentials. He was one of three great grandsons of the founder of DuPont who had rescued the business in 1902 and transformed it into a research-led, well-managed corporation diversifying away from its original core produce of gunpowder into the chemicals sector. DuPont's presence on the GM board gave the bankers confidence, and the organization gained the time to emerge from its crisis. That it did so is thanks to the managerial genius first of DuPont and, most particularly, of Alfred P. Sloan, whose name is the more readily connected with General Motors.

DuPont took over as president until 1923 when he stepped down and made way for Sloan, but it was to Sloan's blueprint that the board of GM worked in turning the business around. That blueprint turned out to be the model of the modern corporate head office function presiding over fairly autonomous divisions. In the head office Sloan located the President, operating and financial officers together with group executives and advisory staff officers who functioned as in-house experts. In the line the general managers were accorded considerable authority over day-to-day operations. This structure welded together the best elements of a decentralized with a centralized business, allowing the board to maintain control without inhibiting the actions and judgments of line general managers. This structure, forty years later, had been adopted by the vast majority of corporations. It ensured, in a large and fast growing environment, that decision-making power was not vested solely in one person but that there were mechanisms for sharing and monitoring decision-making.

Sloan's vision went beyond a suitable structure for the business. Most importantly, he identified a strategy for the business which would differentiate it from its major competitor, Ford. The Ford strategy was to focus on economy and to persist with a model which would appeal to the average customer. Sloan on the other hand recognized that the market could be divided into segments and that different products would appeal to different segments. 'A car for every purse and purpose' became the GM slogan. Indeed, Sloan also launched advertising and sales approaches to reach his market and incorporated the growing used car market into his strategy, bringing out a new model each year and encouraging car owners to trade in – and up. Aftercare was also included in the GM offering, with the company acquiring an excellent service record. Sloan had a strategy for the business, a structure that would support it and, finally, the systems to enable the structure to work. Aside from his overall business vision, Sloan had a vision for how to make the mechanics of an organization work and he invented sophisticated budgeting, planning and control systems. Not surprisingly, GM rapidly overtook Ford and Sloan became one of America's first corporate heroes.

Is Alfred Sloan a leader or a manager? Clearly he had a vision for the business, for GM in particular and for a corporate entity in general. He was also able to galvanize others to support that vision, including his own staff and people outside his direct control. For example, he made it his business to understand the needs of businesses which related to GM, in particular the dealer system ('I would meet them in their own places of business and ask them for suggestions and criticisms concerning their relation with the corporation . . .'). Given his vision and motivational skills and his development of something new, it would seem only just that Sloan should qualify as a leader. Indeed, some of Sloan's statements have the universalizing air of a political leader: 'Today it is clear that every man, woman and child, including generations yet to be born, has a stake in the power of General Motors.' Sloan's primary field of expertise, however, the area where he made his most lasting contribution to business, was not in leadership *per se* but in management. Sloan reduced the complexities of corporate business to a science or a formula that could be learned.

It is instructive to look at Sloan's own background. Born on the East Coast of America in Connecticut in 1875, he was the son of a businessman. His father was in the wholesale tea, coffee and cigars business. After an unremarkable childhood and youth, Sloan completed his studies at the top-rated Massachusetts Institute of Technology, gaining a degree in electrical engineering. He then went to apply his learning at the Hyatt Roller Bearing Company of New Jersey. One of the company's products was soon to become an important component in the motor car. The company was small when Sloan joined it and he rapidly moved through the ranks to take over the management of the business. Sloan grew the business very rapidly, becoming, at one point, sole supplier to Fords. In 1916, realizing that the company had limited growth potential, Sloan sold it to Durant for $13.5 million. Durant put Sloan in charge of a conglomerate within GM called United Motors and from there Sloan moved to become a member of the executive committee in charge of General Motors.

Unlike many of the early, rather maverick figures in business, the entrepreneurs, Sloan's route to the top was one of gradually acquired expertise. First he took a degree, then he entered a business where that degree has some application. He moved to the helm of that small business and then started to diversify and exploit the potential of the business to the full. He had the prescience to see the limitations on the Hyatt business and seized the opportunity to sell, which brought him into the GM firmament. Here Sloan gained first-hand experience of senior business figures, notably Pierre DuPont from whose example he could learn. Unquestionably, Sloan had a fine mind and prodigious energy which led to his rapid progression. Moreover, he had the intellectual skills to analyse the essentials of the automobile industry and to devise an entire operating system to enable a company to exploit the market opportunities to the fullest. A remarkable man and a very significant personality in American public life (he was a noted philanthropist), Sloan almost personifies the model of legal authority (returning to Weber's models) based on rationality and knowledge. Management is just this: a science based on rationality and knowledge. It is fitting that Sloan has given his name to business schools and business programmes since he was, unquestionably, the father of modern management science.

Sloan's legacy to business was an organization based on the three Ss of strategy, structure and systems. His primary concern was with what he described as a paradox: 'How could we exercise permanent control over the whole corporation in a way consistent with the decentralized scheme of organization? We never ceased to attack this paradox.' If that was a paradox, then Sloan's core concern was with maintaining balance and achieving a compromise between the conflicting needs. In his illuminating essay *Managers and Leaders: Are They Different?*, Abraham Zaleznik writes: 'In order to get people to accept solutions to problems, managers need to coordinate and balance continually. Interestingly enough, this managerial work has much in common with what diplomats and mediators do. The manager aims at shifting balances of power toward solutions acceptable as a compromise between conflicting values.' The analogy with the diplomat is an interesting one. Diplomats are facilitators and fixers but they are never central stage; that privileged position belongs to leaders. For all that Sloan introduced extraordinary innovations to GM and the business community at large, his mind-set remained that of a manager rather than a leader. This view derives from his overt concern with control, with systems and procedures (he devised the committee and policy group style of management) and, above all, his attitude to risk.

The manager concerned with maintaining an entity will rarely risk either the company or themselves. Sloan, the diplomat, took few risks. Indeed, Zaleznik explains at some length that in his dealings with others Sloan took pains to cloak his actions in ambiguity in order not to risk alienating any of the parties in conflict. Innately conservative, for all his innovation, Sloan's management genius resided in the fact that he on the one hand enabled GM to achieve its full market potential while on the other ensuring it did so with little risk. Risk, more than any other factor, differentiates managers, leaders and entrepreneurs. Sloan by dint of risk-aversion is indeed the embodiment or exemplar of management.

The terms leader, manager and entrepreneur should not be seen as mutually exclusive absolutes. It would be folly to deny that Sloan had some of the attributes of a leader; his natural style, however, was that of the manager. His stature should lend additional stature to the notion of management. Management is concerned with the maximizing of opportunity and the minimizing of risk. Without sound management no corporation can sustain itself beyond a few years. Without Sloan (and DuPont) General Motors would not have survived beyond 1920. The founder of the business, entrepreneur Durant, took risk after risk and created a corporate multi-headed beast where there was no consistency of strategy or behaviour. The business very nearly foundered on its founder's risk indulgence and his deal addiction. America grew great in business between 1850 and 1950 precisely because it developed a management discipline to balance its entrepreneurial zeal. It also distilled its management discipline into a series of modules which could be taught. In the autumn of 1908 the first students entered Harvard to pursue a two-year course which was the foundation of the Master of Business Administration (MBA). By the middle 1960s, just as a Royal Commission reported that Britain should recognize graduate business studies as a legitimate educational aspiration, the United States produced some 21,000 MBAs from a total of 198 business schools. Little wonder, then, that at the time America's hegemony of worldwide business was largely unchallenged.

Management can be taught because it is, above all, rational and susceptible to logic and the application of rigorous analysis. Management is about optimal delivery of, generally, preconceived aims. It is entirely about predictability so it is no surprise that the managed can learn from the example set by the manager. Management is about the containment of risk. Too much management is as bad for a business as too little. Management alone can ossify businesses, stifle innovation and arrest change. Management must act in conjunction with a vision derived from a leader, although that leader may be long gone from the organization. Eventually a surfeit of linear rather than lateral thought could lead to management squeezing out leadership from the organization altogether. At this point the organization will need to find leadership from outside.

Is management, then, antithetical to leadership? The two should complement one another. Management is the small print of leadership, it supports and qualifies but, if it takes over, confuses and obfuscates. Leadership operates to a different rhythm from management. Where management is manageable and rational, leadership is reckless and intuitive. If we compare the priorities of the manager with those of the leader we find a very different scenario. While the manager plans and budgets, the leader strategizes. He (or she) has a vision for making things happen in the long rather than the short term. The leader must measure the distance between now and the distant future when the vision can be realized, spotting the hurdles and pitfalls along the way which are inimical to that vision. While the manager moves people into position in order to execute a plan to budget, the leader is concerned to move people emotionally, to win their support for the vision and to prepare them for the inevitable series of changes.

This element of the leadership role, described in a few words, is the leader's single biggest challenge. Every word the leader speaks, or act he performs, must be consistent with the overall vision. The leader must come to embody, to personify the vision in so far as that is possible. In a very real sense the leader's personality comes into play and he must create himself anew in accordance with the vision. The outcome for which the leader must aspire is the fulfilment of his followers such that they remain moved and motivated to continue with the realization of the vision. This is not something that can be taught in a module of a business school. The ultimate outcome, the vision made manifest, will be a changed organization, one that is better prepared to meet its particular competitive challenges.

Managers are usually followers. Just as 'management' should not be seen as a pejorative term, nor should 'followers'. A manager may be in ultimate executive control within an organization, its chief executive, perhaps, but the path he or she follows is one that has been pre-ordained by a past leader. Following is always less risky than leading. The leader puts himself on the line, risks his very soul or, in modern parlance, his self-esteem. A leader is not needed in every situation. Indeed, in the wake of leadership it is often a manager that is required, who can consolidate the vision and can translate the vision into sustainable objectives, into budgets and plans. To take a political rather than a commercial example, in the wake of Margaret Thatcher's removal from power the party had had enough leadership. They selected as party leader a competent manager who could be trusted with the better parts of the Thatcher legacy. That John Major lost the election so catastrophically in 1997 ignores the fact that he won, against all expectations, in 1992. To all things there is a season; this applies as much to management as to leadership. Internal wrangling led to total public disaffection with the Conservative Party. There were numerous calls to replace Major, so numerous that he called his opponents' bluff and staged a leadership contest in which he, nothing if not a consummate politician, secured his party's mandate to lead. That he did so was perhaps because leaders do not always beget leaders and when Thatcher fell from power there was a dearth of strong leadership potential waiting to take centre stage. Indeed, one of Thatcher's shortcomings had been her refusal to allow others to build any kind of power base.

It should never, however, be the responsibility of a leader to ensure that there is a successor in place. Indeed, rulers who name an heir apparent (and Thatcher, after all, gave her support initially at least to Major) tend to name a pale imitation of themselves, a favoured protégé, someone who will maintain the flame of their own leadership and not burn any brighter than they. In an organization it is the responsibility of the chairman of the board to ensure that a suitable succession plan is in place. In the case of the successor to the chairman the non-executive directors should form a nominating committee to consider potential candidates.

Business has generated many more managers than leaders because management is linear in a way that leadership is not. A graduate trainee entering a company at twenty-one can confidently look forward to a period in ten to fifteen years' time when they can consider themselves a fully fledged, well-rounded manager. The career path is a fairly established one, with clearly defined stages and for, risk-containers, a pleasing degree of predictability.

Management development focuses on the acquisition of specialist knowledge and managers are invariably experts in their chosen field. The leap to general management can be something of a leap in the dark, although it is at this point that some people will opt to take an MBA to bring some breadth to their experience. An MBA provides a course spanning the business scene. It does offer breadth but does not attempt to – nor can it – bring depth. Some organizations better prepare their young executives for the career milestone of general management than others. Mars, the American confectionery and pet-food business, for example, routinely rotates its best talent through a range of lateral moves before giving people responsibility for a business unit or region or distribution channel. J. P. Morgan does the same in the banking world. Large multinationals which move their cadre of good young managers around the globe also offer some broadening beyond the narrow confines of one function in one parochial business unit. Nevertheless, even when the specialist has the chance to become a generalist and move into general management the emphasis is still one of control.

A recent study concerning leadership in the service sector in the City of London produced by the City & Inner London North Training & Enterprise Council usefully tabulates the differences between managers and leaders as defined by Warren Bennis in *On Becoming a Leader*.

Figure 5.1: Differences between Managers and Leaders

The manager	The leader
• administers	• innovates
• is a copy	• is an original
• maintains	• develops
• focuses on systems and structure	• focuses on people
• relies on control	• inspires trust
• has a short-range view	• asks what and why
• asks how and when	• has a long-range perspective
• has his eye always on the bottom line	• has his eye on the horizon
	• originates
	• challenges it

- imitates
- accepts the status quo
- is the classic good soldier
- does things right

- is his/her own person
- does the right thing

Source: *Leading People*, by Amin Rajan with Penny van Eupen

The last two bullet points in Figure 5.1 are perhaps the most illuminating. Managers are classic good soldiers who do things right, whereas leaders are their own person who do the right thing. Managers conform while leaders are innately iconoclastic. To what extent will a corporate environment tolerate the iconoclastic at junior levels? Or indeed at more senior levels? Most managers who are selected for fast-track development are those who have a history of excellent performance and a generally conformist attitude. The rebel who rebels for the sake of rebelling brings no clear benefits, but the rebel who looks at the world a little differently and can come up with creative suggestions is not someone most corporations would wish to have slip through their recruitment net. Finding a reliable way of measuring this difference has so far eluded most organizations.

Measurement is at the heart of the management / leadership dilemma. One of the primary reasons why managers predominate in business is because management can be better measured than leadership and so can be predicted and recognized in its latent form. It must be said that business needs more managers than leaders and so the focus of human resource development programmes on management has some logic. Indeed, the route to the top of an organization is via management. Few existing chief executives will have attained their position without a track record of excellence in a range of management positions. The opportunity to prove leadership potential will only be possible if the potential leader has first proven themselves in the management arena. Nevertheless, while businesses may need fewer leaders than managers it still needs more leaders than it has currently. Most corporations cross their fingers and hope that a leader will emerge.

John Kotter, in his study of leadership entitled *A Force for Change*, undertook research to identify how a number of senior business figures evaluated the management and leadership skills of their managerial hierarchies. The results were illuminating. Given the option of answering too few, too many or about right, the deficiency of strong leadership is notable:

Figure 5.2

Management (M)

High management ability – low leadership	Ideal combination – strong management and leadership
Many people in this category in large organisations	Very few in this category
2	4
Low management Low leadership Low value	High leadership – low management
	Need more people – great blend with box 2
1	3

Leadership (L)

Intuitively, it is easy to agree with these findings. The magic box is 4, where we find the ideal blend of management and leadership. This combination is found in individuals all too rarely. Corporations frequently construct the combination represented by Box 4 by careful twinning of those in Boxes 2 and 3. This is a clever way of avoiding the problem. Nonetheless it would be highly valuable to develop nascent leadership skills.

Of what might a leadership development programme consist? First we want to encourage innovation and so we need to expose candidates to different ways of thinking. At the very least we should test our best recruits by ensuring that they take on lateral assignments, perhaps in different divisions, countries, functions and ideally at different points in the business cycle. We cannot cater for originality (although we encourage it by exposing people to different experiences) but we can give people direct experience of developing something, of seeing a project through from start-up, perhaps, be it a new business or project. We can expose people to project leadership at an early stage and ensure they are given plenty of feedback on their performance.

More important than the experience we give people is the manner in which we measure and judge them. We should be able to take risks. Where people fail we should understand that failure and learn by it. We should gamble on the ability of promising executives by cutting them a little loose from corporate ties and letting them go and manage a situation at some remove from head office where the supports to which they have grown accustomed do not exist. Removing support in this way will very quickly focus a would-be leader on how to extract the best possible performance from the available staff by the exercise of leadership skills on the group.

Providing a sounding board for new ideas can also be invaluable. I have yet to encounter a first-class leader who has not, in the course of his career, had important mentors whose influence he both recognizes and acknowledges. An organization cannot legislate and insist that one person act as a mentor for another: mentors and mentees must find one another naturally. Nevertheless organizations should create an environment where there is sufficient mobility within the hierarchy for young aspiring executives to gain access to more senior figures.

There are, undoubtedly, some things that organizations can do to bring out the latent leadership skills of their resident executives but no organization can inculcate in people intellect, integrity, a capacity to inspire trust, a forward-thinking frame of mind. These are much-vaunted leadership skills which organizations are ill-equipped to develop in their employees. The level of emotional resilience, the ability to stand alone – these are attributes for which an organization can test (better than is currently the case) but for which no development programme can possibly cater.

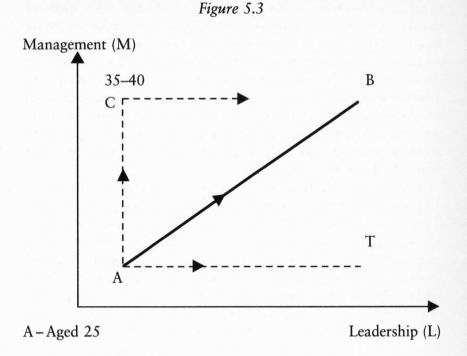

Figure 5.3

Management (M)

35–40

C

B

A

T

A – Aged 25   Leadership (L)

After John Kotter Force of Management

Figure 5.3 helps pinpoint the dilemma for organizations pursuing the holy grail of people who can both manage and lead. An organization will need powerful, effective leadership from the top and many helpful, focused, effective but smaller acts of leadership throughout the organization. These should take their tone from the vision of the chief executive. These smaller acts of leadership should not attempt to disrupt or transform but should be channelled into projects which support the overall vision. As people rise in the organization their leadership quotient can rise too – but must not conflict with, or enter into competition with, that of the chief executive. In reality one of two things tends to happen. Most will become good, or even outstanding, process managers and will play the corporate game. These are in real career danger if the organization undergoes seismic change. A few will not conform, will be regarded as dangerous and will be edged out. Sooner or later, the organization will need to go outside to find its leader.

Kotter's model Figure 5.3 gives some visual representation to this process. At point A the notional twenty-five-year-old budding business executive enters a well-led and managed organization. They must go from A towards C up the management axis. At around thirty-five to forty the nascent leaders should strike out towards point B. The ideal route in this navigation is from A directly to B. Too much leadership without the discipline of management can be an exhilarating ride to nowhere, all charisma, motivation and sheer energy but no outputs or goals met. Management without leadership, however, is sterile. It is possible to reach the top of an organization by moving from A to C and not reaching B, but there must be a very robust vision in place for an individual to succeed without any leadership skills. Indeed, it is more likely that, without any noticeable leadership skills at all, a role as, for example, chief operating officer would be a more realistic pinnacle to aim for. He or she will be an excellent manager. They may bear the title chief executive, but will always be a manager.

Management and leadership are clearly two important dimensions in business, but a central question when reviewing the Kotter model is where does the entrepreneur fit in? Most people, asked to name a business leader, would be more likely to name an entrepreneur than the head of a major corporation: Bill Gates, rather than Jack Welch, or Richard Branson rather than Sir John Browne. Entrepreneurs are at once the most romantic and glamorous of business heroes – and indeed, the most obvious type of businessman. Climbing the corporate ladder does not provide the stuff of headlines, but making many millions from a tiny investment captures the imagination of journalists and the public alike. A successful entrepreneur has the allure of Cinderella. Michael Dell of Dell Computers, not a particularly romantic figure personally, is the local boy made good and a role model for others, proof that it can be done. Few have the skill to make $18 million dollars by the time they are twenty-three and fewer still have the wit and maturity to recognize when they need to import skills that they do not themselves possess. Entrepreneurs all too frequently think they are infallible. This proves their biggest fallibility. The highly successful entrepreneurs, who become the founders of corporate empires, are those who, like Michael Dell, know their limits. Perhaps Dell's wisest single act was to recruit Mort Topfer from Motorola to build the structure of his empire as chief operating officer. Topfer combines managerial talents with entrepreneurial flair and at Dell this must be a winning combination. He can empathize with the aims of an entrepreneur but see how those aims need to be translated into a corporate structure.

Figure 5.4

LEADERS	ENTREPRENEURS	MANAGERS
Charisma	Calculated risk	Analysis
Beguiling	Starting something	Cool
Vision	Building the new	Logical
Strategies	Independence	Process
Motivation of people	Game player	Systems
Catalyst for change	Iconoclast	Conservative
Inspiration	Not constrained	Planning
Energising people	Everything is possible	Budgeting
The longer term	Focus	Controlling
Dreams	Energy	Problem solving
Big picture	Luck	Predictability
Empowerment	Tenacity	Frameworks
Cultural values	Creators of the new	Reduction of risk
Personality centred	Innovation	Rationality
Irrational	Unorthodox personality	Structures and rules
Drive		Detail
Originality		Build an organisation

Leadership, management and entrepreneurial skills all interconnect and each on its own is without lasting benefit unless leavened by one or both of the others. Despite the interconnection of the three skills each is sufficiently independent of the others to be described in distinct terms. Figure 5.4 identifies the salient characteristics of each from which can be seen the areas of commonality as well as the points of distinction.

Management concerns implementation, process, details and outputs. Leadership is being concerned with creating difference and bringing about change, and entrepreneurship concerns the development of the new, built on an appetite for large risk, independence and money. The principal difference between the three resides in the readiness to take a risk. A manager is a fundamentally conservative person who prefers to maintain and work within the status quo. A corporate leader is ready to change that status quo and will do so in quest of fame and to fulfil his destiny within an existing framework. Ultimately, however, corporate chief executives are driven by status and rarely will one take too great a risk with that.

Entrepreneurs, more than either of the other categories, are driven by a requirement for independence which manifests itself as a desire for money and freedom from the control of others. The school rebel is probably the latent entrepreneur, someone who is instinctively different, not afraid to stand out and willing to take any risks to ensure that they can maintain their independence. This freedom of spirit manifests itself very early, as it did with Richard Branson, who started his first venture while still at school, or with Sir James Goldsmith, who as a schoolboy at Eton placed a £10 accumulator on a horse at Lewes, scooped £8,000 and never really ceased gambling. Entrepreneurs do not need formal education, indeed, formal education usually robs them of their originality and innovation. Think of Bill Gates, who was a successful computer hacker as a schoolboy and who quit Harvard because it bored him. Michael Dell reluctantly went along with his parents' plan that he train as a doctor. When, in his first college vacation, he sold $180,000 worth of PCs, he decided not to return. Audacity, willpower, a very strong nerve – these are among the primary characteristics of an entrepreneur.

Sir James Goldsmith, perhaps a classic entrepreneur, was one of the few remarkable people who had strong skills across all three dimensions. He had the attention to detail of the manager, the vision of the leader and the appetite for risk of the entrepreneur. He is rare in so far as he crosses all three dimensions, but most successful people will have a core or preferred style but will combine elements of the other styles in the course of their careers.

Figures 5.5 i) and ii) provide a visual representation of the three dimensions, enabling people to plot the extent to which they combine elements of the three. All the entrepreneurs I have mentioned have founded corporations and so have combined their entrepreneurial skills with others. John Kotter's four-box matrix for managers and leaders can be extended to embrace managers, leaders and entrepreneurs. Point C in Figure 5.5 is the summation of one's quota of management, leadership and entrepreneurial ability.

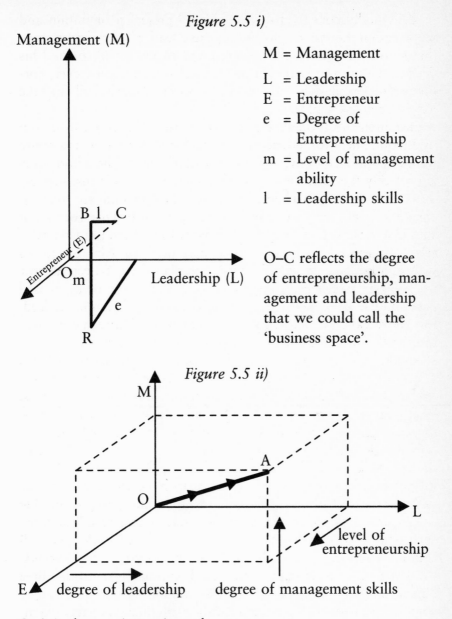

Figure 5.5 i)

M = Management

L = Leadership

E = Entrepreneur

e = Degree of Entrepreneurship

m = Level of management ability

l = Leadership skills

O–C reflects the degree of entrepreneurship, management and leadership that we could call the 'business space'.

Figure 5.5 ii)

O–A is the maximum in each category

A is the optimum where E, L and M are simultaneously maximised. Few, if any, people achieve this optimum but a team of two or three constituent parts should be assembled to reach the optimum point.

If we consider Figure 5.6, which highlights the differences between entrepreneurs and leaders, we find that box 1 identifies those who are low on leadership with some, but limited, entre-

Figure 5.6

Entrepreneur

Smaller family business which will stay small, or frustrated entrepreneur who cannot get bigger	The complete entrepreneur will build a substantial business, the magic combination
2	4
Low entrepreneurship Low leadership One man band – most people in this box	A leader in an organisation which is not his own venture One model of intrapreneur – high leadership/low entrepreneurship
1	3

Leadership

preneurship. They are likely to be one-man bands. They run their own small, often family, businesses – plumbers, hairdressers, restauranteurs. They take minimal risk and have no infrastructure to support and little vision. Box 2 depicts the entrepreneur with few leadership skills who runs a business that is likely to stay small.

Some cultures, notably the Italian and the Chinese, are dominated by businesses of this type, which may produce very high-quality goods or services but which seldom extend beyond the lifetime of the founding entrepreneur. Box 3 represents the individual who has some entrepreneurial skills without the appetite for risk of the true entrepreneur. This can be one model of leadership and can be very useful in a corporate context. Sometimes called an 'intrapreneur', this is someone who wants the safety of the larger organization but is a maverick with a requirement for more independence than the organization needs or can provide. Given appropriate financial backing and support, those who occupy this space can often build new ventures at the edge of an existing structure. Some organizations are particularly strong at allowing people to develop their own businesses: Racal, 3M, Hewlett Packard are three examples which come to mind. Box 4 – the magic one in this case – identifies those who have the capability to build major corporations from nothing, being both leaders and entrepreneurs. The modern media moguls Ted Turner and Rupert Murdoch belong firmly in this box, alongside those other extraordinary builders of empires, Michael Dell and Bill Gates.

Turning to Figure 5.7, we will find that many of the population, with low management and entrepreneurial skills, fit in Box 1. Again, these people may be one-man bands where their only need is to manage themselves, or they may remain junior level employees in an organization. Box 2 represents the well-trained, highly competent corporate manager, with high levels of management skill but no entrepreneurial aspirations. Box 3 is the entrepreneur who has big ideas but does not have the skills to put those ideas into action. This individual is distinct from, but is similarly frustrated to, the figure in Box 2, Figure 5.6, in that he or she does not have the management skills to support even a quite small business venture. The individual who is high on entrepreneurial skills but low on management skills must enlist the support of a strong manager if the initial idea is to bear fruit. Some highly able inventors and designers may fit into this category, destined to see their ideas ultimately put into practice by others with superior management skills.

The entrepreneurial manager, in Box 4, Figure 5.7, on the other hand, is someone who has all the analytical and problem-solving skills that come with management and the desire for money and independence that drives the entrepreneur. He or she lacks the leadership that will often enable them to reach the heights of chief executive in a major corporation. Such people will often be appointed to run businesses backed by venture capitalists (indeed they are not dissimilar in personal profile to venture capitalists themselves). Often quite low-key in style, their desire for money and independence offsets their risk aversion. The risks they take,

Figure 5.7

Management (M)

High quality manager in an organisation	The Entrepreneurial Manager who, for example, runs a venture capital backed buyout from a bigger group. Alternatively, the Intrapreneur is the manager who takes risks. The ideal mix: a manager who becomes more entrepreneurial after working within a large organisation.
2	4
Low management skills. Little or no entrepreneurial flair. Most people in this box	Entrepreneur in a small business or family enterprise. Will stay small. Big ideas but no ideas on structure. Cannot put the entrepreneurial flair into action
1	3

Entrepreneur (E)

however, are often not with their own money. This intrapreneur (strong on leadership and entrepreneurship) will need to be underpinned by a strong manager, whereas the entrepreneur / manager style of intrapreneur will need alongside him someone who can be a figurehead for the venture and supply the leadership, possibly as the chairman. There are fewer figures who combine outstanding entrepreneurial skills with equally outstanding management skills. The absence of true leadership is often an impediment to their ability to build a large-scale corporation. A clear exception in this instance must be Martin Sorrell, Chief Executive of marketing services firm WPP Plc and the man behind some of the most audacious bids of the 1980s. His strongest suits are managerial and entrepreneurial. He first came to prominence as finance director of Saatchi & Saatchi at the time when it moved from boutique to world's top advertising agency. Sorrell is not a qualified accountant but has strong credentials as a manager. He is the son of a businessman, educated at Cambridge University and Harvard Business School, and is well schooled in detail and, moreover, intrigued by it: 'I take it as a compliment to be called a micro-manager.'

Sorrell also has an extraordinary appetite for risk. He left Saatchi & Saatchi and invested in WPP (makers of supermarket trolleys and baskets, the organization was originally called Wire and Plastic Products). Sorrell used this business as a vehicle to acquire an empire that rivalled Saatchi & Saatchi and is now highly profitable. Having acquired the bluest of blue chip agencies, Sorrell was hit by recession and, extremely highly leveraged, almost sank altogether. His managerial skill, coupled with the staying power that comes when a venture is one's own, and a fair measure of courage (some might also mention financial incentive) kept him going. Of course Sorrell is not without some leadership skills; he had a vision after all. Nevertheless the major acquisitions were of fairly autonomous and well-led businesses. Sorrell's primary motivation is that of the financially driven entrepreneur: 'I always wanted to have a significant equity stake in a large company, one that I had founded and built.'

Few people excel in all three dimensions, leadership, management and entrepreneurship, and yet there are few companies which can survive long-term without some blend of the three. This is where team building at the upper echelons of a company becomes critically important. There are numerous double acts in business where pairs achieve success. The extraordinary success story of Coca Cola in the last twenty years owes much to two men. Roberto Goizueta is undoubtedly a true leader, but his chosen heir, now the chairman and chief executive, Doug Ivester, also played a massive part in the overall success of the business. I would characterize Ivester as a classic manager in an equally classic scenario. He has followed a visionary leader who transformed an organization and, as his successor, is someone who subscribes to and helped bring that vision about and will ensure that it is sustained.

Ivester majored in accounting at university and joined what was then Ernst & Whinney, eventually joining the Coca Cola audit team. He then made the common move into the client, joining Coke as assistant controller in 1979, rising to be the chief financial officer by January 1987 when still aged just thirty-seven. Ivester was an important figure in the spin-off of Coke's bottling arm which was to give the business considerable edge against its major rival, Pepsi, which followed the initiative a year later by spinning off its own bottling business. More recently Ivester has grown the business in the home market, against predictions that the market was mature. These successes have been based on the skills of the manager: planning, thorough understanding of the market and the ability to organize the business to deliver to plan. In the long and prosperous double act between Goizueta and Ivester the former was often portrayed as Mr Nice while Ivester was Mr Nasty – a not entirely accurate depiction of the facts. Goizueta, the leader, embodied the vision; Ivester, the manager, ensured its implementation. Now Ivester has his time in the sun as chief executive . . .

Another such double act is that of Michael Dell, the entrepreneur, with Mort Topfer, Dell's vice-chairman. Similarly, at the top of Microsoft there is the man of ideas, Bill Gates, the salesman, Steve Ballmer, and now the corporate manager, Bob Herbold, Gates's number two and chief operating officer. Herbold joined Microsoft from Procter & Gamble, where, somewhat unusually, he headed both Information Systems and Advertising. He is the manager who has instilled the disciplines of a Fortune 500 company into the Microsoft business.

I began this chapter with a statement made by Abraham Zaleznik about the creativity of leadership. The formation of a company on the part of an entrepreneur or the transformation of one in the case of a leader, involving more often than not the creation of a strong and cohesive company culture, is, indeed, an extraordinary act of artistry. A leader must be able to tell a story, create a mood and atmosphere and move others. It requires extraordinary integrity and consistency. One corporate transformation in recent years that called for the highest levels of integrity and consistency has been that of Eni by Franco Bernabè who has recently moved to head up Italy's state telecommunications business. After some six years as chief executive of Italy's state-owned energy conglomerate he has entirely re-invented the business. What was once corrupt, indebted, state-owned, bureaucratic and unprofitable is now profitable, public and highly competitive with absolute operating transparency such that there is little risk of stain attaching to any part of the corporation in future.

Bernabè was a shock appointment in the aftermath of a change of government. Interestingly, he had come from a planning and finance background, although he was originally an academic and then an economist with Fiat. Bernabè was not someone who was seen as a natural for the post of CEO, not least because he had alienated members of the board by calling for change on numerous occasions. When appointed he moved quickly to put his vision in place. He tore out swathes of managers and replaced them with those who shared his vision for Eni as a commercial, viable venture. He took a great interest in the operations of all the businesses, ensuring that they conformed to the corporate strategic plan. He divested the business of any non-core activities, even one of its few profitable ventures, and did so while the entire Italian business community was under scrutiny for corruption. Eni lost twenty top executives, including the chairman, in the course of the investigation. Bernabè persevered with dogged commitment and the results of the business speak for themselves. In 1992 it made a loss of $554 million but by 1997 it turned in profits of $3 billion. Share price has more than doubled.

Bernabè is someone driven with an almost messianic fervour to clean up Italy and develop its businesses into global entities. That vision is supported by a very keen intellect and an ability to see the entirety of the business from a remove. Never an operational manager, Bernabè came the route of the outsider, the adviser. His personality is introverted and his style precise and rather chilly, but the quality of his conviction and the insistence of his message have achieved far more than any amount of tub-thumping and PR could have done. He is that rare person with the vision, appetite for risk, independence of mind and attention to detail who can move between the personae of leader, manager and entrepreneur. Eni, as it stands today, is indeed a quite remarkable testimony to his creativity.

Most companies do not have the good fortune to stumble upon someone with this breadth of skills. Instead, they must use existing resources to construct a composite. What makes Bernabè a useful figure with which to end this chapter is that there is no single element of his skill set which is more important than any other. If he were not a risk-taker and deal-doer he could not have done what he has done. If he did not have a vision he could not have done what he has done. If he could not manage the business so that the vision could be realized he could not have done what he has done. Entrepreneurs, managers and leaders are equally important. The entrepreneur brings something into being, the manager ensures its sustained and successful existence and the leader transforms it. The first and the last are needed far more rarely than those in the middle. This simple matter of mathematics perhaps contributes to our awestruck approach to leadership. However much we may value our leaders and entrepreneurs, their efforts are wasted without those of the more plentiful but no less essential managers.

Chapter 6

Follow My Leader:
The Role of the Follower

'No nation will let its fingers be burnt twice. The trick of the Pied Piper of Hamelin catches people only once.' – Adolf Hitler

'. . . the growing good of the world is partly dependent on unhistoric acts; and that things are not so ill with you and me as they might have been, is half owing to the number who lived faithfully a hidden life, and rest in unvisited tombs.' – George Eliot, *Middlemarch*

Whether it is just or not, society favours leaders over managers, especially those with some claim to charisma. Leaders enjoy immense prestige, but not so those who enable them. Both the Pied Piper and Hitler give following a bad name: they depict followers as a mass without independent decision-making faculties. There is no question that in certain circumstances the act of following can lead to catastrophic consequences. By and large, however, someone who follows is an individual who exercises judgment in considering and acting upon the vision of a leader. Leaders simply do not exist unless their leadership is endorsed by followers. Further, without followers to act as agents for them, the vision of the leader would remain a distant dream. Leadership may be where the accolades lie but following is not an ignominious activity. On the contrary, followers are the unsung facilitators of the leader's fame, as the management literature with its sub-section on followership has come to realize.

George Eliot in her study of a small-town English community in the nineteenth century shows that most of us are obliged to live out our lives in obscurity, having impact only on those in our immediate circle. She ennobles the ordinary. It is not just the ordinary who follow, however. Some people with extraordinary talent may choose to exercise that talent in the service of a leader who may have less raw talent than they. The choice may be motivated by lifestyle issues and a reluctance to make the necessary sacrifices. Following and leading is about a mix of personality, talent and opportunity rather than just one of the three.

Attitudes to risk influence one's preference for leadership, management and entrepreneurship. In the same way, tolerance to risk can be a major factor in the decision to follow rather than attempt to lead. A leader is simply more prepared to take on the burden of risk and personal exposure than the follower who relies on vicarious achievement, enjoying the success of the leader they follow and knowing their own part in that success. The notion of risk is at the heart of some definitions of what it is to be human. No beast would voluntarily risk its life, other than the human beast. Man is defined as man, according to German philosopher, Hegel, precisely because man can take this risk: 'And it is solely by risking life that freedom is obtained.' Hegel believed that in the early battle between men for recognition, the end point of the battle came when the inferior being stepped aside and refused to risk his life, leaving the other who had made no such surrender as the superior. From this battle, so Hegel proclaimed, came the social division between the superior master and his inferior slave. The master who chooses to run the risk of losing his life does so in the recognition that what he can win is altogether worth the risk. He appears to act against his own immediate interests but acts in pursuit of a higher interest still. Through the battle for prestige the superior man demonstrates his freedom of choice.

In a business context, Hegelian philosophy may seem a long way from modern society and the roles played in it by leaders and followers, but in the relationship between leaders and followers there is both choice and a calculation of the level of risk an individual is likely to tolerate. Today we would not see the relationship between leader and led in quite such hierarchical terms as Hegel's master/slave dichotomy. What, after all is a leader without a follower? Little short of a conceited failure. Leaders and followers have the same relationship as locks and keys, the one unlocking the other, the two combining in a useful mechanism. So, while we would be loath to see the relationship in quite such polarized terms we would nevertheless see the decision to pursue power – for what else is the pursuit of leadership – as a matter of clear choice. Many who come to lead are not the most able of their generation. Indeed, we probably cannot begin to judge who is the most able of a given generation since the majority of those who would qualify have doubtless been lost to obscurity. Those who come to prominence are those who have the drive to lead, who thrive on risk.

Entrepreneurs often take grave financial risks. The risks run by corporate business leaders are of the emotional variety. The life of a business leader is not, to my mind, a particularly enviable one. It is characterized by complexity and the appearance of comfort is something of a chimera. A glance at an annual report for a leading quoted company will give the impression that a chief executive should want for nothing, such is his remuneration. The remuneration, however, is – to use the term favoured by Americans – compensation. Strictly, the meaning behind the phrase is that an individual is compensated for their labour. To my mind they must also be compensated for the hardship of a working life which keeps them permanently on show to a range of interest groups which are not all supportive. Answerable to shareholders, a chief executive faces a far more hostile set of critics than the average manager and he is ultimately answerable on all issues all the time. Permanently on call, the chief executive is also permanently on show. Rare is the chief executive who manages to accomplish all his tasks within the average eight-hour day.

On the whole, a chief executive can expect to be at his desk at 8.00 in the morning and at 8.00 in the evening is likely to be leaving it only in time to attend one of the many so-called 'social' functions which go with the job. Few chief executives, however much they talk about 'quality' time with their families, can expect to achieve much in the way of family time, quality or otherwise. Most miss out on the childhood of their offspring, and aspiring chief executives can confidently rely on knowing their grandchildren rather better than their own children. That is if the rigours of the job or, even worse, the absence of those rigours in retirement, do not claim them first. Most of us would wish for a modicum of balance in our lives: the chance to read a good book, dine with friends, see the best plays and films and pursue our favourite sports. The average chief executive will find that life revolves around work. Indeed, over time they often lose interest in anything other than work, hence profiles of business figures always remark, with some astonishment, upon a leader who has read something other than *The Art of War* by Sun Zi.

So chief executives give up what less elevated mortals assume to be the normal comforts of life. But is this really risk? Probably not. The sense in which chief executives take a risk is with their inner selves, their souls. Franco Bernabè, the chief executive at Eni, had a vision to transform the company and encountered immense opposition but he put his reputation firmly on the line: 'It was really war. It was a question of survival. If I had lost the battle to clean Eni of politics and make it a commercial business, both the company and the country would have suffered.' The stakes were very high indeed but Bernabè took astonishing risks in pursuit of a company that any observer would know to be incorrupt. Indeed, he asked all his senior managers to resign when some came under suspicion of corruption, thereby risking the short-term future of the business altogether. He also had to face and counter the inevitable (and, of course, false) charges that he had accepted a bribe. Bernabè risked his belief system.

None of us like failure. Most of us avoid putting ourselves into positions where failure can be either too costly or too public. Not so with chief executives. The generals who lead troops into battle risk the lives of others on an irregular basis. On a regular basis we could, with some justice, claim that the chief executive risks the livelihoods of large numbers of people. Some corporations are so large that they employ many thousands of people. The chief executive is not, clearly, solely responsible for those people, but he is the individual who, in the eyes of the public and interested parties, must be held to be responsible. If he fails, his failure is of a very public nature. A leader leads because he is driven by a need to be recognized and revered by his peers. Failure, then, is anathema. Indeed, failure to someone who is driven by a need to succeed is considerably worse than a similar failure suffered by someone less driven. To make matters worse, by dint of the very difficulty of the task, it is probably as easy to be a failure as a leader as it is to be a success. Most probably achieve something in between, but all take a risk in pursuing success of achieving only failure and, as the old adage has it, the higher they are, the harder they fall. Looked at in this light, the choice to remain a follower in business, rather than strive to lead, seems the wise one.

Some followers, of course, are people who would have liked the chance to lead. Michael Heseltine, a successful entrepreneur in business, would have liked the opportunity to lead the Conservative Party. A charismatic man, beloved of the party faithful, he came to prominence under Margaret Thatcher and was the right man at the wrong time when she was deposed. The party needed, and elected, a manager and Heseltine chose to follow Major. When opportunity did present itself to contest the leadership it came too late and his health would not allow him to put his popularity to the test.

Some are luckier. In Procter & Gamble, the major international detergents business, there was a battle at the top in 1995 to take over from the legendary Ed Artzt, the then chairman and chief executive. The battle was won by John Pepper and lost by Durk Jager, his chief rival, who became instead the president and chief operating officer. People thought that Jager would have to settle for second best and that the support for Pepper, in every way Jager's polar opposite, was a significant vote against Jager. Jager, however, has turned in a supportive performance and his reward in 1998 was to be announced the next chief executive of the business.

Western culture has tended not to depict followers in flattering terms. Instead they are seen as lacking in individuality, being sheeplike and preferring the comfort of the herd to operating alone. Heroism and glamour are reserved for the role of the leader. There have been famous followers, but they have not necessarily been celebrated. Dr Watson is perhaps the archetypal sidekick, at least as portrayed by Nigel Bruce as the key supporting actor to Basil Rathbone's Holmes. The good doctor is seen as well meaning but ineffectual, something of a lovable buffoon. Sidekicks are often servile or so far removed from the leader that it almost calls into question the leader's judgment – one thinks of Batman and Robin, here. Posterity has not treated Captain Hardy, another famous follower, particularly well. Flag captain to Nelson at the Battle of Trafalgar (he was Captain of the *Victory* when Nelson was

Admiral of the Fleet). Hardy went on to be First Sea Lord but is principally remembered for bestowing a kiss on the dying Nelson. This incident, it is now widely believed, is altogether apocryphal, since Nelson's final words are now thought to have been 'Kismet, Hardy', a reflection of fate (kismet) rather than a sentimental show of affection. Nevertheless, the story continues to be Hardy's epitaph as much as it is Nelson's. Occasionally we will celebrate a follower. Captain Oates, of the ill-fated expedition to the South Pole led by Robert Falcon Scott (himself a hero who captivated an entire generation), is perhaps an examplar of a heroic follower. Oates took himself off to die in order that he should not further impede the embattled team.

The master/slave distinction made by Hegel is a chilling one. In our egalitarian days we are, perhaps, inclined to go a little too far in the opposite direction. The notion of leadership is being stretched to include any number of small acts of leadership. Empowerment has become an important concept in the last decade. It is one with which I have considerable sympathy. No one can doubt the efficacy of a practice which offers people the opportunity to take as much responsibility as possible. Empowerment means that at all levels in an organization individuals know themselves to be an integral part of the business with an important role to play. People are given increased decision-making powers and manage many more processes with much more autonomy than previously. Many business writers affirm that running anything, be it a project, or a small team of people, or a process, amounts to leadership and make the claim that leadership is open to all. Indeed, some would claim that these small acts of leadership are excellent preparation for a large act of leadership, such as running a company. Most of these people who are acquiring knowledge and expertise are more likely to be managers than leaders. Put simply, a small act of leadership will lead to a small amount of change. A large act of leadership will give rise to substantial change.

Another common view held by those who want to make leadership available to the masses is that in different situations different people may lead. The business leader, transplanted into a different context, may find that he is become a follower. If he is musically inclined and joins a string quartet, for example, he may find that he is the second violin while someone else takes the lead. This argument is emotionally pleasing: be he ever so mighty he may still play second fiddle and no matter how humble we are we can aspire to lead in some situations. There may be some truth in this argument. Some people may find satisfaction in small acts of leadership which preclude them wanting to pursue leadership with the aggression required in business. For some traditional males, for example, the act of heading the family may give satisfaction, others may enjoy captaining the local sports team. I would dispute whether we are talking about the same kind of leadership, the leadership on a grand scale where the ultimate object is to effect change.

By giving wider access to leadership we further erode the status of following. Today many of the people that we would once have described as followers we would now identify as team players. We would be more likely to commend Captain Oates for his self-sacrifice on behalf of the team, rather than on behalf of the leader. And we may well be right. We feel uncomfortable with any explicit sense of inequality such as exists between those who wield and those who obey power. Leaders themselves must be a part of a team. No leader operates in isolation in a modern business. Instead they are obliged to work closely with others, particularly with their key reports in order to achieve company objectives. A political leader, assuming they operate within a democracy, is similarly placed with a cabinet of ministerial colleagues. The phrase *primus inter pares* has considerable application to modern organizations, be they political or commercial.

In the first 'modern' war, the American Civil War, the great generals were those who understood that they were indeed first among equals. Nowhere is this more obvious than in the case of the aptly named Ulysses S. Grant. A somewhat patrician, highly trained man (a graduate of West Point), Grant was a first-rate soldier who recognized that his troops, largely volunteers, were themselves very able individuals who in peacetime occupied positions equivalent in status to his own. He demonstrated his innate respect for his followers by allowing them to follow their own judgement rather than the view he put forward. Accordingly, they mounted an ill-fated assault only to come to their own belated understanding of their leader's rationale in opposing them. In short, Grant demonstrated to a group of people whom he respected that he was qualified to be their leader.

To speak in terms of those who wield and those who obey power is highly anachronistic, not to mention simplistic. It is not particularly easy to identify where power does reside in a modern organization. Those in control hold the finances and the very future of the company in trust for the shareholders. Board decisions must operate in the interests of those shareholders and both the chairman in his function as leader of the board and the chief executive as leader of the company must provide a service to shareholders. The relationship of the leader of the company to the shareholders is not that of a follower to a leader, rather it is that of the steward of a vast estate to the title holder of that estate. Shareholders may not be able to wield direct power but they can have considerable influence and institutional shareholders in particular are a formidable force in the business arena.

The leader finds himself in the midst of a complex set of relationships and old modes of leadership are not as effective as they once were. The command and control model, where power is centralized and information retained by a select inner cabal, has little or no relevance to a modern business. The autocrat has given way to the democratic leader who empowers others. The democrat does not seek election by his followers (in the true sense of the word 'democratic') but invites them to be increasingly involved in the decision-making process and to participate in the management of the operation. Tacitly, at least, such leaders are open to criticism. They appear to be willing to listen to it and by so doing invite their followers to legitimize their status as leader. By being open in this way, by creating opportunity, respecting the competence and contribution of others, the democratic leader receives more genuine and better-grounded respect than his autocratic forebear. In the late 1990s all institutions are having to wake up to the reality that openness of demeanour, ease of communication and the ability to listen are factors which will win respect and, in some instances, adulation.

Even the British monarchy has had to accept that it must find a new model of leadership if it is to have any relevance to Britain in the twenty-first century. The death of Diana, Princess of Wales, in 1997 and the extraordinary outpouring of public grief which followed took everybody by surprise. Nobody would want to deny that the Princess was a woman with flaws, but it was these which made her human. What mattered about Diana was her belief in people, her ability to communicate to people that she valued them, and her genuine interest in what they had to say. Diana, Princess of Wales, embodied a number of virtues which are not out of place in the modern model of leadership.

Just because the model of modern leadership is a different one from that which held sway in previous generations, does not mean that modern society has any less need of leaders than formerly. Society still needs those rare people who can genuinely effect change by motivating others to act in accordance with their vision. Leaders may occupy a position which is occasionally a little ambiguous (as when they are operating in relation to shareholders) and may from time to time need to demonstrate their humility and their recognition that they do not occupy their leadership position by divine right. This, however, is very little different from the position many leaders in the past have found themselves in. Great leaders have seldom been those who have not been able to make themselves loved, as well as respected, by their followers.

If we still need leaders, we certainly still need followers. There is a case to reclaim the role of the follower from the ignominy into which it seems to have been cast. Doctor Watson seems as good a point as any at which to start. Numerous film representations of the good doctor have reproduced the bumbling caricature that I conjured above. Conan Doyle's original character, inclined to be misguided in his interpretation of crimes, was a much more important figure than the stock Watson of the cinema. Watson was a medical man and his medical knowledge was directly important in the solution of crimes. Certainly there is in Conan Doyle's text a sense in which Watson is a foil to Holmes but, most importantly, it is Watson who keeps Holmes rooted in the real world. Holmes's genius inclines him to eccentricity and self-destructive behaviour (in particular his penchant for cocaine). Without Watson to cajole him into maintaining some degree of equilibrium Holmes could not function at all. The follower, rather like the manager in the previous chapter, is someone who makes something happen.

In Freudian dream symbolism the key represents knowledge. The follower as the key that unlocks a leader's potential very often ensures that the leader gains the knowledge he needs. Leaders must maintain their mystique, which they do, in part, through the maintenance of a certain distance from those who follow. On an emotional level this is essential but on a practical level it can be problematic. Leaders need to be in a position to make decisions, they need to be in as full possession of the facts as circumstances allow and they must depend on others to furnish them with the knowledge. Followers are often in a position to provide the leader with this type of intelligence. T. S. Eliot understood this well. In *The Love Song of J. Alfred Prufrock* he notes, with considerable irony:

> No! I am not Prince Hamlet, nor was meant to be;
> Am an attendant lord, one that will do
> To swell a progress, start a scene or two,
> Advise the prince; no doubt, an easy tool,
> Deferential, glad to be of use;
> Politic, cautious, and meticulous;
> Full of high sentence, but a bit obtuse;

There is more than a little playfulness here. The observer, politic, cautious and meticulous – the civil servant, perhaps – can find considerable more intellectual stimulation in the act of observing leadership than in leadership itself. For a number of years the BBC screened a situation comedy in Britain that parodied the foolish leader's dependence on his wise counsel. *Yes, Minister* was immensely popular, striking a chord with a populace largely comprised of followers.

There are some very gifted people on the periphery of leadership but not actually in a leadership position who have chosen not to move into a role that would bring the spotlight of attention entirely on to them. The most obvious case in the UK is Ian Duncan, who is the Deputy Chairman and Managing Director (Finance) of Tomkins plc. Tomkins is a conglomerate in the age of the focused business and, as such, has become unfashionable. Greg Hutchings, the maverick and entrepreneurial leader, has built the business from a market value of £6 million to £3.5 billion in the thirteen or fourteen years he has been with it. He would not have had this success had it not been for Ian Duncan, recently described in the national press as 'one of the unsung heroes of British business'. Duncan is a first-rate operator with a tough mind who insists on the highest standards from his colleagues. It is he who has kept the glory-seeking, deal-doing, arch-competitor Hutchings on his mettle and, in a situation where change is more familiar than stability, he has provided a vital fixed point for shareholders and investors. In common, I imagine, with some other headhunters I have on occasion tried to woo Duncan away but, so far at least, he has elected to stay. We must presume that he takes his satisfaction from knowing that the achievements of Tomkins could not have happened but for his pivotal role. Management and following can give rise to as much satisfaction for a certain – non-egotistical – person as can leadership.

In my working life I spend a great deal of time contemplating the role of the independent non-executive – or outside – director. In the last few years I have been a principal agent in the construction of a large number of boards, putting together teams of both executive and non-executive directors. I have also contributed to the governance debate. The role of the follower has some affinity with the role of the independent non-executive director. I insist on putting considerable emphasis on the word independent. Too many directors who serve in a non-executive capacity are still not truly independent. They may be former executives, friends of friends, or friends of relatives, indeed in some cases they may be relatives (relatives do not necessarily share the same name, after all). Such people are sometimes chosen because they represent a safe option and can be relied upon not to act against the wishes of (usually) a very strong chairman. Such people correspond to what I have somewhere in the business literature seen described as bad followers.

The word follower should not imply slavish devotion on the part of the follower towards the leader. On the contrary it denotes someone who follows a leader because they recognize the authority of that leader (as Grant's men recognized that he was qualified to lead them), who shares the vision and wants to participate in the realization of that vision. A follower should be someone who will facilitate and that may involve being a critic. A leader cannot be right all of the time and must be able to rely on some people to dispute and criticize. In the case of the chairman that role is institutionalized. Independent non-executive directors serve as a check upon any excesses on the part of the chairman. The role is not exclusively that of a watchdog. The non-executives are there to debate issues around the boardroom table and to bring to the debate a different perspective, brought from their own experience outside the confines of that particular business. Increasingly, far seeing chairmen and nominating committees are looking to appoint independent non-executive directors from very different businesses and different cultures in order to bring real breadth to the board room. The chief executive who is a leader may find in his chairman the confidant, check and control and adviser that the chairman finds in the non-executive team. If he does not (and a non-executive chairman, for instance, cannot be as close to the business as someone who is employed in its service every working day), then he must look to his followers for that all important check and control.

His followers, if they are to fulfil this function adequately, must have outstanding qualities of their own. They must have quality of judgement, a rigorous sense of justice, the self-assurance to make and persist with their point and the independence to do so in the knowledge that, to a certain extent, they are hostage to their leader. A follower must risk himself that far. History throws up followers who took one risk too many. Sir Thomas More, Lord Chancellor to Tudor King Henry VIII, torn between following his God and following his King, gave Henry VIII his candid opinion regarding Henry's opposition to the Pope and proposed divorce. He paid for his conscience and his candour with his life. A follower, despite the negative connotations which attach to the word, is *not* a sycophant. Absolute monarchs, like Henry VIII, often preferred flattery to sincerity. In *King Lear* Shakespeare presents an honest follower who speaks his mind to an egotistical king under cover of his role as the court jester or fool:

> That sir which serves and seeks for gain
> And follows but for form
> Will pack when it begins to rain
> And leave thee in the storm.
> But I will tarry; the Fool will stay,
> And let the wise man fly:

> The knave turns Fool that runs away;
> The fool no knave, perdy.

Shakespeare's wise fool offers a moving paradigm of the disinterested follower. A leader who surrounds himself with sycophants is likely to be a bad leader or, at the very least, a leader who sets too much store by his own word. A leader who surrounds himself with highly able advisers who stretch that leader and challenge him is far more likely to be successful than one who does not.

The follower's skill set may be every bit as sophisticated as the leader's. Indeed, the leader should hope that this is the case. One of the exponents of the translation theory of power, Bruno Latour, writes: 'The problem of power may be encapsulated in the following paradox: when you simply have power – in potentia – nothing happens and you are powerless; when you exert power – in actu – others are performing the action and not you.' In short, a leader is not personally responsible for seeing to it that the actions he initiates are performed. He is entirely at the mercy of the competence and reliability of those who translate his or her initial message. Latour continues: 'The obedience to an order given by someone would require the alignment of all the people concerned by it, who would all assent to it faithfully, without adding or subtracting anything. Such a situation is highly improbable.' Latour's point is that in the process of transmission the initial message will be interpreted by each follower in accordance with that follower's own particular interests. Inevitably, in the course of transmission one person will use different words, the message will be subtly altered and, once it has been through any number of translations, may barely resemble either its form or content at the outset. A leader needs to have confidence in the integrity of a follower if the message being relayed is to remain, in spirit at least, faithful to the original.

There is, of course, a hierarchy of followers as a message cascades down an organization through successively more junior managers. In a business environment a leader who is managing a complex change programme will take steps to ensure that he or she is not endlessly at the mercy of those interpreting the vision/ message. In the first place the vision will have a certain simplicity. Second, it will be conveyed in the same form through many different media and will not depend entirely on word of mouth. The leader will maintain some control, but followers will have some freedom of interpretation. The two sides are locked into a relationship of mutuality.

Power is, of course, at the heart of the subject of leadership and attitudes towards it form one of the primary distinctions between those who lead and those who follow. The leader is intoxicated by power; the follower prefers to (or settles for) influence rather than direct power. Here, of course, I am referring to a senior follower or someone who is close to the leader, rather than someone at the base of the pyramid of followers. Power is much more immediate than influence. Someone with power can see the effects on the instant, whereas the effects of influence are far more insidious. Power can be crude, whereas influence has the scope for far greater subtlety. Power brings recognition. Influence may lead to acknowledgement, but often not even this much. On the face of it, a preference for influence over power would appear to be perverse. A quick exercise shows that influence is not always the poor relation to power.

Figure 6.1

Powerful figures in the twentieth century	Influential figures in the twentieth century
Lenin	Freud
Hitler	Einstein
Mussolini	Picasso
Stalin	Schoenberg
Churchill	T. S. Eliot
De Gaulle	Alexander Fleming
Chairman Mao	Crick & Watson
John F. Kennedy	Jean-Paul Sartre

Few would dispute that the achievements of those in the column on the right will have a longer-term, more beneficial effect than those of the individuals on the left. Some few people such as Nelson Mandela manage to bring together both power and influence; perhaps Mahatma Gandhi is another such and Mikhael Gorbachev is probably someone who, ultimately, had more influence than power although by rights he belongs in the left-hand column. The powerful may have extraordinary personal fame or notoriety which the influential cannot match. The powerful are, however, trapped in history. The influential – especially those whose influence has, like Newton's, radically altered our understanding of the world – can be said to stand outside time. The quartet of Galileo, Marx, Darwin and Freud have probably had a more lasting effect on the way we live our lives in the twentieth century than have Alexander the Great, Genghis Khan, Napoleon and Hitler. Power appeals to the man or woman of action. Influence is of more appeal to the contemplative individual than to the sensationalist.

Some relationships in history throw out an interesting commentary on the seductiveness of influence. Eva Perón did not hold power. She was never more than a consort to her husband. Her effect on the people of Argentina was nevertheless extraordinary. So great a figure was she that her body was embalmed and three copies were made of the embalmed figure in order to confuse would-be grave robbers. She has given rise to a box-office-breaking musical which has been filmed starring one of the icons of pop music, Madonna. Her name is known far beyond the country of her birth. Who remembers her husband?

In starting out in their career some people take the decision that they want to influence rather than wield power. In recent years professional services firms have become the destination of choice for many top graduates of university and business school. Some go into these organizations with the hope of using them as a stepping stone to an accelerated corporate career, but many enjoy the stimuli and status of being advisers. Moreover, the accountants and management consultants have a very well-developed mechanism for recruiting, developing and retaining talent. They seldom lose those they wish to hold on to. Some of the best brains of the last twenty or thirty years have probably been applied to a host of business problems in an advisory rather than a leadership or even a managerial capacity. Of course, some of these highly able advisers go on to run companies in their turn. American Express, for example, has at the helm a former McKinsey consultant in the shape of Chairman and CEO Harvey Golub, and a former Bain consultant in President and Chief Operating Officer Ken Chenault. Both, however, had long exposure to operational roles and did not move into these front-line positions directly from consulting.

Firms of professional advisers occasionally throw up leaders who can, in turn, transfer to the corporate sector and replicate that leadership. Harold Cottam, who led Ernst & Young through the merger between Ernst and Whinney and Arthur Young in the UK, has subsequently taken on several non-executive roles, most recently as, nominally, the non-executive Chairman of Britannic. I say nominally simply because over the last eighteen months, during which time he has led the business through a turnaround programme, taking it from being a Cinderella in its sector to a budding princess, he has worked a four-day week. He is a rare example of someone who, apparently an influencer, has shown equal (probably superior) flair as a powerful leader figure.

It should not be a matter of undue concern that many of the better-educated brains move into professional advisory roles. Successful leadership is not a matter of mere brains, or for that matter of education. The well-educated are often almost over-educated. They may be quite brilliant critics but their creativity may be

Figure 6.2

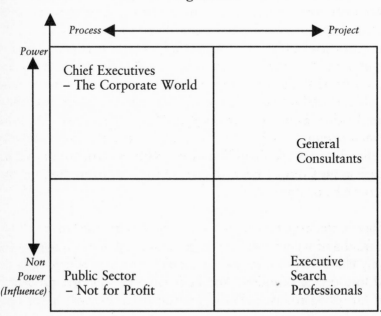

disabled by that very critical faculty: they will see the glass half empty whereas a less critical person would see the glass half full. Leadership is a matter of personality. Those whose talents reside in the intellectual area are likely to find the chance to exert influence more seductive than the opportunity to wield power.

Figure 6.2 depicts the choices that people make regarding the nature of their career. Power or influence represent one clear choice, process or project another. Some, notably professional advisers, enjoy the deadline-driven environment of the project, whereas those who thrive on both power and process are much more likely to choose a corporate environment. Public service organizations appeal to people who enjoy process and influence. Interestingly, those who favour projects over process and influence over power are less willing followers than those who welcome process. Consultants are fickle and answer many masters and professional services businesses, home to consultants, are notoriously difficult to manage and unwelcoming towards leaders.

The different approach to power and influence discernible in leaders and followers is intimately connected with the psyche of the individual. Leaders are often outsiders. Followers tend to be insiders. Indeed, they tend to be comfortable working in and around a network, building strong relationships, gathering intelligence as they do so. Leaders are often first-born children. Followers, conversely, may be middle children or the younger children of larger families. Their position in the family will have accustomed them to getting things done by developing good relationships with their siblings and pleasing, rather than particularly forceful, interpersonal skills. Followers are people who invite trust. The old-fashioned notion of a follower conveys a strong sense of loyalty and reliability. US President Woodrow Wilson wrote of one of his chief advisers, Colonel Edward House (whom, ironically, he was later to sack for duplicity):

House has a strong character – if to be disinterested and
unafraid and incorruptible is to be strong. He has a noble and
lovely character, too, for he is capable of utter self-forgetfulness
and loyalty and devotion. And he is wise. He can give prudent
and far-seeing counsel. He can find out what many men, of
diverse kinds, are thinking about, and how they can be made to

work together for a common purpose. He wins the confidence
of all sorts of men, and wins it at once, by deserving it.

These positive virtues remain very much a part of the follower's
tool kit. They are not particularly fashionable terms, at least in
business where there tends to be a greater focus on being a hard,
driving character. Nevertheless, corporate followers do seem to
embody some, if not all, of these attributes. A follower is someone
who invites the trust of the leader but also of his own peers and so
can develop a far more immediate grasp of the mechanics of an
organization or situation than can the leader. Woodrow Wilson's
assessment of House gives too much credence to qualities of self-
effacement. A follower must have good judgement to be effective,
for which there is some need of strength of personality and a core
sense of self. What a strong follower should lack is an over-
demanding ego. Followers should be able to subsume their own
ego to give space to the persona – and ego – of the leader.

Followers are, by and large, comfortable with the notion of
belonging. They are likely to be proud of belonging. *Business Week*
ran a report recently about Steve Ballmer of Microsoft, who clearly
relishes belonging to the business. The article reported how, at an
annual sales meeting, Ballmer received a five-minute standing
ovation for running on stage shouting: 'I love this company! I
love this company!' Given the general fetish for leadership which
operates to the disadvantage of followers, I hesitate to label someone a follower. Nevertheless, Ballmer is a clear contender for the
title. A college friend of Bill Gates, he is described in the same
article as Microsoft's 'wildly thumping heart'. Recently elevated to
President, Sales and Product Development, it has been Ballmer who
has inspired and corralled the troops at Microsoft and it is Ballmer
who provides a key sounding board for Gates: 'We trust each other
and understand how the other one thinks,' says Gates of Ballmer.
He is a devoted father, son, colleague and friend. He rushes home
to put his children to bed each evening, and last year took three
months off work in order to care for his ailing parents. He joined
Microsoft at Gates's invitation and has stayed there, despite being
passed over for the role he now holds some five years ago. The son
of a demanding father and a mother whom he adored, Ballmer
grew up needing to perform to please. He has taken these values

with him into adulthood. Neither the chief executive nor the chief operating officer, Ballmer is a very important factor in the success of Microsoft and the equilibrium of its leader.

Some people found businesses. Some join a company on graduation, or in early career, and spend the greater part of their career within it. Others achieve success in one environment but then move to another, sometimes at mid-career, and replicate or extend their success. These founders, lifers and migrants are three core categories into which people divide. In my experience lifers are good managers and excellent followers where as it is more likely to be among the migrant community that one finds the leaders or the would-be leaders. Lifers and followers are, of course, in the majority in the population. Most of us, after all, become accustomed to following from a very early age. We follow our parents or our siblings, we look up to our elders at school and we exist within a hierarchy where we can fix our position in terms of age, social class, intelligence, sporting ability or whichever parameters are deemed important.

If leaders seem to come more often from family situations where there has been an experience of loss, followers tend to be the product of happier homes. For those who have had a happy childhood, especially those who are disappointed with their adult existence, the past can take on an important symbolic aspect. Just as in the post-industrial age numerous writers looked back wistfully to some mythical organic society, so disappointed adults look back to a golden childhood era. To a greater or lesser extent most of us find some appeal in the notion of having a parent figure to take full responsibility for our well-being. Followers are people who take comfort from the notion of belonging and, in part at least, the leader offers a renewal of an early relationship where another person takes ultimate responsibility.

Jacques Lacan, a practising psychoanalyst for some fifty years and one of the discipline's leading thinkers, said that the analyst was the person who was *supposed* to know, the person who as a proxy parent has the answers. Followers regard their leader as someone who has this knowledge. Military historian John Keegan, writing of leaders who must lead men to risk their lives on the battlefield, makes a similar point: 'What [followers] know of him must be what they hope and require.' The relationship between the leader and the led must supply the needs of the follower. Keegan calls his study *The Mask of Comnand*, because leadership must be a pretence. Leaders, like parents, are fallible; but they must conceal their fallibility at all costs, for part of following is indulging in the fantasy that there is such a thing as certainty and security.

It is this child-like requirement that there be someone on whom we can rely, someone in this world to whom we can turn, that makes cults so effective. Indeed, cults and their figureheads appeal to a broad cross-section of the population, not simply the particularly vulnerable and gullible. One such guru was Georgei Ivanovitch Gurdjieff, who in the first couple of decades of this century built up a following among the intelligentsia and middle classes in Europe and the United States, although his written works were utterly incomprehensible.

Anthony Storr, in his illuminating study of gurus, *Feet of Clay*, refers to Gurdjieff's beliefs as a psychotic delusional system and recounts an anecdote about this confidence trickster which smacks of the children's fairy tale *The Emperor's New Clothes*. Gurdjieff diluted a bottle of *vin ordinaire* with water, made the bottle seem old by covering it with sand and cobwebs, and passed it off as a rare vintage to two distinguished guests. Both apparently pronounced the drink the most delicious they had tasted. Storr sums up Gurdjieff's appeal in terms reminiscent of Lacan's statement that the analyst is *supposed* to know.

'Gurdjieff's picture of the universe, whether learned from esoteric sources or constructed by himself, provided him with his own myth, his own answer to the problem of the meaning of life . . . It was his own conviction that he had discovered *the answer* which made him charismatic and persuasive. Even if some of his followers could not accept or understand all his cosmic doctrines, they still believed that he knew.'

Our early childhood experiences have as much impact on our role as followers as on our role as leaders. Indeed, in the *Interpretation of Dreams* Freud wrote: 'In the unconscious nothing can be brought to an end, nothing is past or forgotten.' Nowhere is this more obvious than in our predisposition to refer any new relationship with authority to our original relationship with authority, to transfer the present situation back to the past, or to transfer our past experience on to the present. The psychoanalytic term for this practice is *transference*. The term was first employed by Freud when he found that the analysand responded to the analyst in the way he or she had responded to a parent or similarly influential person. Steve Ballmer grew up with a great respect for his parents. He indeed cites them as the people that to this day he admires most. Keen to please them and win their approval, he carries that same desire into his working life.

Most human relationships reflect a certain degree of transference as well as of realistic reactions. Manfred Kets de Vries is an academic whose study of business is undertaken from a psychoanalytical standpoint. What follows owes much to his work. De Vries identifies three main forms of transference, the first of which is *idealizing transference*. Here the follower looks to his leader to fulfil a role as omnipotent and perfect. He puts the leader on a pedestal and worships him. The leader comes to have a huge influence over the follower's life. He moulds himself in the leader's image and replicates, faithfully and uncritically, the leader's message. Initially an egotistical leader may find some gratification in a follower who idealizes him but ultimately the relationship will act as a constraint rather than a release on the leader. The follower who idealizes the leader can be devastated by any form of conflict and requires constant praise. He (or she) will need to be the sole focus of the leader's attention and when a colleague or peer competes for time or space there is likely to be conflict. Followers who follow this pattern are likely to have had early experience of distance from a beloved parent. Indeed, it is possible that the distance may have been brought about by death, which, we have seen, is a circumstance that can often give rise to leadership.

Different personality types deal with similar circumstances in very different ways; subject to the level of emotional robustness and the quality of opportunities and support on offer, the early death of a parent may give rise to a leader, a strong follower or, as in this case, a poor follower. One of the principal weaknesses of the follower who idealizes the leader is that when they are disappointed by their leader the feelings of disenchantment are acute. Indeed, the follower will feel betrayed and let down. In such instances the follower can turn against the leader and, in a spirit of rebellion, become a very negative force. Gurdjieff, for instance, was brought to the attention of the intelligentsia by his disciple Ouspensky. From being the guru's most devoted disciple, he became disillusioned by 1917 and 1924 severed relations with Gurdjieff entirely. Ouspensky forbade his pupils to have any further contact with their former leader. Ouspensky kept the religion, but ditched its focal point. Gurdjieff's decline dates from this rift with the man who had so popularized him.

In business, the type of leader who can attract followers of the idealizing type is the entrepreneur or founder who has the willpower and force of personality to develop a new enterprise from a standing start. Such people do not have the luxury of a vast resource of highly able followers on whom to draw. Often they must simply make the best of what is available and the loyalty of the idealizing follower can count for much in a start-up situation. As the business matures, however, and the vision and force of the founder's personality are no longer sufficient to sustain the business, then the passive follower (for such is the idealizing follower) who follows without questioning will find themselves challenged in a more professionally managed environment.

The second form of transference is the mirroring variety. *Mirror transference* is an attempt to restore oneself to an original state of bliss in which one is perfect and all-powerful. It is an attempt to regain the period prior to socialization. Mirroring takes place when an individual has a grandiose sense of self and is highly narcissistic, needing constant attention and praise and demanding that he or she be at centre stage. Followers whose self-image is inflated in this way can be very difficult subordinates to manage. They will constantly want to demonstrate their superiority to their peers and, by implication, to the leader and will be political in the sense that they will manoeuvre to show themselves in the most positive light and will seek the highest form of rewards possible. Theirs is a desperate need for recognition and will, on a positive note, lead to a productive level of drive and energy. Unfortunately, however, such subordinates tend to be a little unscrupulous in their desire for recognition: they will steal a colleague's ideas or go over the heads of immediate superiors to a higher level of management if they sense that recognition lies along that route. Richard Rich, in Robert

Bolt's play *A Man for All Seasons*, falls into this category. Disappointed in Sir Thomas More's service (for More judges him and sees his shortcomings all too clearly), Rich insinuates his way into the King's favour and while he is on the rise he passes his former master on the descent.

Finally, de Vries identifies a third transferent type which is persecutory. Here an individual re-enacts an early experience where he or she felt persecuted and prepares a range of defences against the repetition of this conflict. Overwhelmingly negative in either a leader or a follower, *persecution transference* manifests itself in hostility, envy or moral masochism, where the individual feels guilt about wishing to persecute and so turns the persecution inward upon the self. A hostile subordinate is an uncooperative follower whose manner registers a lack of trust, a generalized suspicion towards the environment and, apparently, gratuitous opposition toward the leader. Where the reaction is one of envy the subordinate will focus on a presumed injustice which has led to the subordinate in question having less in a way of rewards or being less well regarded than the leader that is envied. Iago, in Shakespeare's *Othello*, is driven by an act he perceives as an unjust one (he is overlooked for promotion) and the ensuing trick played upon Othello, leading to Othello's murder of Desdemona and his own suicide, derives entirely from his envy. Either a hostile or an envious reaction in a follower can have damaging cultural repercussions, as an atmosphere of mistrust and injustice will over time be corrosive of the trust and the goodwill of others. The transferent who favours moral masochism is a liability either as a leader or a follower, since they will court failure and inefficiency and put themselves in a position where they can be punished.

By their very nature followers remain in the shadows, so it is hard to focus on the part personality plays in their make-up unless the leader they follow is such a monster that all his followers come under suspicion. The twentieth century has seen totalitarian states led by dictators surrounded by an intimate circle of disciples. The Third Reich must be the most obvious example. Perhaps one of the most interesting of Hitler's inner circle was one who, once considered as a successor to Hitler, nevertheless escaped the Nuremberg trials with his life, serving a twenty-year sentence in Spandau prison instead. Albert Speer was Hitler's architect, who stage-managed the early Nuremberg rallies and, a brilliant organizer, ultimately rose to be second in command, in charge of armaments and munitions. It was Speer who organized the traffic in slave labour, although one of his juniors was hanged for the crime of having recruited that labour.

Speer is an example of a follower who through his relationship with Hitler found a paternal role model which he had lacked in his childhood. His parents were very unloving towards Albert, favouring his two brothers and disregarding him completely. A Catholic priest who knew Speer in later life, when Speer used to go on retreat at a monastery, said: 'I often wondered what happened to him as a child to make him into what he was, a brilliant man incapable of abstract thinking and, I think, incapable of sensual love and thus, finally, an incomplete man.' The priest had read the man with uncanny accuracy. It was the deficiencies in personality which made Speer love Hitler in the first place and follow him without any exercise of empathetic imagination throughout the war. For all he was cold, Speer was a first-rate follower in that he had expert knowledge and critical faculties combined with the courage to express his criticism. Towards the end he alone stood up to Hitler to try to persuade him out of the scorched earth campaign and, when he could not do so, he took (uncharacteristically) to intriguing to achieve his ends.

For many of us, those who followed Hitler cannot be forgiven, whatever sentence they may have served, and I would not select Speer as paradigmatic of the follower. He is, however, an interesting case study. Above all, of course, he shows that early life experiences are as important in a follower as in a leader. Gitta Sereny, in her fascinating study *Albert Speer: His Battle with Truth*, sums up by saying: 'There was a dimension missing in him, a capacity to feel which his childhood had blotted out, allowing him to experience not love but only romanticized substitutes for love.' Hitler was the ultimate romanticized subject whom Speer, the classic transferent, idealized. Speer demonstrates the power the follower can have. It was he who saw it to that the machinery worked which put Hitler's diabolical vision into practice. Without Speer, Hitler's power would have existed *in potentia* rather than *in actu*. For all he was a devoted follower, Speer never doubted his own expertise and genius as a logistician and nor did any other member of Hitler's inner team. Goebbels wrote of him: 'Speer is not only approaching his huge task with the finest sense of idealism, but immense expert knowledge. He is beginning to rationalize the apparatus; will get rid of all the far too many dilettantes . . . streamline the whole operation . . . What luck to have Speer . . .'

An able, indeed expert, follower can have tremendous impact on the course of an institution or organization and in terms of knowledge, at least, if not in terms of personal charisma or ambition, can surpass the person they follow. Following is not about slavish adherence to a master. Even Speer, who claimed to Hitler that he stood unconditionally behind him, defied his master at great personal risk in order to try to stop the lunacies that, with war so evidently lost, could only have further hurt what remained of the German people and those in German occupied territories. The power of the follower is such that, when that follower ceases to believe in the leader and what the leader is trying to do, they have the means of bringing that leader down. Whether Speer, who had made Hitler's power possible, contributed to his downfall is more than a little doubtful, but certainly in disobeying Hitler he at least put an end to some of his final excesses. Speer demonstrates how much the leader depends upon the follower. The follower will not have the same degree of fame or notoriety as the leader but through giving or removing support the strong and able follower can both make and break a leader.

All leaders have, at some point in their career, been followers. To a leader, therefore, a follower may present a threat as someone who covets their job. In some cases, the follower is a partner in achieving a vision and when they succeed the leader there is both natural logic and justice in the promotion. The relationship between Roberto Guizueta and Doug Ivester fits neatly into this scenario. An insecure leader might, however, neutralize the competition and simply surround himself with sycophants, leaving a vacuum in his wake. The follower who turns is a relatively rare (or rarely acknowledged) phenomenon in business. Domenico de Sole, a tax lawyer at a prestigious Washington law firm, who was hired by the Guccis to sort out an investigation with the US revenue service and, having fallen out with Maurizio Gucci over strategy, went on to lead the empire as its Chief Executive and President, comes close to this. A follower who seeks to overthrow the leader will not succeed if the leader's vision is the right one for the business. If it is not, then the follower is not obliged to subscribe to it and, if he or she has a better vision, then in the interests of the business an act of usurpation must be acceptable.

In *Richard II* Shakespeare depicts, and approves, the usurpation of a monarch who is ill-suited to rule. Richard has no understanding of the importance of the people over whom he rules. Bolingbroke, the usurper, has. Richard observes Bolingbroke's popularity and sneers at it:

> Ourself and Bushy
> Observ'd his courtship to the common people,
> How he did seem to dive into their hearts
> With humble and familiar courtesy;
> What reverence he did throw away on slaves
> Wooing poor craftsmen with the craft of smiles . . .

Richard has misunderstood the requirements of the entity he leads (in this case a country). Bolingbroke, the follower, fully understands the needs of the nation and has, therefore, a better right to lead it. Most importantly, Bolingbroke, the follower, knows the importance of followers, which Richard fatally underestimates.

Followers free leaders but they can also fetter them. They can endorse and enable a leader's vision but they can sap a leader's strength. Leaders must satisfy the emotional demands of their followers, recognizing, even deferring to, their expertise on the one hand, while on the other providing a fixed point of ultimate authority. Followers demand a certain schizophrenia in their leaders alongside complete consistency. To date leaders have tended to lead fairly uniform groups of followers. In the main followers will be united by a common concern or a common background. The most common banner under which followers group has traditionally been a national one. In an age where national boundaries have become more fluid, the global leader is becoming more commonplace. There is no such thing, however, as a global follower. In the business environment, where the global leader is a much-needed reality, followers remain the polyglot group that ever they were. For the future leaders can expect to face a community of followers with increasingly complex and often conflicting requirements. More than ever before leaders must understand the importance of sustaining and nourishing the symbiotic relationship which exists between them and their followers.

Chapter 7

The Global Leader

'Nationalism is an infantile sickness. It is the measles of the human race.' – Albert Einstein

His father died before he was born, his mother when he was six. He was brought up by relatives in poverty and obscurity. He had a vision which, in his forties, he communicated to others by means of great oratory and his personality was such that he won and retained the loyalty of those who came into contact with him. Not least among his skills was a gift of oratory and a sense of humour. He knew poverty, mockery and disappointment but overcame all three. He was, perhaps, driven by all three. A classic leader's background. He was Mohammed, the founder of Islam and one of history's most influential figures.

Mohammed was both a religious and a political leader. He united his followers under a warring banner which led them to expand their territories in the name of Allah so that a century after his death his followers ruled an area that was larger than the Roman Empire at its height. Mohammed founded a religion which was to become a truly global movement, as of course did Jesus of Nazareth. Christianity and Islam have been extraordinary movements, embracing peoples essentially unlike, of different nationalities and races, under a single banner. As their founders and figureheads, Christ and Mohammed have truly global appeal.

There have, of course, been leaders who have led numerous peoples across many territories: Alexander the Great and Napoleon, by dint of their imperial ambitions and extraordinary campaigning skills, provided leadership in just such a way. Those who submitted to them did so involuntarily and so we are stretching a point to describe conquerors as global leaders, in the sense of leaders who are acceptable across numerous boundaries. There are of course many cross-border movements, both political and cultural. Marx was the founder of an ideology that took root in Europe and Asia but while he was of immense influence and changed the course of history he did so at a remove and over time, depending upon his interpreters as much as on his own thinking. Nationalism, Romanticism – these trends certainly crossed numerous borders but scarcely generated leaders as such. Various art forms, particularly those which are non-linguistic, have proven accessible across different cultures. Mozart's music may not have universal appeal but it certainly transcends many barriers of nationality and class. Nevertheless, we can hardly regard Mozart as a leader.

The notion of global leadership is becoming increasingly important as the world shrinks. Whether or not one believes in the concept of globalization, there is no doubt that the world is becoming a smaller place, linked by increasingly sophisticated technologies so that distances in time and space are becoming meaningless. The Internet, cable, satellite and digital communications have brought people into immediate contact with one another. The media which gives birth to trends creates international tastes for brands which become global. Levi jeans, Coke, Disney – these brands have cachet across the world and, irrespective of sector, companies are obliged to operate across a huge international spectrum. Few can afford to remain parochial in outlook.

The form of internationalism that is acceptable today differs substantially from that which has prevailed in the past. Until relatively recently a large multinational would rely for its top managerial talent upon executives from the country in which the organization's head office was based. A company that had its origins in the US would tend to be run by Americans across all territories, while one that was British would be run in all locales by the British. It remains the case that very large multinational organizations send their cadre of top managers on international assignments as a matter of routine. The difference, today, however, is that nationality is no longer a barrier to promotion. Indeed,

Harvey Golub, Chairman and Chief Executive of American Express, is particularly proud that his senior managers around the world are of a range of nationalities instead (as would once have been the case) of being solidly American.

There has been a very strong revolt against colonialism across the globe. The practice of colonizing territory and treating the indigenous population as inferior has come to be seen as an abuse of power and an abuse of fundamental human rights. Starting at the political level with the break-up of the nineteenth-century European empires following the Second World War, the attitude has permeated into all aspects of life. The end of the Cold War, which has led to the break-up of the former Soviet empire, has intensified the reaction, as has the end of apartheid in South Africa. No wonder that Lech Walesa, Vaclav Havel and, most particularly, Nelson Mandela have gained such heroic status – they are liberators who have stood up for justice, ethnicity and the right to maintain a different set of beliefs and customs from the prevailing political regime.

Little by little the notion of respect for other peoples has become an important principle underpinning modern society. It would be naïve to suggest that the scourge of racism has been eliminated: racial or religious prejudice remains an all too prominent part of international relations. The term *ethnic cleansing* is, after all, a new one. Nonetheless among the young in particular there is a growing sense of 'one world'. Youth culture has done much to promote internationalism. Black musicians dominate popular music. 'World' music is a respected category in every record shop. The notion of respect for others and 'ethical' trading is not unimportant in commerce. Consumers are increasingly offered the chance to invest their money in organizations which will not reinvest it in any vehicle which cannot withstand public scrutiny. We may buy furniture which is made from the wood of sustainable forests, cosmetics that have not been tested on animals and coffee where the profits go directly to those who have been involved in its production. Commerce has had to show a conscience because consumers have.

The business model which has prevailed for the greater part of the twentieth century has been that of the corporation. Most likely to have its headquarters near the home of the original founder of the business, the head office traditionally did much to define the nature of the company. If the company had a US base, a German base or a British one it would be decidedly American, British or German in style. Imperial Chemical Industries and British Petroleum have been British and Imperial in style for much of their existence, sending respected British-born and trained managers out to distant parts of the Empire to manage operations there. Known as multinationals, few would have doubted that these were British companies any more than they would have doubted that Coca Cola is American.

Since the Second World War it has been American companies which more than the companies of any other nation (with one major exception) have exported their operating culture lock, stock and barrel to sites outside the US. The American style of doing business internationally was as heedless of local sensitivities as the European imperial regimes had been a century before. American businesses set up shop and local governments and competitors were obliged to put up or shut up. The new American businesses operated much as they did on home territory. Run by Americans, the management did not alter their ways of working to take account of different cultural types. On the contrary, Europeans had one option, to bend to the way of their American masters or risk the removal of the venture from their shores altogether. The American parent would have little hesitation in abandoning the venture if it did not appear to be prospering.

Subject peoples have a way of rising up against their subjugation and very often they do this by selectively taking the best elements of their masters and then using them in their battle to break free from dominion. In India, for instance, those who fought against the Raj were themselves the recipient of some of the benefits of British rule. They partook of an education that was, in part, made available to them through their Imperial masters and came to an understanding of the value system and British way of working in order to be able to use that in their own fight for freedom. In much the same way, the best European managers learnt from their American masters and then put their knowledge to use in the service of European companies. The example of the European who joins a US company, is sponsored by them through several assignments and, perhaps, an MBA but returns to his or her original homeland to achieve their fullest potential is an extremely common one. With very few exceptions, it tends to be Americans who make it to the top in American companies. In the recent past the ambitious European would need to turn his back on a US company if his aim was to make it to the very top in business. The pattern is changing, but slowly.

What the Americans did in the fifties and sixties (some companies considerably earlier than this), the Japanese were to emulate in the seventies. The Japanese method of doing business was different from the American but similar in one important sense. It was uniform and markedly Japanese, not bowing to any alternative way of doing things. Japanese managers ran Japanese businesses outside Japan and Europeans seemed to have rather less opportunity than they had under American rule of moving through the corporate hierarchy. American and Japanese businesses had a confident business culture that derived from a confident or at least united national culture. Allied to such assets as scale and production efficiencies, the homogeneity of management style did much to help the wholesale commercial conquest of large swathes of the international business arena.

In the face of competition, Europe did what it was obliged to do or go under altogether – it fought back. On a local level organizations borrowed first American and later Japanese techniques to improve the quality of their outputs and the manner in which they marketed and distributed those outputs. Management training became far more prevalent than previously and reward structures slowly came to recognize that incentivizing key staff could lead to important performance improvements. While on one level European businesses simply emulated a foreign model, on another they proved highly innovative, taking their commercial lead from a political precedent.

The European Union is an extraordinarily ambitious project. Arising from a desire to avert the enmity which had given rise to two world wars, it has sought to bring political unity and economic well-being to all its citizens. The only truly international political experiment of its kind, it has given a very clear message to Europeans: that it is possible to combine and to overcome abundant differences in the interest of achieving a shared aim. Put simply, that shared aim is peace and prosperity. As with any idea that is new and especially one that seems to fly in the face of the empirical experience, the Union has not been universally welcomed. The idea, however, has persisted, been embellished, worked and reworked through some five decades and has offered an extremely useful template for European business.

One thing that first American and then Japanese business hegemony brought forcefully home to Europeans was the benefits of economy of scale. The vast domestic markets for both countries underpinned the endeavours of their various economic enterprises. German, French and British businesses could, undoubtedly, compete as individual entities with their American and Japanese counterparts but few would be able to muster the might to triumph in their particular sector. A pooling of resources and expertise, however, between European businesses might give the Japanese and Americans a run for their money. A spate of high-profile mergers between European businesses has created businesses that are better placed to compete in global markets: GEC Alsthom, Arjo Wiggins Appleton, Reed Elsevier and, perhaps the most innovative of all, ABB are just a few obvious examples.

Alongside the recognition that this pooling of resources may provide a better platform from which to compete has come a far greater respect for cultural difference leading to much less ethnocentricism by management. Indeed, Europeans seem to have left behind their fierce nationalism. This is evident outside the strictly political or strictly commercial arenas. Take football, a sport of massive popular appeal, which has come to be highly international. Football players are sold to the highest bidder irrespective of nationality, thus many of the best players in the English Premier League are not British. The cult that surrounded Eric Cantona showed the extent to which the British fan can dispense with old enmities. Ruud Gullit, who seemed to have heroic status at Chelsea, was unceremoniously ditched only to reappear in Newcastle. His place at the London side went not to a British manager but to an Italian. Arsenal, which in 1998 carried off the double, winning both the League and the FA cups, did so under French management.

Curiously, while football has become highly international, popular music has not. With the exception of ABBA, a group which rose to international acclaim in the light of victory in the much ridiculed Eurovision Song Contest, no European group seems to have enjoyed the ascendancy of Anglo-Saxon bands and artists. Perhaps the key to this riddle lies in language. Football does not depend on language for its appeal. Popular music, dominated by the song, does. More than this, soccer, though its origins may be British, has become very much a European game. What it is not is American. America provided the template for popular music and all subsequent popular music has made some reference to that American heritage. American sporting obsessions have not, however, been successfully transplanted across the continent, and vice versa, reflecting the fact, perhaps, that international sporting competition coexisting with domestic competition does require geographical proximity. Whatever the causes for the Europeanization of the British game of football and the presence in various countries of non-national footballing heroes, the results are worthy of record. Heroes can come from another culture, speak another language but excel in a quite different culture provided there is a common aim.

There are numerous reasons why Europeans are coming to have increasing tolerance for one another. The increasing affluence of many Europeans has led to the extraordinary expansion of the leisure industry and, in particular, to the habit of taking foreign holidays. Most Europeans have gained, however briefly, first-hand experience of other peoples and other nations. Indeed, that experience is gained at one of the most beneficial of moments, when the hard-working European is taking time out and is predisposed to be positive towards his or her foreign hosts. Unlikely cultures meet through the medium of the holiday, with the Germans and the British vying for space around Spanish poolsides. Young people are obliged to study one European language (often two or more) during their school years. Exchange programmes between schools encourage an understanding of different ways of living, and the popularity of the European tour among students and the newly graduated or those in their gap year has also helped erode nationalism. Astonishingly, only 9 per cent of Americans have a current up-to-date passport but Europeans move with increasing freedom between the various states of the Union and of the continent.

European companies, even those which have not undergone complex mergers, show growing levels of internationalism in the way they do business and in the way they construct their boards.

Reckitt & Colman is a business which Heidrick & Struggles has worked with closely in recent years. Once it would not have been unfair to have called it an old-style British colonial business. Certainly it had operations in many countries overseas but the style of those operations was, like their management, unvaryingly British. Today the business has been recast as a genuinely international one where non-nationals hold positions of influence right across the organization and, indeed, on the board. The example of Reckitt & Colman is not an isolated one. Indeed, as in football, British businesses need no more be run by the British than Swedish businesses need be run by Swedes. In the UK a Frenchman is currently running ASW, a South Wales-based steel business, a Swede is running Rexam the paper and packaging business and an Italian American is running BBA. Another client of Heidrick & Struggles is Kvaerner. Originally a Norwegian business, it moved its headquarters to London and when my colleagues went out to find a divisional chief executive for them they found a Thai-speaking, Singapore-based Englishman whose family home remains in France. For the record, his references were taken up in Denmark. It would seem that, in business at least, the international barriers are coming down.

The old models for doing international business, the American and Japanese ones, are outdated and being found so by both nations. A newer model, European in origin but global in application, is undoubtedly gaining prominence. In keeping with the current belief in the importance of ethnic experience, business is giving much greater importance to the other, the different, than ever before. This new model has some implications for both managers and leaders. To take management first, it is generally the case that management skills are transferable from one culture to another. Different fiscal, legal and accounting regimes will pertain in different countries but, allowing for these differences, the organization of a corporation, its day-to-day management, need not differ very substantially. The same principles, mainly those of maximizing profits and minimizing costs, will apply in any commercial venture irrespective of its country of origin.

At Heidrick & Struggles we work extensively in the finance function. Over recent years we have observed that the nature of the function is changing to encompass the increasingly international activities of most successful organizations. Fifteen years ago it was reasonably rare for a business to operate in the countries of Eastern Europe and unheard of to do business with the Chinese. Since the downfall of the Soviet state few organizations do not consider the potential for their products in East Europe. Similarly, there is a scramble to do business in China. Looking just at Western Europe, the equity markets are expanding very rapidly and the prudent organization is increasingly raising money around Europe rather than just in the domestic market. A truly able finance director or CFO needs to be cognizant of the potential operating advantages and disadvantages in this international arena. A recognition, for instance, that the tax regime in some Eastern European states is highly ambiguous and misinterpretation of it can have substantial impact on an organization could prove a very valuable skill. This is not to say that every budding finance director needs to ensure that they have fully understood the minutiae of tax legislation in Kazakhstan, or for that matter, to know in detail the range of products available in the German equity market. He or she will, however, need to know where to go to find this information and will have a sufficiently broad world view to understand the type of knowledge that will be increasingly useful. The finance manager, or for that matter the human resources manager, of the future will take an aerial view rather than, myopically, focus on the local and domestic.

Where management functions change those in the function can change with them, for management is a skill that is learned. Where information is missing there are abundant resources to which an executive may turn to supply that information. For leaders, sadly, there is not this option. Leaders become necessary where an organization must embrace change. A company that is confronting a global market place and changing accordingly is in urgent need of leadership. More than ever, in this instance, the leader must be imaginative, psychologically penetrating and highly persuasive. However, the leader is, perhaps for the first time, addressing a very diverse community of followers and must find a language in which to address them which is not culturally specific. The leader, in this context, must be a superb storyteller.

It is worth considering whether leadership itself is irredeemably culturally specific. The answer to this question lies in the extent to which a leader represents issues that are universal. Margaret Thatcher, very British in style, nevertheless appealed to people around the world. In part this was gender-related. Certainly much of her support came from other women who rejoiced in such a powerful role model. Her appeal, however, was broader than this. She represented the individual, and private enterprise. She also represented a distinct break with the past, a move away from privilege towards merit. In power she was someone who dared to be different and who stood firm in the face of conflict. Her gender, class, ideology and personal resolve, in their different ways, appealed to people across a range of nationalities.

Political figures are less likely to be revered cross-culturally than the idols that emerge from film and pop music. James Dean and Kurt Cobain appealed to young people around the world and became iconic of the struggles of youth, as Marilyn Monroe symbolized the feminine contradiction between overt sexuality and equally overt vulnerability. Early death, of course, does much to promote iconic status; one clear reason why Kennedy came to represent so much. The notion of promise cut short, of what might have been, is a powerful and romantic one. Where individuals represent issues of universal appeal they can transcend the culture which has formed them.

Mohammed and Jesus Christ were universalizing (if not universal) leaders. Both were undoubtedly master storytellers. More than this they were, of course, visionary in the literal sense of the word. What is particularly important about both these figures is the nature of the vision that they shared with their followers. In both cases they offered people a new and radical belief system. Jesus offered, to those who believed in his God, forgiveness of sins, life ever after and, importantly, everlasting love from God. Moreover, his God did not discriminate between rich and poor but, if anything, looked more kindly on the outcast, the outsider than on those in society's comfortable positions. Mohammed's vision made the Arab, rather than the Jew, God's standard-bearer on earth. The role of the devil (Iblis) was greatly reduced and believers could look forward to a heaven which was a far more sensual place than the ascetic Christian vision of paradise. Mohammed's vision dispensed with original sin altogether.

Both Jesus and Mohammed offered people hope, a sense of

aspiration, a sense of certainty and a sense of being special. These factors are not particularly culturally specific but reflect the human condition. Small wonder that the visions of both have been immensely portable. Islam moved far beyond the Arab peoples and travelled to Malaysia, Indonesia, China and, of course, India. Christianity is the largest single religion in the world, with some 1,000 million adherents to the faith. Mohammed and Jesus were then truly global leaders in so far as they offered their followers (or the followers of the faith they founded) something that went beyond nationality or race. They offered potential escape from the bonds of human existence, they gave a point of aspiration and, most of all, a sense of meaning to life.

Pity the poor chief executive of an international business if this is the paradigm he or she should seek to replicate! Absurd though it may seem, however, there is something that the would-be global leader can extract from these spiritual examples. In the first place, the message needs to be simple and in the second it needs to be compelling. It needs to be presented in an imaginative way, as a story in which all those listening can find a point of reference. A leader who aims to transcend national barriers must find a supernational construct around which peoples of many nationalities can rally. The corporate leader has one huge advantage, a ready-made supranational construct which can provide this supranational totem – the corporate culture.

A company's culture is the set of core values which have gained ascendancy in the business over time and which are shared by those within the business such that people who embrace those values come to feel a profound sense of identification and belonging. The culture is not forged overnight nor is it fixed but, since it is in the hands of people, inevitably is fluid and capable of being recast. Company cultures can ossify. A set of beliefs which helped a business to a pre-eminent market position can be a factor in the loss of that leading market position. IBM is perhaps the ultimate example of a business where the culture became so entrenched that the organization came close to collapse and had to be reborn through the corporate midwifery of Lou Gerstner, whose case I shall return to shortly.

The custodian of culture must inevitably be the person at the head of the organization, most likely to be the chief executive.

There must be no mistake, however. The chief executive is the custodian only – the person who holds the culture in trust. He or she is empowered to change that culture but can do so only with the trust of the people within the organization. The root of the problem for the global leader is how he or she is to gain the trust of the people within the organization if that organization crosses multiple borders. How can the embattled chief executive find a way to communicate a vision which resonates with people whose lives have been formed by very different forces? Can one person speak with one voice to the workforce of a company made up of Italians, Swedes and Irish employees, to choose at random? Many commentators would argue that national differences can be so great as to preclude any such act of communication.

The nationality of the leader is of course an extra factor to complicate the issue. Leadership styles are to some extent culturally specific. The best way of illustrating this is to look at a culture which has bred a very different type of chief executive officer to those that emerged from the American system. The culture in question is, of course, the Japanese one. The Japanese business culture in its current form is a mere fifty years old. While it is clearly true that the Japanese can be galvanized into extraordinarily swift and effective action, theirs is a culture which values a measured, reasoned approach to a problem. Famously, like other Asian cultures, the Japanese have a strong measure of respect for seniority: older probably does (or certainly did) mean better. For an emerging economy this can only be a good thing, guaranteeing stability at the top of companies and a clear career path for succeeding generations. The belief in the sublimation of the individual in pursuit of a higher goal has manifested itself in a willingness on the part of the individual to identify strongly with the company. Self-interest has taken second place to the interests of the company as a whole. This has meant that Japanese industry has not been bedevilled by huge wage claims by workers wanting to participate in the enjoyment of the wealth they are creating. The loyalty and trust placed in companies by workers is repaid by an unprecedented degree of care for the worker by the company. While Europe has struggled to finance the social welfare systems created in the aftermath of the war, the Japanese citizen has looked for support not to the state but to the company. This has eased some of the potential burden on the public purse.

The attitude of mind which has helped make Japan a great economic nation is apparent in the constitution of its managerial class. Strikingly, the community of Japanese business leaders is on average considerably older than European or American counterparts. Research in *Tokyo Business Today* undertook some useful analysis of the profile of company bosses. This found that 62 per cent of company presidents are in their sixties, 22 per cent in their fifties, 7 per cent in their seventies and a mere 4 per cent in their forties. Equally striking is the fact that over 99 per cent of these chief executives have been with the same company for the whole of their working life – the exceptions are founders of businesses or heirs to family concerns. Further, these CEOs are all male, all Japanese and typically (although not exclusively) the product of the top four universities in Japan – Tokyo (415 presidents), Keio (208 presidents), Waseda (152 presidents) and Kyoto (106 presidents). A further sixty-four budding CEOs were trained at Hitotshubashi University. There is little evidence, among the upper echelons of Japanese business, of overseas evidence being strongly valued or a particular signal of success potential. Indeed, the homogeneity of the Japanese business culture is such that the ex-pat Japanese is unlikely to integrate in a culture outside Japan but remains suspended within the culture capsule of the organization with which he has been stationed abroad.

Consistent with the belief in long- rather than short-term returns, the Japanese executive has enjoyed financial rewards considerably lower than those of his European or American counterpart – a Japanese executive will typically be earning about one third of the income earned by an American. Indeed, $500,000–$700,000, a fairly routine salary for an American CEO, would be a very significant, headline-hitting salary in Japan. Within a company the compensation differentials are not as great as elsewhere in the capitalist world – a factor of around 20. Compensation in Japan, however, is not simply a question of cash. An executive can expect some significant social benefits in kind – housing, cars, club fees (golf club fees are substantial in Japan), holidays, schooling for children, pensions – a range of perquisites that neither Americans nor many Europeans would expect. For those who make it to the very top of a company there is the additional compensation of very high status. The fortunes of the state and the business world are closely intertwined in the Japanese mind. Attaining the top job in a substantial enterprise is a form of serving one's country – a view particularly held by the current generation of business leaders who were themselves witnesses of post-war reconstruction. Baby-boomers (*shinjinrui*) identify less strongly with the state, having a clearer sense of generation than nation.

It is wrong to assume that the hierarchical system in Japan is a facile one whereby power is vested in those who have served longest. Power is vested in those who have served best. There is an abiding concern in Japan with competence and with excellence and respect is conferred on those who demonstrate these qualities – at whatever level in the organization. Unlike many European and American organizations, the Japanese appear to have, effortlessly, achieved this end. All workers dress alike, to a similar standard, and so there are not the easy distinctions of blue- and white-collar workers. Senior and junior managers work alongside one another to solve a particular problem. The emblems of differentiation which are common outside Japan, different canteens (the directors' dining-room), better office space, superior secretarial support and bigger and better cars are not to be found in Japan or Japanese operations abroad. Boss and worker alike are judged on results – a simple but, to date, eminently satisfactory system.

The structure of a Japanese company, not surprisingly, is modelled on the American model. There is a unitary board structure with a chairman (*kaicho*) and a president/chief executive (*shacho*). At the next level down the company will have a senior managing director/chief operating officer (*senmu*), who in turn will have reporting in to him the divisional managing directors (*jomu*). It is normal for the chief executive to move into the chairman's position and to nominate his successor from within the business. In Japanese businesses peer evaluation is the norm. The person selected by this procedure will have been assessed continually – and to exacting standards – throughout his career in the business. The outgoing chief executive, assuming he is moving on to be the chairman (and if he were not then he would in all probability not be in a position to select his successor), will have a vested interest in appointing someone of equal – or indeed – superior calibre to himself. Western individualism is such that not all outgoing chief executives want their successor to perform better than they have done themselves. In Japan this is not a concern that would be understood, since one's own fortunes are so intimately bound up with the fortunes of the organization.

There is, however, considerable evidence that the profile of the Japanese chief executive is changing. A new style chief executive is coming to the fore in response to several years of recession and the recognition that a new model of leadership is required. Indeed, perhaps this is the first time, when Japanese companies need to be transformed, that leadership skills have become more important than management skills. A quick survey of a couple of emerging chief executives in Japan is instructive. Minoru Makihara is the president and chief executive officer of Mitsubishi Corporation, which has sales of around $123 billion. In age he matches the profile of the average president (he was sixty-two when appointed five years ago), but there all similarities end. Makihara was born in England, went to St Paul's, a top English public school, and then on to study at Harvard in the United States, in which country he spent twenty-two years – including running the American subsidiary of Mitsubishi. He has a cosmopolitan outlook on life, a son working for Goldman Sachs and a daughter for *Time* magazine, and recognizes the value of truly international experience in these days of global markets. His appointment represented a sea change in Japanese recruitment policies. He says: 'Technologies are now moving so fast that it is impossible for the top manager to know all the details. Companies are now looking for generalists who can understand the broad changes, delegate and *provide leadership*' (my italics).

In 1995 Toyota appointed Hiroshi Okuda President. A sales expert who pioneered his company's expansion into the United States, his aim is to turn Toyota into the world's premier car manufacturer. Okuda is a sixty-six year-old who has spent his life in the business, but, for all that, he definitely represents a departure from the standard chief executive. The first non-family leader of the business, he is six feet tall and immensely energetic. He is a fighter, and his attitude, far from the self-effacing polite stereotype, is best described as combative. Outspoken, driven, in control – he test-drives every new model and vets all advertising – he is largely a self-made man who has not benefited from family connections. Deeply intellectually curious, his horizons extend far beyond Japan. He is an avid reader and is known to have read, in translation, the political memoirs of Henry Kissinger and Margaret Thatcher. To relax he reads the works of Goethe. He is indeed international in outlook.

International Japanese chief executives running Japanese companies are rare. Japanese chief executives at the helm of non-Japanese businesses are rarer still. I am indebted to Richard Hill's book *EuroManagers and Martians* for the following example. He dedicates this book to Hayao Nakamura and tells, by way of explaining the book's title, the disturbing story of this Japanese executive's efforts in running a European company. Nakamura – an Italian resident – was invited by Italy's state-owned steel company ILVA to sort out the problems that had defied the best efforts of native-born Italians. Nakamura did so, but ultimately in a consulting rather than an executive capacity and, for his pains, was dubbed by the Italian work force 'the Martian'. Nakamura was no more complimentary about the Italians. The cultural gap between the Italians and their Japanese boss was immense. It would seem apparent that leadership styles are culturally specific and it will be some time before a Japanese-trained chief executive translates readily into a European or American context. Nevertheless, a style of leadership which served the nation well for half a century seems to be less relevant than previously and shows signs of being changed.

The gap between the Japanese and Europeans in business is not entirely surprising. There is a vast geographical space to bridge. The cultural differences between the neighbouring peoples within Europe are perhaps more surprising given the geographical proximity. However, that proximity led to a sequence of shifting alliances and has given rise to several distinct cultural types. Some of the work undertaken by Geert Hofstede, F. Trompenaars and most recently by a team from Cranfield School of Management, Kakabadse, Myres, McMahon and Spony, can be instructive. There is some consensus that different types of organization emerge in different cultures. The Cranfield team offer a neat summary of the various different types in their essay 'Top Management Styles in Europe', from which text I have assembled the data below.

Figure 7.1

	Anglo-Saxon	Germanic	Asian/Latin	French	Scandinavian
Hofstede	*Village market model*	*Well-oiled machine model*	*Family model*	*Pyramid model*	
	Low on hierarchy and rules. High on responsiveness to particular situation.	High on rules, low on management intervention.	Owner manager is a family member.	High on hierarchy.	Not included in the Hofstede model.
Trompenaar	*Guided missile model* Task orientated culture. Team or project group driven.	*Eiffel Tower model* Formal, de-personalized, strong rational/legal basis.	*Family model* Power-orientated, leader seen as a 'caring father'.		*Incubator model* Fulfilment of individuals more impor-tant than organization. Responsive to new ideas.
Cranfield	*Leading from the front* Emphasis on an individual leader, on charisma, self-motivation and a distrust of rules and procedures.	*Towards common goal* Functional expertise, authority, clarity, discipline and systems important.	*Leading from the front* Emphasis on an individual leader, on charisma, self-motivation and a distrust of rules and procedures.	*Managing from a distance* Value strategy and concepts not discipline, and commun-ication. High ambiguity and focus on personal agendas.	*Consensus* Team spirit important, com-munication, organizational detail, open debate, consensus decision.

The models above are based on a significant body of research undertaken by all three sources. It is interesting to note the broad similarities which exist and which cohere quite well with the intuitive, or perhaps simply stereotypical, views that abound in relation to the various national types. It is, for instance, common-place for people to complain that the British in an international team will favour action over contemplation, while the French are much more comfortable working through the intellectual aspects of a problem. Naturally these categories cannot be seen as fixed and applicable in all cases. There will be British executives who want to explore all sides of a question before acting, just as there will be Frenchmen who take their business forward without much forethought. These categories reflect the most common responses in the relevant groups.

Psychologists have done considerable work in analysing different personality types. One of the best-known classification methods is that devised by a mother and daughter team using a technique based on the work of the psychoanalyst Jung. The Myers Briggs indicator produces a range of personality types. It goes on to indicate how people who conform to type will respond to different situations and other personality types. The cultural grid operates in the same way. In my business as a search consultant I find Myers Briggs an invaluable tool. I know my own personality type (INTJ) and how it relates to others and I have become adept at spotting the prevailing characteristics of those around me or of those I interview. The technique does not help me to form a judgement. On the contrary, it helps prevent the unnecessary intervention of prejudice. In such a way should the cultural grid offer some help to the beleaguered international executive trying to understand where misunderstandings habitually arise with international colleagues.

It may seem hopeless, given the range of different types, to aim for any kind of reconciliation between them and therefore impossible to pursue the notion of a global leader. In discussing the question of international leadership it is all too easy to over-complicate the question. Simplicity is at the core of leadership. A good leader makes the complex seem simple. A leader who complicates and obfuscates does so to hide his lack of fundamental talent. Leaders who successfully transform businesses do so in a manner which is basically quite simple. The career of Lou Gerstner provides an excellent case study here. Gerstner is someone who has transformed not one but three different businesses, all of them household names.

In his seminal study considering the differences between leadership and management (*A Force for Change*), John Kotter offers an illuminating study of the first corporate turnaround enacted by Gerstner, that of American Express and its Travel Related Services division. Joining the business from McKinsey, Gerstner had the advantage of knowing the business from a consultancy perspective. His tactic, however, was not to go into an ailing business and dictate terms but to go into an ailing business and ask questions of its managers. In true McKinsey style, he forced all those in any decision-making role in the organization to study the premises on which their decisions were being made. He took the company back to first principles and insisted that, through rigorous debate, the team would agree on the organization's key products, competitors and competitive advantages. Gerstner led many such strategy meetings and hijacked many other meetings scheduled for different discussions in order to arrive at a consensus that – we can infer – chimed with his own vision.

Like a psychoanalyst working with a patient, Gerstner took those in the business to the point where they understood that they were labouring under important misapprehensions. In the first place, the product was not mature but had substantial growth potential and, in the second, the company need not be a one-product business. The vision to which Gerstner led the entire team was that Travel Related Services was a dynamic and growing enterprise. It was a business which could withstand competition and which had significant potential for profitable, serving newly identified customer segments within the core customer group with new products to an industry-leading level of service. Gerstner saw to it that the entire company arrived at the strategy collectively. As a consequence, this empowered workforce moved as one to bring about the necessary changes to implement that strategy. It was to be a formula that Gerstner rolled out across the business, with a focus on recruitment of top-quality staff, elimination of bureaucracy and the empowerment of a risk-taking, entrepreneurially inclined workforce. Moreover, collective strategizing was to be a strategy – in leadership terms – that he was to revisit not once but twice over.

In 1989 after some eleven years with American Express, Gerstner made a surprise move to RJR Nabisco. When he took over, the business was in a state of turmoil with net losses of £1.1 billion. When he left in 1992 he had turned this around to a net income of £299 million. The *Wall Street Journal* reviewed his progress after a couple of years in the post:

> The food company was a financial success, but showed more infighting and complacency than Gerstner wanted. Gerstner aired

his strategic thoughts to groups of employees: Cut bureaucracy. Act with a sense of urgency. Emphasise quality and teamwork. He printed up pale grey cards with eight such points and mailed them to all 64,000 employees.

The *Wall Street Journal*'s slightly cynical tone is deceptive. Where Gerstner is said to have aired his strategic thoughts, it might have been better to have said he 'shared' his strategic thoughts. Certainly his methodology was the same as that which he had employed while at Amex – a strategy of involving those within the business in defining the necessary strategy, a process of collective, creative problem-solving. The success formula was based on a combination, in the words of the *Wall Street Journal*, of 'teamwork, urgency and a Japanese-style fixation on quality'.

In 1993, following an approach by Heidrick & Struggles, Gerstner took on one of the biggest corporate challenges of all time – to turn around the ailing fortunes of IBM. After he had been just six months in the post, commentators were critical. There was little sign of action, merely a reversal of some steps taken by his predecessor (such as the abandonment of a break-up of the company into thirteen operating units, and the return to the old nomenclature of 'divisions' rather than 'line of business'). What he did do in the first six months, however, set the stage for the plaudits he was to receive in a further twelve months. He re-shuffled top management to improve the working relationship between operating units. He also created a corporate executive committee and a worldwide management council. In short, he created an environment in which he could pursue his simple but effective strategy of a shared strategic debate. A year later he came up with a five-pronged strategy based on the fundamental recasting of the company's product line from top to bottom. The strategic initiatives showed that a very thorough survey had been conducted of the entire business. 'If we fail' Gerstner said at the time, 'it will be because we got in our own way'. After just eighteen months with the business, Gerstner engineered a remarkable turnaround in financial fortunes, turning in four consecutive quarters in profit after three years of losses. In 1997 Gerstner, by then aged fifty-five, announced that he would remain a further five years as Chairman and Chief Executive.

Gerstner is a remarkable man to have replicated his success three times over. He has done so by using a methodology of repeatable simplicity based on analysis, debate, empowerment and eradication of all barriers to inefficiency. A first-rate intellect (a Dartmouth graduate and a Harvard MBA, not to mention thirteen years with McKinsey, where he was their youngest ever partner and their youngest ever senior partner) and the ability to engage with people have been the core skills that have helped Gerstner. The businesses which he has turned around are all international, none more so than IBM. In transforming one of the most entrenched and ossified of corporate cultures, Gerstner has had to engage on a global basis. He must then be a global leader.

What, then, enabled Gerstner to speak with one voice to businesses which encompassed so many people of so many different cultural groups? In the first place it is worth noting that Gerstner took on RJR and IBM at a very distinct point – when they appeared to be on the point of collapse. The people he inherited were, inevitably, strongly identified with that collapse. The consequences of collapse would have been job loss and uncertainty. Gerstner was the white knight who came and offered a demotivated work force a point of escape from their otherwise inevitable fate. He gave the workforce a sense of hope, a sense of possibility, a sense that they held their own destiny in their own hands and gave to their corporate lives a sense of purpose and meaning.

Gerstner had one major advantage – the weight of the cultures to which he succeeded. American Express has its origins in the mid nineteenth century, when it introduced a money order to the market in an effort to thwart robberies by the likes of Jesse James. RJR Nabisco brought together a range of known brands, whereas IBM's cultural force is legendary. The people within the businesses identified strongly with this supranational construct, the cultural identity of the business. All three businesses were older than the workforce within them. Those who joined them did so with a reasonable knowledge of how they operated. All three businesses were American in style, and wherever in the world people signed up to one of them they will have done so in the knowledge of what it is to be an employee in an American corporation. Nationality could not, in any of these instances, have overridden the other concerns of workers. Gerstner came in and offered to revive a culture and

brands in which the workforce had made an investment; he offered
to help them secure their own jobs and gave them back a sense of
pride. In all the three environments where Gerstner has led a
turnaround, national identity has been less important than cultural
identity. There are, however, an increasing number of cases where
national identity is at least as strong as corporate identity. In
particular this is the case in cross-border mergers of businesses
where the people within the merging businesses find themselves in a
state of great uncertainty. Will jobs be duplicated? Will they be
eliminated? Which company will have the upper hand? On what
basis will hiring and firing decisions be made? Faced with this level
of uncertainty people cling to the few certainties on offer. One of
these will be nationality, the very thing that a cross-border merger
may appear to be undermining. The more it seems to be under
threat the more important it becomes. If a French and a Norwegian
business, for instance, come together, those who have not been
involved in the merger decision (the bulk of the workforce, in other
words) all become more aware of the personal differences among
themselves than they are of any business synergies. The new entity
will not have one strong corporate culture on which the workforce
can depend, so national cultures will slip into this breach.

Sometimes even those who have forged an international alliance
find that nationalism gets in the way. The alliance (not a merger)
between the American Northwest Airlines and the Dutch carrier
KLM brought together several parties who were essentially unlike:
the reserved and private KLM president Pieter Bouw and the
high-flying American investors Gary Wilson and Al Checchi
who live like film stars (Checchi living in Sidney Poitier's former
home in Beverly Hills). Of the ensuing clash of cultures, Bouw said,
'It's the European way versus the American,' and he clearly saw his
US partners as carpet-baggers and speculators: 'We're airline
people, they're not. These guys are here for the short term . . .'
For their part the Americans were suspicious of imperial designs by
the Dutch: 'They can wrap themselves in tulips all they want. Their
real agenda is controlling Northwest Airlines.' Clearly, where there
are differences it is easy to fall back on national stereotypes.
Remarkably, given the bitterness of the boardroom battle, the
two parties resolved their differences, aided by the insistent refusal
on the part of Northwest's Executive Vice-President, Michael E.

Levine, to let go of a clear moneyspinner. The persistence has paid off and in 1997 the two carriers split an estimated $150 million in profit.

Cross-border mergers are on the increase as companies recognize the benefits of economies of scale when competing in a global marketplace. There is no doubt that there will be a growing need for leaders who can evolve a new corporate culture through a form of leadership which evades the entire issue of nationality. The new global leader should be someone who can force other issues on to the agenda to the exclusion of nationality, unless the issue of national identity can be harnessed as a positive asset. This superman (or superwoman) among leaders must find a way of uniting a disparate workforce around a set of common goals which are unlikely to bear any more relation to nationality than they do to gender or social class. We are fortunate in that we have in Europe a paradigm of such cross-border leadership. Few books on either the subject of leadership or, indeed, of European business can fail to make at least passing reference to the singular figure of Percy Barnevik.

Barnevik may indeed be a one-off. Six foot three inches in height, he is an imposing man of extraordinary energy who is rumoured to relax by ten-hour jogging sessions. His career is by no means over at fifty-five, but he may have achieved his masterpiece in the merger and subsequent remodelling of ABB, which might well provide an organizational template for other future cross-border mergers. The architect of a truly global organization, he grappled with the inherent contradictions of how to combine large and small, local and global, economies of scale and intimate market knowledge in the process of putting together ABB as we know it today. He maintains his position as chairman of the company but has relinquished the role of chief executive in order to take on the role of running the holding company of the Swedish Wallenberg dynasty, Investor.

When ABB was created out of the merger of the Swedish ASEA and the Swiss Brown Boveri, Barnevik took a step which some must, without the benefit of hindsight, have thought to be a false one. He dispersed both the Swedish and Swiss headquarters which between them employed some 6,000 staff and divided these operations into a string of smaller operating units. Today ABB boasts some 1,300 companies and 5,000 profit centres, all run from a head office in Zürich numbering no more than 135 people. This first step of Percy Barnevik's was a great one for the global leader. The head office is, famously, the site of political machinations and the cauldron in which national concerns can brew. By dispensing with the old-style head office with such aplomb, Barnevik dispensed with the old-style nationalist in-fighting as well.

A hero to students of corporate leadership, Barnevik has not always appeared in this light to the Swedes and the Swiss, who have had to accept that the vision for ABB has not included a resolute dependence on the resources in the developed world. Indeed, Barnevik switched a huge portion of the business's manufacturing from the developed to the developing world, in particular to Eastern Europe. Barnevik's genius lies in his recognition that giving people a sense of control in their business as well as in their private lives can unleash an extraordinary degree of energy and talent. His vision is not so very far away from that of Lou Gerstner. He has transformed two businesses which were highly centralized into decentralized organisms where decisions are taken on the local level, with authority devolved to the heads of the 1,300 companies. Across the 5,000 profit centres, Barnevik has ensured that he has given full rein to the entrepreneurial skills of, at least, 5,000 managers. This is empowerment on a global scale. Barnevik communicated his sense of purpose to his managers in person as he rushed around the globe spreading his own corporate gospel. Those managers in turn cascaded the sense of drive, energy and purpose through their own business units. Barnevik gave his people a sketch and allowed them to refine it, add colour and dimension. His great gift, in short, has been to trust people to act in their own interests and the best interests of the entity called ABB.

Of course, it may be easier to bring together the Swiss and the Swedish than to bring together some other nations. The cultural model that I tabulated above does not explicitly characterize the Swiss. It does, however, offer a Scandinavian and Swedish model which suggests that they might prove good business partners. The Swedish or Scandinavians are seen as being concerned with team spirit, with achieving consensus, and are responsive to innovation. There are, moreover, some links between the two nations. Both, for instance, chose not to engage in the Second World War but to assume a stance of neutrality. This shared distance from a cataclysmic event which set asunder the rest of the continent must have some bearing on the way in which the Swiss and Swedish interact.

Barnevik's identity as someone from a flank power is also interesting. People from nations which are not seen to have been imperial aggressors are often more acceptable, internationally, than those who, in the last couple of centuries at least, have striven after a position of political dominance. The Belgians, Dutch, Danish and Swedish are more likely to be acceptable senior players on the European stage than their German, French and British counterparts. Similarly, the Irish are very acceptable in Europe. These are all outsider nations, on the flanks of the great powers. The importance of language skills should not be underestimated here. If a Belgian, Dutchman or someone from one of the Scandinavian countries wants to succeed on the international arena they are obliged, as the French, British and Germans are not, to master several languages. This mastery of foreign tongues inevitably brings insight into other cultures and insight often leads to acceptance.

There is, I believe, a model for a cross-border leader which has been pioneered in Europe (for more on this see my book *The Culture Wars*). The model is one of cultural dexterity or cultural neutrality and certainly involves experience of more than one culture. A typical profile might be someone who is the child of parents of different nationalities, or who is raised or educated away from the country of their birth. They will probably have endeavoured to gain early international experience in their career and will be accomplished linguists. Quite possibly they will have married someone of a different nationality to themselves. Certainly their home is unlikely to be redolent of the country of their birth, rather it will reflect a cosmopolitan lifestyle. The most notable thing about a cross-border leader of this type is the fact that nationality is one of the least notable things about them. Their internationalism runs sufficiently deep for nationality to be a non-issue.

Robert Louis-Dreyfus does not, naturally, conform to all the above criteria but is certainly a leader in this mould. Scion of a wealthy Parisian grain trading and banking family, Louis-Dreyfus seems far removed from the French cultural type suggested by the work of Hofstede, Trompenaars, *et al.* Born in Paris, Louis-Dreyfus rounded off his education with an MBA from Harvard before entering the family business, where he spent nine years developing new ventures for them. In 1982 he joined IMS, which was to become the US's second largest research house, and, becoming president two years later, he played a vital part in the turnaround of the business. It went from a value of something in the region of £100 million to one of £1.7 billion, the price for which it was sold to Dun & Bradstreet in 1988.

After an eighteen-month sabbatical, Louis-Dreyfus took on the immense challenge of restoring the fortunes of Saatchi & Saatchi. This was not a particularly enjoyable period for Louis-Dreyfus: he did not find the egotistical nature of the advertising business to his taste. But it was a successful one. He restored the financial fortunes of the business (in company with Charles Scott, who accompanied him from IMS to Saatchi & Saatchi) and instilled greater business awareness, stronger financial disciplines and a better organizational structure into the operation. This brief interregnum between the periods when the Saatchi brothers held sway over the business did much to prolong its life.

From running one of London's go-go businesses of the 1980s, whose fortunes were intimately connected with those of the Conservative Party and its leader, Margaret Thatcher, Louis-Dreyfus went on to buy a share in and run one of the world's best-known brands and a major German business, Adidas. He took over in 1992 when the company turned in losses in the region of $80 million. By the end of 1997 it registered a net income of $255 million and revenues of $3.6 billion. Like Lou Gerstner he can boast a hat-trick of turnarounds. Rather than sticking with French businesses which, as a member of the French establishment, he might easily have done, he took on successively an American, a British and a German business. French by birth with an international education and early overseas experience with the family firm (in Latin America), he keeps a home in Switzerland and is married to a Russian wife. He is nothing if not cosmopolitan. Articles often refer to Louis-Dreyfus as enigmatic. The word is a fitting one both for a business leader and a global leader: neither should be someone who can be too closely known by their followers.

Nationhood has been a subject that has dominated the nineteenth and twentieth centuries with catastrophic results. On the brink of the twenty-first century nationhood remains important in the construction of an individual's identity in the same way as gender and family background, but is becoming increasingly irrelevant beyond this as people of all nationalities mix together to enjoy sport, music or in the course of higher education. In outlook people are much more tolerant of other nations and of difference, in part because, with the increasing sameness brought about by the prevalence of global brands, difference is something to be cherished rather than something to be feared. Those who take an international outlook, however, very often do so consciously, rationally and intellectually. When threatened, people rarely behave rationally and are more often motivated by the heart than the head. In cases where workers (of any level) of one nationality feel threatened by those of another, the emotional response is likely to be based on national prejudices which remain programmed into most of us, no matter how, with our intellect, we resist them. For this reason it is vital that the business world develops mechanisms for bringing the people of different nations into a cooperative culture where the predominant culture is that of the corporation, a supranational construct, rather than of any one nation state. Percy Barnevik has offered one such model.

The relation between leaders and followers is not rational. The decision to follow a leader will very often be made on the basis of feeling rather than of thought. All the more important then, that where a situation exists of potential conflict between people of different nationalities, there be a leader *in situ* whose vision and persona transcends national considerations. There is, I believe, a template of sorts for such a leader as exemplified by Robert Louis-Dreyfus.

We cannot expect to overcome centuries of nationalism in one generation but there are signs that the current generation of up and coming world leaders in politics and in business are increasingly aware of their responsibilities as global leaders. The initiative by the World Economic Forum (which is financed by the membership fees of the top 1,000 companies in the world) to elect Global Leaders for Tomorrow is an encouraging one. According to the World Economic Forum, Global Leaders for Tomorrow are 'individuals born in the second half of the century, holding positions of considerable power, influence and responsibility, and are 'global' in terms of their accomplishments and potential. They come from business, politics, public interest groups, the media, the arts and sciences'. To date some 600 individuals worldwide have been named as Global Leaders for Tomorrow. To what extent they will truly prove to be cross-border leaders is a matter for debate; what matters most is that the notion of global leadership is firmly on the international agenda.

Chapter 8

Why Leaders Fail

In my beginning is my end.
*

What we call the beginning is often the end
And to make an end is to make a beginning
                        T. S. Eliot *Four Quartets*

We have always been demanding of our leaders but are becoming more so. In the age of the global leader we require our leaders to be all things to all people and we set them under the microscope of the media so that we can spot when they fail. There is almost a sense in which our demands can be so great that we set people up to fail from the outset. The excessive demands we make on our leaders are matched by a certain excess in leaders themselves. Many are larger than life; their drive and appetites are far greater than those in the average person, who is content simply to follow.

Leadership on one visceral level is about excess: excessive drive, excessive application, excessive energy. This basic excess needs to be matched by an excessive intelligence and ability if it is to lead anywhere other than frustration and disappointed hopes. Leadership is about dreams: dreams of splendour, of recognition, of being the best in one's field, of being admired, respected, worshipped, even adored. These factors, unmitigated by a sense of perspective or a recognition of the need for balance, can, in business, lead to individual and, by extension, corporate failures. Very often leadership is about proving oneself, especially where one has been or believes oneself to have been disadvantaged either physically or emotionally. This need to prove oneself never goes away.

The leader, having reached the top, finds that this is still not enough and extends himself further and further until, eventually, he extends himself too far. He may experience burn-out or destroy his health altogether. Hubris, the Greek notion of over-reaching, must be one of the most common reasons for failure. On the other hand, it is only by making an excessive effort that one has any chance of capturing success.

Tied up with the notion of hubris is that of narcissism, of self-love and a belief in one's own mythology. Failure is often brought about by a lack of proportion, the absence of any real and sustained grip on reality. The narcissist has no sense of his own limits, does not know himself. The role of the ego, of deep-seated personal vanity alongside deep-seated insecurity, these are not to be underestimated as likely factors in the make-up of a leader. They will give rise to success but, equally, will impact on a leader's ability to survive the inevitable knocks. For some they will give rise to the leader's eventual downfall. The poet is right, all too often the end is in their beginning.

Success is the drug to which many leaders are addicted. They crave it and, in some instances, will do anything in their quest to grab hold of it. Success acts on the mind and body of the leader in much the same way as a powerful drug. It can provide extraordinary highs but give way to abysmal lows. An overdose of success can destroy the personality. Leaders come to expect that they will always be centre stage. The side effects of success may destroy the body, for a lifestyle of long hours, little rest, high stress levels and constant corporate entertaining is not conducive to good health. Remove success, however, and the result is agonizing withdrawal. Of the numerous risks a leader takes, the principal one is that of failure. Fear of failure can, in some cases, drive people almost as much as a desire for success.

We need to be clear what we mean by successful or failed leadership. Successful leadership is not merely a matter of being followed by a large number of people. Jim Jones and David Koresh both succeeded in winning the allegiance of groups of people such that they participated in mass suicide in Jonestown in 1978 and Waco, Texas, in 1993. Successful leadership involves winning the support of others to enact a necessary change to bring about improvements to an institution or organization that will bring benefits to the stakeholders in that institution. Success or failure is not always immediately obvious. During his lifetime many thought that entrepreneur Robert Maxwell was immensely successful. He built a very successful publishing empire and provided employment and opportunity to a significant number. At the height of his success, however, he was using the pension fund of those employees to finance his own overblown business ambitions. His abuse of power became apparent only after his death (a death assumed to be at his own hand in the face of inevitable exposure).

Failure in leadership can embrace a vast number of situations. Catastrophic corporate collapses such as that of Yamaichi Bank is business failure at its most extreme. This was a collective failure brought about by a long chain of wrong decisions and a conservative, non-reforming top management team. There are, however, individual failures. In the complex operating environment of business today, people are required to act with tremendous speed and to bring about change, or to create success in as short a period of time as possible. Shareholders demand rapid returns or evidence of forthcoming returns and so it is almost commonplace for chief executives to be removed from their position if these are not delivered promptly.

Sometimes it seems unfair to castigate an individual chief executive for the failure of a business when that business seems to have been doomed in any case. When the shareholders at British retail group Sears finally decided that enough was enough and dispensed with the services of its beleaguered chief executive Liam Strong, there were some who thought that no businessman, no matter how accomplished, could rescue the operation which was in terminal decline. Certainly the business has needed some extensive surgery and the services of a company doctor to give it any chance of survival, and its survival is by no means yet guaranteed.

While some unfortunate chief executives face very public dismissal, others are never held to account for their failure. Indeed, too many people who should have been judged to have failed go on to enjoy lavish rewards, all too frequently receiving huge pay-offs and going on to take on board seats in other businesses. Success in a quoted business involves delivering strong and sustained improvement in share value. No matter what other successes a business leader may score – how well he develops subordinates, for instance, if he cannot deliver profits then he cannot be deemed successful. There are, of course, many more stakeholders in a business than just those who hold its shares. A business leader should take account of the needs of those who work for the corporation and should attend to their corporate welfare, and similarly should be cognizant of the needs of suppliers and the wider environment affected by the business.

The leader of a business is obliged to ensure that those working within the organization are enabled to maximize their potential and be given a fair reward. In managing the talent that resides in an organization the successful leader will, effectively, be attending to the interests of future shareholders and ensuring future profits. It is not enough to have a pipeline of good products. Businesses have a duty to ensure they also have a pipeline of good managers, if good performance levels are to be sustained or enhanced. The leader who turns his or her back on the future high earners in a business runs the risk of turning his or her back on future high earnings altogether.

Power corrupts; absolute power corrupts absolutely. This maxim need not always be true, but inevitably there are people in positions of power who routinely abuse that power. In a business environment the combined chairman and chief executive may have the potential to abuse power, especially if the non-executives are in his pocket and not, therefore, independent. As a consequence elimination of the combined role became an early focal point of the corporate governance debate in the UK. In a few well publicized cases powerful leaders abuse their power in an obviously criminal way. One or two executives have been given jail sentences for defrauding their shareholders, others simply disgraced. Usually, however, abuse of power is a little more insidious than this. Some business leaders will stint on the rewards given to those who have worked alongside them, while ensuring that their own portion is more than their just reward. Remuneration committees endeavour to ensure that this does not happen, but in companies where there is not a strong team of non-executive directors or in cultures where the chief executive has considerable freedom of action, such abuse can go unchecked.

Abuse of power by no means always involves money. Unfortunately, there are numerous corporate bullies whose success is bought at the expense of the careers of those who work with them. Some corporate bullies sap the confidence of their colleagues, or set people up to fail, or simply overload them with work to such an extent that they buckle and fail in both their health and work. It is to be hoped that organizations will take action against individuals who squander the talent which is not theirs to squander, but too often these people are menacing and unjust towards their subordinates and nothing but honeyed in their tone to superiors. Bullying of this kind can go unnoticed for years and can do untold damage to an organization, both in terms of the reputation the business enjoys (disaffected employees rarely speak well of a business) and the calibre of people it is able to retain. As word spreads that an organization has a punitive culture or a revolving door, good people will not consider taking up positions within it. Good people usually have other options. Over time, therefore, the business will suffer at the most fundamental level.

Abuse of hierarchical power can often be conducted in the company's name. A leader might disguise his own personal agenda as the company's agenda and so extract incremental effort from staff on false pretences. The current trend to empower the workforce, for instance, allows some of those who actually hold power to delegate an unfair level of responsibility to subordinates who will not be properly rewarded and who will suffer unfair stress levels. Empowerment should release people from undue pressure and stress by giving them a sense of control over their own lives and fortunes. Where empowerment is a sham, however, the effects on loyal employees can be devastating.

Some leaders are insecure and when confronted by an individual whose talent poses a threat they will seek to destroy their potential rival. An executive at a leading financial services organization enjoys a reputation for developing young, gifted managers in their twenties and early thirties. A superb mentor of the young, he is known to be without prejudice in relation to race, class or gender. At more senior levels, however, he is a consummate bully who will consciously wreck the careers of those who appear as potential rivals. He simply will not let others near the flame of success. Indeed, such is his insecurity that he will turn against even those people with whom he has built up strong personal friendships over the years.

Failure can be individual or collective, accidental or deliberate, acknowledged or undisclosed. In the context of business it is wrong to focus exclusively on individuals. With the demise of old command and control structures and the emphasis on empowerment, the failure of a venture is no more the sole responsibility of one individual than is the success. It may take the vision, energy and mind of one person to motivate and re-focus a group of people to effect change, but the change that is brought about will be the collective responsibility of the team, including those at the very base of the organizational pyramid. Similarly, one person at the top of a business may make a series of mistakes but if they lead to the ultimate failure of the business then that failure cannot be laid solely at the door of the one person.

Accountability is not necessarily a matter of strict justice. The individual who is deemed ultimately accountable will luxuriate in the praise that accompanies a collective success and so must bear the consequences of collective failure. A leader must be prepared to be the focus of criticism when a business fails as much as of praise when it succeeds. Over the last decade there has been an increasing level of interest in the notion of governance in public life. The Nolan Committee (now the Neill Committee) in the UK looked into standards of those in the public sector, in government and affiliated bodies. It has been matched, in the private sector, by various committees, the Cadbury, Greenbury and Hampel committees, the outputs of which have now been brought together as the Combined Code. In Europe the UK has undoubtedly led the way in terms of the governance debate, although most continental countries are now following suit and issuing guidelines, with Spain the latest to do so. Key words emerging from the debate are transparency and accountability. Company boards should display transparency in terms of their procedures and should also be accountable for all that occurs within a company.

The debate in the UK was launched after a spate of high-profile corporate failures which significantly undermined public confidence in the probity of publicly limited companies and those who ran them. One such case was the fall of British and Commonwealth. This was a family-owned business transformed by John

Gunn from a company that had lost its way into a £2 billion empire with interests in fund management, broking and leasing. Gunn had already made the Cayzer family millions at the helm of Exco, which he ran until a boardroom split in 1985. It was a reasonable bet that he would make them still more millions at the helm of British & Commonwealth (B&C). All the early signs were good but Gunn was caught out by the stock market crash which decimated the value of the business. He went on to make an ill-advised and expensive acquisition which in turn led to the ill-fated bid for computer company Atlantic, which was to bring down B&C.

A governmental report by the Department of Trade and Industry found that the responsibility for the fall was not exclusively Gunn's. Indeed, the responsibility had to be shared among the bank's board and the wider community of people who advised it. Ultimately, the failure of British & Commonwealth was a failure in corporate governance, with fingers being pointed at the original auditors of Atlantic as well as B&C's banking and consulting advisers, not to mention other members of the board. Responsibility was collective although punishment, ultimately, was meted out on an individual basis.

This may not seem entirely just but leadership operates in an environment that is not predicated on rational considerations. Had the British & Commonwealth acquisition of Atlantic been proven to be prescient and taken the organization on to staggering new successes, John Gunn would doubtless have enjoyed plaudits and rewards which were disproportionate to success. Leaders in a business environment are paid to succeed and expected to face the consequences when they do not, irrespective of mitigating circumstances.

There must be any number of checks and controls within the boardroom to ensure that a company cannot reach the point of meltdown. The chief executive is monitored by the chairman and the chairman by a strong team of independent non-executive directors. A senior non-executive will chair various committees focusing on audit, remuneration and nomination (succession). Important decisions are made collectively and advisers are subject to fierce scrutiny. No matter how well run a business there will always be a risk of failure, and sometimes no amount of talent can second-guess irrational forces in the market place. Eddie George,

Governor of the Bank of England, remarked that in a market system there will always be some failures. He made the remark at the time of the collapse of Barings, a 200-year-old banking dynasty at the centre of the British financial establishment.

This collapse appears to have been the result of a complete vacuum of leadership, management and administration. Some observers are still incredulous that a twenty-eight-year-old trader could bring down an institution that had existed for some 230 years and mutter that a conspiracy to defraud might be a better explanation. Rigorous inspections by independent regulators suggest otherwise. A series of ludicrous oversights and crass incompetence seem to be at the heart of the affair. The Barings management was warned in August of 1994 (some seven months before the crisis point) that the rogue trader Nick Leeson represented a serious risk. Nonetheless, management accepted that the situation could be contained in Singapore and did nothing to ensure that management procedures were tightened. How was it, for instance, that Leeson was able to both make and settle his deals? Such a situation is unheard of in other banks.

There is no question that Peter Baring personally bears any direct responsibility for the failure of the family institution of which he became chairman in 1989 (ironically the same year that Leeson joined the bank). As the chairman at the time of the collapse, however, he must ultimately be accountable. There is, perhaps, something a little anachronistic about a chairman such as he. The scion of the Baring family, Peter was a thirty-year banking veteran when he succeeded to the chairmanship. The role was, effectively, his birthright, and the downfall of the bank smacks a little of the downfall of the British aristocracy. Peter Baring is a gentleman, educated at Eton and Cambridge. He is a reserved man and a far cry from the flashy traders who did so much to build the wealth of the bank. It is curious to think that his forebears who founded the bank might have rather more in common with the flashy nouveau riche trader than their namesake.

The Barings scenario represents a culture clash in which old money met new money and found it to be an uncomfortable liaison. It was under Peter Baring's stewardship that Barings moved into the futures and derivatives market, but it was not, apparently, a world that he understood. The dirty work of raising huge sums of money was left to the traders. The gentlemanly chairman would not inquire too closely into the means by which increased profits were generated and, besides, he paid others in the complicated hierarchy to oversee the activities of those actually generating the wealth. The workers did not want for rewards. Nick Leeson and Peter Baring earned broadly similar figures in 1994.

The patrician remoteness, however charming, of a Peter Baring is inappropriate to a modern financial institution. He is reminiscent of Ashley Wilkes, the man Scarlett O'Hara favours over Rhett Butler in *Gone with the Wind*. Of the Civil War Wilkes says: 'If we win this war . . . we will become like the Yankees, at whose money-making activities, acquisitiveness and commercialism we now sneer.' Modern financial institutions may not need a Rhett Butler at the helm, but they do need people who are familiar with the complexities of the operation and can see to it that those below them in the hierarchy can identify and contain the risks. The crucial question must be this: how could any institution tolerate a chairman who did not understand the principles of the business over which he stood accountable?

Failure is insidious. It can build up over time without anyone spotting its source or being able to stem its flow. Perhaps the ultimate mistake made by Barings was to go into a market for which the upper echelons of the company were temperamentally ill-suited. Perhaps a different personality was needed in the chair. What is certain is that its downfall was due to a deficit of both leadership and management. Not so much a corporate failure as a corporate tragedy. Perhaps the truly prescient might have predicted something of the kind for Barings, but a decade ago no one would have predicted that Courtaulds would be in a lacklustre state and sold to a foreign company.

Courtaulds was a business that was run, until 1996, by one of British business's most able leaders, Sir Christopher Hogg. Since 1996 its chairman has been another of UK business's outstanding figures, Sir David Lees, the man who refocused and so rejuvenated GKN's operations. Both are gifted men. Sir Christopher Hogg has the rare gift of spotting and grooming talent. Several of his protégés have gone on to head up, or sit on the boards of, quoted companies. A first-rate strategist, Hogg was also behind the innovative de-merger which led to the creation of Courtaulds Textiles, which model has been copied by others since. For Courtaulds, however, the de-merger was not to be the prelude to a period of greater strength. Indeed, the company has consistently under-performed since the textile and chemicals businesses went their separate ways.

Hindsight is, of course, a marvellous thing and it allows us to see some of the reasons behind the declining success at Courtaulds. During the 1980s a two-decade reliance on synthetic fibres gave way to a return by consumers to natural materials. Raw material prices have been volatile since then and new Asian economies have undercut the established players. Ironically innovation lies at the heart of the poor performance. Tencel was to have done for Courtaulds what Lycra did for DuPont. Courtaulds consistently over-invested in a product which has failed to ignite the market as expected. This deflection of resources has been to the detriment of some of Courtaulds' better performing businesses, notably the coatings division which is widely recognized as one of the best operations in its sector.

Poor succession planning, however, may also account for the declining fortunes of the business. For all his gifts as a young talent-spotter Hogg seems to have been a little less successful at retaining talent than at finding it in the first place. Few would probably quarrel with the view that Courtaulds has fared a little better in its chairman than in its chief executives. Certainly, neither of Hogg's successors as chief executive seems to have developed a vision for the company. The latest chief executive, Gordon Campbell, is an excellent manager, but Courtaulds needed a leader to restore its flagging fortune.

Courtaulds proved, once again, fortunate in its chairman. Sir David Leas has been the leader who found an innovative solution. It was Leas, apparently, who masterminded the complex three-way de-merger which was announced a month before the bid, and it was Leas who took the business into the merger with Akzo Nobel. Courtaulds is now poised to become a truly European business and will have the strength to fight in a global marketplace. There are some who regret the absorption of an old British business (Courtaulds was founded in 1816, in the heart of the industrial revolution) into a European one, just as they fear the loss of sovereignty in the involvement of the United Kingdom in Europe and a single European currency. The future for the business within the various states of the European Union must lie in precisely the type of innovative merged structures that we see in the Akzo Nobel take over of Courtaulds.

Business failure is the consequence of various factors. In Courtaulds we have quite a few of them: the volatility of the market; vulnerability to changing fashions; over-confidence in a new product; loss of focus; and, arguably, less than perfect succession planning. In the end, however, a leader with vision has emerged to carry the business forward into a new operating environment. Courtaulds is an interesting case study of a business that has been built and salvaged by the insight and leadership skills of individuals and undermined, in between times, by blunders made at the corporate and collective level.

Business is complex. So much so that it seems perhaps facile to credit or blame one individual with the development, turnaround or decline of an organization. Periodically, however, individuals do come to prominence who can, as in the Courtaulds example, transform the fortunes of a business. The increasing complexity of business requires more rather than less leadership and a different blend of courage and risk.

One sacred cow of the search community is that top people can transplant their skills from one environment to another and, given an appropriate period of settling in, suffer no diminution of their success. Leading a modern business is quite difficult enough, however, without adding the additional requirement that the chief executive learn an entirely new industrial area. For instance, the skills required when leading a consumer business are very different from those in an organization which operates in the business-to-business environment. Perhaps organizations when considering the appointment of a new chief executive or chairman would do better to look inside their own businesses and perfect their ability to develop talent internally rather than repeatedly resorting to looking outside? Perhaps the trick is to identify the outsiders on the inside.

PepsiCo has done this well with the appointment in 1996 of Roger Enrico to CEO. The day after his appointment the company's value grew by a substantial $2 billion. Enrico had had a successful and varied PepsiCo career but has always been something of a maverick. A would-be actor, turned Vietnam vet, he

joined PepsiCo as a twenty-seven-year-old. His main mentor was
the last but one president of the corporation, Don Kendall. To a
large extent Enrico has done what he wanted to do, taking on the
Japanese operation because it would be an interesting experience
rather than because it would be career-enhancing and later, in the
early 1990s, taking time out from the line to work in a staff role
coaching the company's young hot-shot managers. To most, including Kendall, this was a bizarre move. Perhaps, in fact, it was
simply far-sighted. It is to the credit of PepsiCo's management that
they have recognized the worth of someone who is not entirely
made in the corporate mould, and by promoting the outsider on the
inside they stand an excellent chance of securing the next generation of top talent. Enrico has something to prove, certainly, but
unlike an outsider from the outside he does not have to spend time
proving his right to the role.

An insider promoted to run a company has a difficult job. An
outsider appointed as CEO with no experience of the company but
an understanding of the sector has a very difficult job. An outsider
who knows neither the company to which he or she is appointed or
the sector in which it operates has an almost impossible task unless
he or she has extraordinary intellectual gifts and utter self-belief.
The complexity of business today demands more leadership but
leads to a restricted number of sources from which leaders might
spring.

In general, good people hire good people. Really good people –
those who are confident in their own success – hire people who are
better than themselves. One aspect of good leadership is about
being fearless in the hiring and development of truly good people.
Too often an outgoing leader wants an organization to be their
personal memorial and so they, perhaps unconsciously, manipulate
the succession in such a way as to ensure that there is no successor
to match their personal achievement. A strong leader sometimes
prefers to be followed by a weak one so that his or her own
achievements are thrown into even sharper relief. More insidious
than this, however, is the fear of rivals for power. In developing a
handful of internal candidates for the succession a chief executive
is, potentially, conniving at his own usurpation.

Fears of this kind are generally misplaced. A good chief executive
who develops people who are potentially more able than him or

herself commands loyalty and respect and is valued for holding the future of the business in trust. A failure to secure strong succession is a failure in trust. Recruiting a CEO from within an existing business has to be the most attractive option to a nominating committee. If an executive has grown up through the business or, at the very least, spent a reasonable number of years in the organization they have had the opportunity to understand the culture and have themselves been assessed in a number of different roles and situations.

Going outside the business should be the last resort but, given the rapid pace of change in businesses, may be increasingly necessary. The recruitment of talented people, the ability to spot the potential, not just to manage but to lead, involves a high degree of imagination and insight. Organizations that take a risk on the ability of an outsider to understand their specific operating dilemmas will find that the pay-off can be very substantial rewards in the future. They must, however, be confident that the outsider in question is truly talented, bringing a combination of intellect and personal qualities such as resilience, confidence and self-belief. Ironically, in order to succeed today companies may need to take more risks in the appointment of those who will lead them tomorrow.

Of course, in the ideal world of perfect corporate governance the development of the next generation of business leaders will not reside with one person alone. The chairman must be judged on the basis of his ability to recruit or develop a strong chief executive but the decision will be a shared one. It will rest with a well-qualified nomination committee. Campbell Soup, seen as one of America's governance pioneers, has gone one better and put the recruitment of its new chief executive entirely in the hands of the outside directors, creating a new model for CEO hiring.

We do not yet inhabit the ideal world of perfect corporate governance and the failure of companies frequently lies with one strong individual who can control the board. It is interesting to note that when a reign comes to an end a number of directors will leave the board along with the outgoing ruler. The chief executive who surrounds himself with fawning courtiers is not uncommon.

Corporate governance, like management, is rational; leaders like markets are not. Nor are the people they lead. There will always be leaders in business who sidestep the principles of good governance and manipulate a business for their own needs. This is not to say that a failed leader is one who sets out to defraud a business for financial gain. On the contrary, leaders who abuse their position are more likely to do so for some obscure emotional gain. In many ways leaders fail for precisely the same reasons as they succeed, brought down by the very neuroses that took them to the top.

Failure is not an altogether easy thing to measure. There are some heavyweight figures who, by one set of criteria, have been enormously successful and, by another, have failed significantly. One of the most influential figures in British business in the post-war period has unquestionably been Lord Weinstock. When he finally announced his successor as chief executive of GEC the share price of the business soared. Yet in a culture which is fairly intolerant of business and businessmen (the British do not look to business for their heroes) Weinstock has already had two biographies published to celebrate the legend.

The son of Polish Jewish immigrants, born in London's East End and orphaned early in life, Weinstock went to university (the London School of Economics, which during the Second World War decamped to Cambridge) and thence to the Admiralty. After a brief civil service career he moved into estate agency and thence to his father-in-law's business, Radio and Allied, which was taken over by GEC in 1961. By 1963 he was the managing director of the merged businesses and set about reforming and streamlining what had been a moribund operation into one poised for great performance. His fierce intellect and undisguised ambition were such that his meteoric rise came as little surprise within the industry.

Weinstock's timing was also excellent. In the early 1960s Britain was changing. The year 1963 saw the Profumo scandal which was to be the downfall of the Conservative administration; it was also the year when the Beatles started their rise to extraordinary fame. Youth culture had burst into existence and there was little truck with the old ways of doing things, with the old school tie dominance in British public life. Borrowing heavily from American best practice, Weinstock forced professionalism on to GEC, his battle cries being return on capital and return on sales. One of Weinstock's biographers describes GEC as a 'cold unforgiving place animated by intellect and logic', and there can be little doubt that

Weinstock was ruthless in his pursuit of success for the business he led.

In 1968 GEC merged with Associated Electrical Industries, making it one of Britain's biggest manufacturers of radios, televisions, washing-machines and other household equipment with brands such as Hotpoint and Morphy Richards. Weinstock's baby became the darling of the stock market. In the 1970s Weinstock successfully refocused the business on defence and power generation. Both were areas where Weinstock could make good use of his extensive government contacts. In defence the government financed research and the business proved enormously profitable for GEC. Weinstock, an outsider, had taken a company that was nothing to a pre-eminent position in British industry. Meticulously managed and highly profitable, it seemed that it could not fail.

So much for the success, but what of the failures? GEC was to suffer at the hands of Japanese competitors and Weinstock did little to stem the business's slow decline in consumer products. Worse than this, he withdrew from the semiconductor business altogether, leaving the way free for competitors. In the 1980s he was obliged to reinvent the business. He did so, but only by repeating a well-known formula. He presided over a series of powerful international mergers with Siemens in telecoms, with GE in consumer goods and with Althsom in power engineering. In the late 1980s GEC bought its competitor Plessey but lost the government's backing for the Nimrod project. Margaret Thatcher took issue with the status of GEC as virtually a nationalized business. The company's shares peaked in the early 1980s and have been in clear decline ever since. This is not entirely fair (but the market is, of course, nothing if not fickle).

The merger programme of the 1980s showed remarkable foresight, a recognition that in the new economic order there would be little place for parochialism. Weinstock was careful, too, to hedge his bets, with alliances both in the United States and in continental Europe. For all this prescience, however, Weinstock is accused of buying or merging businesses but seldom building them. Worse than this, he seems to run the businesses for the benefit of someone other than the shareholders, for he sits on a substantial cash pile which is neither reinvested in the business nor is it directed towards the shareholders.

Weinstock's persona is not, on the face of it, a particularly appealing one. His parsimony and concern with cost-cutting is legendary. The former headquarters of GEC at Stanhope Gate had always been notoriously shabby, and Weinstock has been pathological about turning out the lights, once becoming enraged at the sight from a train window of a fully lit GEC factory at night, only to be reminded that it was working shifts. The ultimate micro manager, Weinstock would, apparently, scan telephone bills to identify if staff were making private calls. His distrust and disdain for others is scarcely concealed and is best exemplified by his decision to have an announcement of 5,500 redundancies made over a company tannoy system.

Weinstock is, of course, a much more complicated man than this. He is an intensely private man, blessed with a marvellous sense of humour and capable of great passion for horses, for the opera and for his family. One of the man's redeeming features has been his great love for his son, but this, more than any other aspect of Weinstock's personality, was to become a thorn in the side of shareholders. Weinstock's fervent desire was that his son, Simon, should succeed him. With this in mind he brought him into the business and on to the board as commercial director, and would not listen to the various murmurs that Simon was neither a suitable successor nor a suitable commercial director. Weinstock did bring other young directors on to the board but his heart was set on Simon taking over from him. Tragically for the family, Simon's early death in 1996 eliminated what had become a significant problem within the business.

Unable to have his own son as his successor, Weinstock flirted with the notion of merging GEC with businesses which would bring in a suitable proxy son as a successor. Carlton Communications and Michael Green was one candidate, Amstrad and Alan Sugar another. These were men like himself. Both were Jewish Eastenders, people with whom Weinstock could feel some cultural affinity. In the end George Simpson of Lucas took over as managing director with Weinstock still on the premises as emeritus chairman. Simpson has been busy, however, dismantling much of Weinstock's team.

Did Lord Weinstock fail? It seems churlish to accuse him of failure in the light of some extraordinary achievements. Nevertheless, in the eyes of the City of London and shareholders he certainly outstayed his welcome and treated the company as though it were a family business, his own to do with as he pleased. How much more successful might the company have been had he developed a strong presence in the semiconductor industry and built a platform from which the United Kingdom could compete with the Japanese and Americans? His innate conservatism and financial caution led him to back defence, which, with the end of the cold war, left the business with the classic dilemma of how to turn swords into ploughshares. Weinstock impressed his personality on the business a little too closely, flaws and all.

Manfred Kes de Vries, psychoanalyst and professor at INSEAD business school, in an illuminating article, 'The Leadership Mystique', produces a table identifying the various characteristics of neurotic organizations. Among them he lists the 'Suspicious organization' of which the leader in charge demonstrates the following characteristics:

> 'Vigilantly prepared to counter any and all attacks and personal threats; hypersensitive; cold and lacks emotional expression; suspicious, distrustful and insists on loyalty; over-involved in rule and details to secure complete control; craves information; sometimes vindictive.

This seems to me an uncannily close description of Lord Weinstock. The leader of a business has responsibilities to a range of stakeholders. Shareholders are clearly a very important group but so too are the staff and employees, and both communities over the years will have had cause to regret the control Weinstock had over GEC. As a psychoanalyst Ket de Vries believes that our psychic composition has its origins in our early childhood. What were Weinstock's early life experiences which led him to conform to this 'suspicious' type? Here I must simply speculate.

Born in the late 1920s, he was an outsider twice over: the son of immigrants and also Jewish. In the East End, of course, he was among one of the UK's principal Jewish communities, but even if Britain can make the proud claim that we have been one of the least antisemitic nations of Europe, Weinstock would nevertheless have been on the outside of the British establishment. Moreover, despite my claim that Britain has been less antisemitic than many European nations, the young Weinstock might not have thought so. He grew up at the time when Oswald Mosley and his blackshirts assaulted the very community of which Weinstock was a part. A poor immigrant from a persecuted race, Weinstock's innate conservatism and native suspicion seem entirely comprehensible.

The most formative influence on Weinstock's life must have been the early loss of both parents. His reported coldness and analytical nature smacks of someone who retreated early from too great emotional commitment, while his very genuine love for his family (at his last AGM he appeared with his thirteen-year-old granddaughter) shows a desire to replace what he lost. Career and family, however, seem constantly intertwined. He married, fortuitously, into a business which was to give him a managerial platform and, as I note above, GEC rapidly became an extension of himself, his domain. Kets de Vries notes that someone who is suspicious has as their guiding theme the notion that 'Some menacing force is out to get me; I had better be on my guard. I cannot really trust anybody.' This conforms to the experience of the young Weinstock, who was an outsider in a hostile environment whom fate chose to orphan. He became the centre of his own world and anything outside himself that he valued he saw simply as an extension of himself.

Weinstock is not alone in wanting to hang on to power. Coca Cola's succession was not clear on the outside until Roberto Goizueta's death in 1997. Despite his extraordinary achievements at Coke (the value of the business rose from $4 billion to $150 billion during Goizueta's sixteen-year tenure as chairman and chief executive officer), there was growing concern that he should stand down. Tony O'Reilly, one of the most flamboyant of business heroes, has been a star rugby player in his native Ireland, the boss of Heinz (that seemingly quintessential American business) and is now fulfilling a long-held ambition to be a newspaper proprietor. These credentials, notwithstanding, O'Reilly also came in for criticism when he was rather dilatory in handing over the reins of Heinz.

Timing is critical both to a leader's success and to their failure. Many would-be leaders never realize their potential because their particular skills were not those required at the point when they were called upon to take on a leadership role. Nowhere is the importance of timing seen to better effect than in the instance of Winston Churchill. Had he died in 1939 aged sixty-five he would have received very mixed obituaries. On balance he would not probably have been seen as a success. It took extreme circumstances to give validity to his grandiose vision.

On a lesser scale many senior directors experience the disappointment of not achieving the top job within the organization to which they have devoted the greater part of their working lives. Very often this will not reflect upon their competence *per se*, nor their commitment, merely that their particular style and experience was less well suited to the particular circumstances in which the organization found itself at the point the appointment was made. Who would have predicted that William Hague or Tony Blair would be the leaders of their respective political parties five years ago? While there is no doubt that most political observers will have thought that William Hague would be a contender for the leadership of the Conservative Party at some point in the future, most would not have expected the point to come in 1997. The decimation of the Conservative Party in the General Election led to many of the more obvious candidates being removed from the frame. Added to this, the health problems of Michael Heseltine removed one of the party's more charismatic potential leaders. Both issues also had some impact on the type of leader the party required. The collapse of the party was so extensive that it became clear a complete overhaul was required. It became imperative for the party to appeal to a broader community, and in particular a younger community and one where there was less prejudice and more openness. In selecting William Hague the party skipped a generation, just as a handful of years previously the Labour Party had done in appointing Tony Blair.

To all things there is a season. Corporate fashions change with the economic cycle. For some their downfall or failure to secure success is linked with the changing taste of the market. Yesterday's business heroes suddenly become tomorrow's blinkered villains. In the UK at the moment we are watching with interest to see whether Greg Hutchings of Tomkins will retain his superstar status or sink into the abyss of corporate failure. In the 1970s and 1980s through to the early 1990s the conglomerate was the beloved of the financial institutions. Some of the UK's top industrialists, Lord Hanson, Tiny Rowland and Owen Green (of BTR), were the architects of sprawling empires in the diversified industrials sector which gained a reputation (as Weinstock did) for taking old, under-performing businesses and applying rigorous cost-cutting techniques to extract top performances from them. It was a strategy which spawned other smaller conglomerates of which Greg Hutchings' Tomkins (and Hutchings was a Hanson-trained man who worked directly for Lord Hanson) was one of the finest.

Times have changed and markets have expanded. There are now many fewer under-performing businesses for the hungry titans to buy up. Those that do exist are rarely of a size to have much impact on the performance of the acquiring parent. The entire strategy behind the conglomerate, of developing a presence in a range of niche markets, is now antithetical to the trend towards globalization. The prevailing view of analysts is that since businesses must act on the world stage they must be world class, not merely regional class. Competition is so tough that few organizations can risk trying to compete across a host of different sectors. The trend today is to focus on a handful of core areas and to spin-off or de-merge non-core businesses. Greg Hutchings has assiduously avoided following this trend. In his defence he points to the fact that two current stock market darlings, Rentokil and Granada, are, to all intents and purposes, conglomerates (but, critically they are in the still dynamic services sector rather than the matured industrial manufacturing area) and carries on regardless.

Will Hutchings win his battle and carry the company on as he wishes? Will he agree to change or will he lose the battle altogether and become just another corporate casualty? Much probably depends on his personality. It seems, however, that he is deeply sceptical about the fickle nature of the market. He has said: 'In the next recession, companies such as ours will continue to grow, while the cyclical companies will be doing badly. As the climate gets tougher, the market will start to appreciate the virtues of diversification again.' He may be right, but in his obstinate disinclination to satisfy what he sees as a whim on the part of the financial community I see an interesting adherence to one of the neurotic types of executive detailed by Kets de Vries.

The guiding theme of the *compulsive* organization and, by implication, its founder and/or head is: 'I don't want to be at the mercy of events; I have to master and control all the things affecting me.' In his rejection of what he clearly regards to be mere fashion, Hutchings seems to embrace this attitude wholeheartedly. Kets de Vries identifies the strategy of the *compulsive* organization as: 'Tightly calculated and focused, exhaustive; slow, unadaptive; reliance on a narrow established theme; obsession with a single aspect of strategy, e.g. cost-cutting or quality; the exclusion of other factors.' Can it be possible that this is true of an organization that went in a matter of a few years from being a £6 m company to a £3.3 billion group? City analysts would probably say that this is a fair reflection.

De Vries's analysis of the typical executive in a *compulsive* organization (in this case the defining executive) gives further cause for alarm: 'Tends to dominate organization from top to bottom; insists that others conform to tightly prescribed procedures and rules; dogmatic or obstinate personality; perfectionist or is obsessed with detail, routine, rituals, efficiency and lockstep organization.' Without a close knowledge of the man's psyche who am I to judge whether Hutchings fits this description? What I can do is assemble some of the clues from what is known about him. He certainly takes a very close personal interest in the performance of each of Tomkins's subsidiaries, meeting the managing and finance directors during performance review of each subsidiary in turn. This has the air of a man who likes to control and is most comfortable with adherence to procedures. He is a known perfectionist, not least with himself. This is demonstrated by his reputation to be extremely competitive and to fight to win. He is also meticulously organized in his life. He exercises for the same period each day, runs several times a week, and maintains a strict routine in relation to his office hours.

Hutchings is an only child. His father was a Gulf Oil executive who spent much of his time overseas. At the age of eight, Hutchings was sent to school in England and saw his parents for only one month a year for the following five years. His background, then, is that of someone who has had to manage by himself, find things out for himself and, having learnt one way of doing things that works, sees no reason to change the formula. He says of himself: 'I have always had to survive on my own which is why I am a loner. I don't share my problems much.' Of his schooldays he says: 'I had my own ideas about things, as I do in everything, so I got either black stars or gold.' It remains to be seen whether he will get a black or gold star in the final judgement of the City, but the fact that it could go either way shows how thin is the dividing line between extraordinary success and catastrophic failure.

Failure for some, however, is a spur. Indeed, it may be a repetition. Those leaders who have in their early life suffered and overcome particular hurdles have often developed a mechanism for dealing with adversity which stands them in good stead when hit by adversity in later life. Take the flamboyant Jurgen Hintz. He was one of the top three executives in Procter & Gamble and a close friend of Ed Arzt when he was fired. This was a tremendous body-blow but he survived it and went on to become the Chief Executive of Carnaud Metal Box, an Anglo-French merger which needed both his first-rate brand skills and understanding of quality and his cultural neutrality. An East German-born naturalized American, he was a suitable intermediary for the two disparate sides of the business. Then, with his task still incomplete, the business – much against Hintz's desires – was taken over by the American Crown Cork. Hintz, by now in his fifties (an uncomfortable time to be looking for a senior job in the UK), might, reasonably, have decided to shelve his ambitions. Instead he had the resilience to withstand a period in the wilderness and was rewarded with the role of Chief Executive of Caradon Plc. Admittedly, this is not a business that could rival P&G and it may be that Hintz has had to tailor his ambitions to match his opportunities, but he has certainly had the resilience to overcome ill fortune.

This is a habit he acquired in early childhood. Hintz was born in Tilsit in Germany (formerly in East Prussia) in the middle of the Second World War. When he was just two years of age he accompanied his mother, grandmother and great-grandmother in their flight west, as the collapse of the Third Reich seemed as inevitable as East Germany's annexation by the Soviet Union. After a journey of several hundred miles the family reached a refugee camp where they remained for the next five years. Eventually an uncle and his grandfather joined them, but Hintz's own father remained in a Russian prisoner-of-war camp for some years. Finally, in 1954 the family emigrated to America, where Hintz quickly mastered the language. The extreme difficulty of his early years was mitigated by the closeness of his family, which gave him a strong sense of emotional stability and self-belief.

This emotional stability deriving from a family background is a common factor in what I term the Lazarus effect, the habit some people have of coming back from the brink. Take George Davies, who transformed Conran's ailing Hepworth business into Next, the paradigm of best practice in the UK retail sector in the 1980s. Davies went on to over-extend the business and was eventually ousted by the board. This was not his first experience of a board-room coup. At Pippa Dee (a clothing business sold through parties in much the same way as Tupperware) he fell out with his chair-man, who sold the business over his head. After Next, Davies has gone on to design Asda's highly successful clothing range. There are rumours that that relationship is under some strain, but there is every reason to suppose that, whatever the outcome, Davies will fight back. His survival instinct comes in part from having had the unstinting support of a strong mother whom he has described as 'a real dynamo, always behind me'.

More spectacular still is the resurgence of Paul Reichmann, who lost a fortune with the collapse of Olympia & York Devel-opments over the Canary Wharf project, which many blame on the British government and banking institutions. At one point Olympia & York controlled assets worth around $25 billion, the Reichmann family being worth $10 billion. His was one of the biggest bankruptcies of our time. He lost all but $100 million. Nevertheless, O&Y Properties Corp is back and thriving, even holding 5 per cent of Canary Wharf. It is not on the scale of its enormous predecessor, but in time and with care may yet be. Paul Reichmann is hugely respected as a man of great integrity. An intensely private man, he is a strict Orthodox Jew who trained as a rabbi and along with the rest of the family is a benefactor to Jewish charities. His faith and the strength of his family allegiance gives him the moral resilience to overcome even the most spec-tacular of failures.

Some do not so much experience failure as disappointment. The executive who comes second in the race for the top job in a company experiences disappointment but cannot be judged a failure. Some have the emotional maturity to turn it to good effect. When Alan Shepherd beat Antony Tennant to the top job in Grand Metropolitan in the mid 1980s, Tennant did not sit back, lick his wounds and give up. On the contrary, he took what at the time was something of a risk, joined Guinness (a company which came back from the brink), and, under Tennant's astute leadership, the business took on Grand Metropolitan's brands, beating them in many markets. It is a moot point which has been the more successful and, if Grand Metropolitan has the upper hand in Diageo (the merger of the two companies), that cannot reflect on Tennant. Charles Miller-Smith's achievements at ICI, where he is the chief executive, may one day overshadow those of Niall FitzGerald, to whom he came second in the race for the top job at Unilever.

A victim of disappointment will be a happier and a wiser figure if he or she can reconcile themself to that disappointment and confront it, head on, for what it is. One of the most moving accounts of disappointment that I know was recorded by Harold Nicolson. The husband of Vita Sackville-West, Nicolson was bisexual and in his youth both brilliant and beautiful. He was rich and enjoyed success early on, but disappointment came to him in 1941 when Churchill requested his resignation as Minister of Information in the wake of criticism of mismanagement. Nicolson wrote in his diary:

'I mind more than I thought that I should mind. It is mainly, I suppose, a sense of failure. I quite see that if the Labour leaders had been pressing to have my post, that is good cause why they should have it. But if I had had more power and drive, I should have been offered Rab Butler's job at the foreign office, which I should dearly have loved. As it is, I come back to the bench below the gangway, having had a chance and failed to profit by it. Ever since I have been in the House, I have been looked on as a might be. Now I shall be a might have been. Always up til now I have been buoyed up by the hope of writing some book or achieving a position of influence in politics. I now know that

> I shall never write a book better than I have written already,
> and that my political career is at an end.

Nicolson was wrong. The achievements of his long life were not over. Against his original promise he may, ultimately, have under-achieved but his ability to analyse his emotions and to acknowl-edge his shortcomings with painful candour can only have helped him move forward from this low point. Nicolson, of course, was not a businessman but a diplomat, politician and author. He had many talents and was something of a polymath.

Business cannot boast too many polymaths. Most businessmen I meet are fairly monolithic in their interests. The individual who can call upon a wide range of experience (and Nicolson, for instance, had an international career as a diplomat before becom-ing a journalist) can often find a way forward more easily than someone who has focused on a narrow range of interests. The irony here, however, is that in order to succeed in business there is very often a requirement for tunnel vision and obsessive attention to the operation in which one is employed. Similarly, too much self-knowledge can be a disadvantage to an aspiring businessman, if that self-knowledge spills over (as it so easily can) into self-doubt. A further factor against business people reconciling them-selves to disappointment or perceived failure is that they find themselves called upon, at times of disappointment, to operate in the emotional domain. This goes against their training. Their business career has very often forced them to focus on their logical skill set to the detriment of their emotions. When disappointment comes they find themselves with few resources with which to combat it.

Outstanding leaders are unlikely to suffer an emotional deficit. The very best are those with a fine-tuned intuition, to which they listen. Such people have an ability to understand the feelings of others without words, to grasp what others value, and so are able to get the best out of people because they know how to appeal to them. Such skills are extraordinarily rare, the more so in men. Across most societies men are expected to take action rather than to engage with their feelings. Men in business devote an inordinate amount of time to action and their emotional lives very often suffer as a consequence. The middle-aged man who ditches his wife of long standing in favour of a younger model, rather like his junior colleagues trade in their cars, is merely demonstrating the difficulty he has sustaining an emotional bond. Rare is the businessman whose second wife is not younger or more attractive than his first. Wives become status objects, rather like cars. I say this, not in a spirit of criticism, but rather with some sympathy for the plight in which many men find themselves when confronted by disappointment or, worse, by failure. They are, very often, emotionally retarded.

Women tend to be very much more attuned to their feelings than are their male counterparts. Companies are increasingly keen to bring women on to their boards, not out of a desire to be seen to be doing the right thing but because they recognize that women operate in a different way from men. There are many fewer women at senior levels in business than there are men, and one small factor in this phenomenon may be that women are less adept at suppressing their emotional side, less capable of the single-mindedness that, during the managerial phase of a career, is well nigh essential. Finding it harder to succeed in business in the first place, they may, ironically, cope better with disappointment than men.

There are, in business, a number of quite senior figures who have little self-knowledge and little reference to points of stability outside themselves. Such people, in positions of leadership, can become dangerous. They start to believe their own myth, to see themselves as invincible, and start to take decisions which reflect their belief in their infallibility. Gerald Ratner, who ran the Ratner's jewellery business until an ill-judged joke brought the share price tumbling, falls into this category. By referring to a cheap item sold by the shop as 'total crap', he demonstrated extraordinary arrogance and disregard for his customers. Most customers were people on lower incomes who gave Ratners products as gifts and needed to believe that they were purchasing quality items. Ratner's disregard for the pride of his customers was profoundly offensive.

Of course it was not the joke alone which brought down Ratner – that was a symptom rather than the problem. The problem resided in a sense of his own invincibility. He had started to do things alone and without the support of the board. The other directors feared that he was over-extending both himself and the business. Ratner's belief in his own invincibility may have come from the fact that he usurped his own father as managing director of the business. Perhaps unconsciously he did not believe that there was an authority figure that could get the better of him.

Some people, for whom the attainment of status is of paramount importance, grow bored with the status quo and look constantly for sensation and new experiences. It is leaders like this who, looking for more and more excitement, take risks which can eventually be their downfall. Ralph Halpern, another retailer, transformed the flagging fortunes of Burton during the 1980s, insisting that 'constant innovation' was his key requirement. A dynamo of energy with it, it seemed, not a shred of self-doubt, Halpern came under scrutiny for the huge sums he paid himself (to be fair he operated a good share scheme for all employees) and became a laughing stock for his taste for rather indiscreet young models. He became a liability rather than an asset for the group and once removed from its boardroom seems to have removed himself entirely from the upper echelons of British corporate life.

There are three clear stages in the decline and fall of leaders. The first stage comes when the leader loses his, or her, grasp on reality. This comes after a period of sustained success when that success, quite literally, goes to the head of the leader. This stage is often marked by a sudden shift in behaviour. Where once the enterprise formed the primary focus in the business leader's life, suddenly he (or she – but most commonly, he) becomes more detached from it than formerly and acquires new interests. This is not simply a matter of taking on a couple of additional board seats, more a matter of suddenly indulging a new passion. All too often that passion may be of a sexual nature. The leader who, in his twenties, was too focused on making his way to the top to spare much time for romance can wake up in his late forties and fifties to the fact that he has something attractive to the opposite sex – money and status. Believing that the business venture cannot fail simply because it is his, he devotes his time to extra-curricular activities, leaving the business to others.

The second phrase in the downfall of a business leader is the period when he stops listening to his advisers. His own interest has moved away from the direct concerns of the business and yet, so tenuous is his hold on reality, he still believes his own version of the truth – that the business is prospering and will continue to prosper. The brave subordinate who seeks to burst the bubble of the leader's inflated ego will find that he or she is simply not believed. Sometimes the leader who is drunk with success finds himself mixing in more elevated circles than previously. Suddenly he is one of the great and the good and, as such, he is no longer satisfied with the counsel of any one who is not of their number.

The misguided leader may listen to other leaders, or to people whose expertise he respects (senior partners in leading consultancies, for example), but will no longer pay attention to those who really have expertise in the business itself, those who are working within it. The team are very often the leader's own creation but the deluded leader in this second stage of decline comes to see the team as Victor Frankenstein came to see the monster he created. The team is out to get him. He comes to despise them and stops hearing any of their messages.

The third, terminal, phase in the decline of a business leader comes when the board lose faith in the leader and come to believe the evidence of the team and, all too often, the evidence before their own eyes of insidious failure. One or two things will have gone very wrong while the leader's attention was elsewhere. The leader himself, however, still does not seem to be facing facts. He has no strategy for remedying his wrongs because, as yet, he has not perceived them to exist. If the leader cannot be called back to reality (and very often he prefers the state of unreality in which he is living) he will be sacrificed, painfully and publicly, by the board. In the interests of the shareholders the board will have little other choice but to sever the relationship.

Such high-profile failures are relatively few and far between; they occur among the larger-than-life personalities that carry one fatal flaw – usually an emotional one. More often failure is down to a fundamental lack of competence in a key area (not infrequently intellect), a failure to deliver against targets or an inability to adapt to a different culture or set of economic circumstances.

Sometimes, having attained the much desired top position, an executive will rest on his laurels and cease to innovate. Jack Welch, Chief Executive of General Electric and one of America's most respected (if not the most respected) businessmen, has said: 'Some CEOs think that the day they become CEO is the high point of their careers. They ought to feel they're just beginning.' Leaders must be prepared to strive continually to improve the performance of the organization and to improve upon their own personal best. This requires stamina, extraordinary drive and the inventiveness to find new ways to tackle difficult situations. Leaders should also know when to stop. The inability to hand over power undermines the success of many business leaders. Indeed, it is so uncommon for people to hand over power while they are at their peak that people were initially suspicious when Andy Grove announced his intention to hand over the role of CEO of Intel to his successor Craig Barrett. In fact, the Intel board and Grove had taken a mature approach to the matter of succession and wanted to give Barrett the opportunity to make his mark on the business. Grove remains as chairman but that ability to stand back and allow others opportunity is a rare act of vision.

Leaders cannot court success eternally, hence the virtue of quitting while at the top. F. Scott FitzGerald's novel *The Great Gatsby* chronicles the transformation of lowly, insignificant Jimmy Gatz into the enigmatic, fabulously wealthy Jay Gatsby. In the end Gatsby's luck ran out. It seemed recently as if Bill Gates's luck might have run out. His leadership position in the global business arena seemed unassailable but he has been under attack for monopolistic and non-competitive activities and started to look vulnerable. The issue seems to have been resolved but for Gates it must have been a glimpse of the mortality of leadership. Gates is clearly sensitive to the potential tragedy of leadership, for he is said to have the closing passage of *The Great Gatsby* (whose name is so eerily like his own) by heart. It deals explicitly with the pathos of ambition, the probability of failure, the inevitability of effort and the absolute lack of control one has over one's destiny:

> He had come a long way to this blue lawn, and his dream must have seemed so close that he could hardly fail to grasp it. He

did not know that it was already behind him somewhere, back in that vast obscurity beyond the city, where the dark fields of the republic rolled on under the night.

Gatsby believed in the green light, the orgastic future that year by year recedes before us. It eluded us then, but that's no matter – tomorrow we will run faster, stretch out our arms further . . . And one fine morning –.

For Gatsby, as for so many, the origins of his failure and of his success are the very same. As the playwright, Samuel Beckett, observed 'The end is in the beginning – and yet you go on.'

Chapter 9

The Leader of the Pack:
Leadership and the Board

'Never doubt that a small group of thoughtful, committed citizens can change the world. Indeed, it is the only thing that ever has.' – Margaret Mead

For some, their ultimate failure is, seemingly, pre-ordained; their end is, indeed, in their beginning. Consider this commonplace set of events in business. A senior figure who has enjoyed some success in his career moves from a large organization to a small one. He finds himself heading up a team of some twenty-five or so people. It is a good team, packed with able people who are proud of the company they have helped to create and keen to ensure that it will fulfil its potential. Bright, innovative, forward-thinking, the team has taken extraordinary risks which have so far paid off. The co-founders who have been the scientific innovators have no aspirations to continue in a managerial function and have had the wisdom to stand back from the business to allow for a new chief executive. They remain on the board and maintain a significant shareholding. The arrival of the senior figure represents something of a coup. It is a mark of the promise the business holds and his appointment has resonated in the sector and in the financial community. The auguries are good.

For the director himself his situation is equally auspicious. Having missed out on a much coveted role in the multinational where he built his career, he finds considerable satisfaction in his new incarnation as a chief executive of a business that is going places and will give him, in time, the level of recognition he wants.

When he bows out of the multinational where he started and always assumed he would end his career, he does so with a strong sense that he is taking a substantial step forward. He appreciates the slightly envious approval of former colleagues. He is taking a gamble going to a young company, but he can make its name and it will make his name. No matter how long or hard he might try, he would be unlikely to do as much in a large multinational, whether or not he were chief executive.

A year on finds all parties disappointed in one another. Life as a chief executive has been found to have its frustrations. His team are forever questioning decisions, wanting to be informed of minutiae which do not concern them and wishing to be consulted on matters outside their immediate domain. They question his authority and, in his turn, he is obliged to question their competence. There is considerable dissension among the staff, which is being felt in reduced productivity and the loss of a couple of important managers to competitors. The chief executive senses that the board is losing confidence in him, but is bemused as to why this should be so. He had expected the boardroom to be a welcome intellectual island in the sea of operational concerns that represent his daily life as a chief executive. He had thought his board colleagues would help him work through the problems in the business. Instead he finds that they merely expect to approve the solutions he has devised outside the boardroom. The chief executive is baffled. The board seem not to want to debate whereas those on the operational side seem not to want to act. Where has he gone wrong?

The answer takes us into an area which is a potential minefield for the chief executive and can make the difference between successful leadership and downright failure – that of group dynamics. It is doubtless the case that a small group of committed directors can change the company provided – and it is a big proviso – each of those directors understands how the group interacts. Our beleaguered chief executive has, at fifty-two, failed to alter the style that was appropriate to a division of a multinational to suit a small group and has misunderstood the nature and function of the board. With a small group where he should have sought to build consensus he demanded obedience and instant approval, without debate, of any of his dictats. When this was not forthcoming, his self-image suffering, he hectored the group, undermined them, used sarcasm and cynicism and demonstrated an inability to respect subordinates who did not share his view. Moreover, he mistook the boardroom for a forum for debate rather than a decision-making council. He came across as vacillating, indecisive, out of control. An everyday tale of corporate calamity based on misconceptions and poor communication.

So far we have considered the leader in isolation, as an individual. Seldom, however, do those who lead act in isolation. Solitude is the preserve of the intellectual leader, the artist who depends upon subtle observation of the world but expresses his findings at a distance from that world. Artists need to develop their own voice, tone and style and in order to do so must be at a remove from others and from the pressure to conform that is an inevitable consequence of interaction with others. Individuals who resolutely stand their ground, making no move to bend their personality to better harmonise with their companion, are rare. At an unconscious level we rapidly identify those factors in our personality which will please or enable discussion and those which will have the converse effect and, in the course of conversation, we suppress the second in the interests of bringing the first to the fore. These social skills are learned at our mother's knee and put into practice from earliest childhood. The production of art that is arresting and has a profound impact on those who encounter it calls for an exaggeration of self on the part of the artist which is better achieved away from the world than within it.

The business leader, like the political or military leader, while having a decided personality must not demonstrate that personality such that it overshadows the cause or interests of the body he represents. Indeed, leaders are often vessels who represent a party position, a political regime or, in the case of a company, a complex set of values which cohere as the company's culture. Only in the case of founders and entrepreneurs where the leader's personality may be an important part of the culture can personality be overtly displayed.

Military and political leaders, and the leaders of corporations represent something other than themselves, are accountable to others and are obliged to interact with others on a daily basis. Business leaders must meet with the board, with the management team, with major customers and major suppliers. In practice a business leader will spend relatively little time outside a group environment, be that group large or small. The business leader needs to energize and motivate, explain and, sometimes, adjudicate. Personal magnetism will be an enormous aid to a leader in these circumstances but charisma and personality are not the same thing. The business leader may continue to be charismatic while subsuming elements of his or her personality in the interests of the successful working of a group. An understanding of group dynamics then (and very often this will be instinctive) is a critical element in the success of a business leader.

Groups vary in size and with difference in scale comes a very different leadership requirement. Managing or leading a group of two, three or four people will call upon the ability of the leader to demonstrate sensitivity to individual needs and to achieve a style of speech which is intimate and inclusive. At the other end of the spectrum, leading a very large group of hundreds or thousands calls for stature and self-confidence and an ability to articulate a message in such a way that its appeal will be universal. These are, of course, very different skills. The person who is compelling on a one-to-one basis and in groups of twelve or fifteen is frequently a very disappointing public speaker. Similarly, an ability to move a multitude is no sure guarantee that the speaker can form a bond with a group of ten. A style that suits one situation, palpably, will not suit another. The leader who is at ease on a large stage, addressing a largely anonymous crowd, is likely to be ill at ease when expected to achieve intimacy. This is especially so if he is male, since men are frequently uncomfortable giving of themselves as intimacy demands and fear such an act to be an expression of weakness. Conversely, women who can excel in motivating small groups can be considerably disconcerted in a large environment where they cannot establish a relationship with individuals. Clearly, the level of comfort an individual can achieve with a particular size of group owes something to psychology. There is, however, another way of considering group dynamics which I believe to be illuminating in the context of a study of business leadership, and that is an anthropological approach.

Anthropologists study human behaviour, finding common behaviour patterns between humans who are divided by many miles or, indeed, many centuries from one another. An obvious example of this is the tendency among people to mythologize and create stories around mysterious events in order to give them meaning. In this way, the sacred stories of most religious faiths include a story about a flood. The human being is constrained by biology to react in similar ways, so just as there is a variant of the Noah story in all religions, so all societies outlaw incest. It may seem imaginative in the extreme to find similarity between the workings of a modern corporation and the habits of primitive peoples. However, in an article entitled 'Hunters and gatherers in corporate life – why CEOs succeed and why they fail' (*Strategy and Business*, Fourth Quarter 1996, Issue 5, published by Booz Allen & Hamilton) the authors, Edward F. Tuck and Timothy Earle, make precisely this analogy. They offer some convincing insights into the vulnerability of corporate man. Their central thesis is that when modern man or woman finds him or herself in a group situation they unconsciously revert to patterns of behaviour laid down over the centuries from the time when people first came together in primitive social organizations.

This chapter begins with a vignette featuring a hapless chief executive who, in the space of a year, loses the confidence both of his team and of his board. He is a figure who might be said to have failed prior to joining the smaller business. He had, after all, missed out on a major prize within the multinational. It should not be assumed that he had failed. It is not uncommon, after all, for the person who misses out in the race for succession in one company to go on to another organization and be as successful, sometimes more successful, than the person to whom they lost in the original company. So the chief executive was by no means predestined to fail. It is unlikely that his failure will have been a matter of technical competence. At the heart of his failure lay an inability to recognize that in moving from a large divisional role in a major multinational to a much smaller structure he needed to make a most fundamental shift in his approach to people, to the group. He moved, in the terms employed by anthropologists, from a hierarchy to a camp, with neither acknowledgement nor alteration to his style of operating. Borrowing substantially from the excellent work of Tuck and Earle I should like to explore the group types they identify and which are of clear relevance to corporate life today, principally the working group, the camp and the hierarchy.

The working group comprises some two to six people and amounts to a small project team of individuals who have come together to perform a particular task or solve a specific problem. The working group operates as a democracy. The members of a working group meet on equal terms, and share their expertise in the interests of completing the task. Such groups do not need leaders. Individuals may take on the mantle of leadership for a limited period dictated by their particular expertise but the status of the group and the individuals within it is subordinated to the satisfactory conclusion of the task or solution of the problem. Those of unequal status outside the working group will be equals within it.

In modern corporations, working groups may be established and a leader named by the hierarchy beyond the group. Within the group itself little credence will be given to this. When the problem is solved the group disbands. Working groups can operate in this casual, democratic fashion because they have no need of internal controls, for the group will cease to exist once the task which brought it into existence has been accomplished. If another task needs to be tackled then another working group will be formed. Working groups are small in size and short-lived associations.

The camp is a more settled entity than the working group. Consisting of somewhere between ten and thirty people, in early societies these would have been collections of families who lived and worked together. Camps would fragment into working groups to undertake the necessary business of hunting, finding shelter, preparing food and so on, and these working groups would be highly flexible. As with the working group, a camp is a broadly egalitarian structure. There is unlikely to be a designated leader but a figure, often an elder, will come to embody the character of the camp in such a way that observers will see the camp as that person's, say John's camp. Camps give rise to more complex decision-making requirements than working groups which focus on one specific task. They therefore need a facilitator who will ensure that decisions are reached in an appropriate fashion. In keeping with the general egalitarianism of the camp, all members are informed of the options for action and all take a keen interest in the outcome.

Camp members are highly informed but are also subject to

strong peer pressure to conform to the prevailing view, so they are somewhat utilitarian. Camps are consensual but decisions are not made collectively, they are made by a few designated members (the elders) but with the full consent of the group. If consensus is not reached, the likely outcome will be that the dissenting group will detach itself from the camp, either to chance survival as a separate camp or to attach itself to another. The collection of Sicilian families in Francis Ford Coppola's film *The Godfather* is a classic example of a camp, in which Don Corleone becomes the head or elder of the camp by dint of his superior expertise. Constituent parts of the camp do break out and set up on their own with mixed success and eventually the camp reaches a size at which it can no longer be sustained. The camp headed by Don Corleone (Marlon Brando) becomes a tribe or hierarchy when Michael (Al Pacino) takes over as the new Don.

A hierarchical organization is one that holds together a range of camp-sized groups, having a clearly defined leader and recognized strata of authority. It is understood that consensus cannot be the aspiration of a hierarchy and instead decisions are made at the top and communicated and monitored through clearly understood lines of command. In becoming a member of a hierarchy an individual gives up his autonomy, thus there must be a significant motivation or common interest to bring people together in an apparently restrictive social structure. One common interest, which led to the emergence of the extended group, was defence – another was worship.

The hierarchy works most effectively where there is a clear need for cohesion, as when under threat. The hierarchy brings together large numbers of people and so must be concerned with control. While there is this element of restriction on the members of the hierarchy, there is the freedom for individuals to develop a particular specialism and expertise which is less frequently the case in the camp, where only a handful of people would have that opportunity. Hierarchies can go from fifty to thousands and can evolve a complex organizational structure. A hierarchy is a complex structure that evolved to enable large numbers of people with common interests and needs to coexist in a controlled fashion. The individual, in return for a degree of restriction of his personal freedom, is offered other outlets for his personality and needs.

The three categories of group enumerated above (and Tuck and Earle identify in the State a fourth which is less relevant to our corporate analogy) have developed in response to the growing complexity of human needs. The point at which a new structure is required is directly related to the size of the existing one. The working group ceases to function at about the point that the seventh person joins it and a camp will splinter at around fifty. Drawing on research by Gregory A. Johnson, Tuck and Earle report that the human brain cannot manage too much complexity and can not process more than six or seven items of information simultaneously. The maximum number a camp can tolerate is broadly seven times seven and in the hierarchy the multitude is broken down into a range of camps and working groups. Importantly, the ultimate decision-making forum in the hierarchy is a council or management team which operates in precisely the consensual manner of a camp. The board of a modern corporation is the camp-like council within a hierarchy.

The hierarchy evolved much later than the working group and the camp, which are primitive forms of social organization. Mankind has had innumerable generations in which to adapt to working groups and camps. Indeed, the working group mirrors the nuclear family, the camp the extended family. Hierarchies are more modern and more troubling because human kind has had a shorter period in which to adapt to them and they do not equate to a close and knowable unit such as a familial one. But it would be wrong to see hierarchies as alienating structures. They fulfil an important role in supplying the emotional and material well-being of modern men and women. With mankind's increasing sophistication has come a desire for more than mere physical comfort and security.

Man as a thinking, as well as a feeling, being has come to want to understand and know the world around him and to find his place within it. Naming and labelling are important activities to mankind. At one stage in the Christian faith the child who died before his formal Christian baptism could not enter the kingdom of heaven and could not be buried on consecrated ground. Hierarchies with their strata of named levels provide a structure around which a large unknowable world can be understood, categorized and controlled. Myth provides a way in which early man, striving to make sense of his surroundings, did so by converting the inexplicable into poetic fantasies and stories which we now call myth. Giambattista Vico, an Italian living in the eighteenth century who was the first thinker to make an anthropological study of myth, explains the emergence of Jove in Roman mythology as a fear by primitive man of the extreme light and noise of a thunderstorm. He writes that early men:

> . . . were frightened and astonished by the great effect whose
> cause they did not know, and raised their eyes and became
> aware of the sky. And because in such a case the nature of the
> human mind leads it to attribute its own nature to the effect,
> and because in that state their nature was that of men all robust
> bodily strength, who expressed their very violent passions by
> shouting and grumbling, they pictured the sky to themselves as a
> great animated body which in that aspect they called Jove . . .
> who meant to tell them something by the hiss of his bolt and
> the clap of his thunder.

It is a human habit to think in metaphors. If we analyse daily language, how often do we express our ideas by comparison of things essentially unlike except in one salient detail? Simile, metaphor, antithesis, oxymorons – these are all figures of speech which most of us use routinely to convey the complexity of our meaning. Most of us use them without knowing we do so and without being able to put a name to them. Language is a rich formula for expressing the felt and the thought. It takes us beyond the immediate, the here and now, and opens up an imaginative other world. All societies engage with art, with adornment, just as music is as much a feature of primitive as of so-called civilized man. The urge to step beyond the confines of daily life, to engage with beauty, is clearly a feature of humanity. To be human is to aspire to be more than merely human. Religions have been built on this principle. To be human is to aspire.

It is with this requirement to move forward in life that hierarchies can assist, especially in a world where the secular has taken over from the spiritual and many people are more concerned with achieving greatness in this life rather than postponing greatness to some after-life which may not materialize. Hierarchies can be immensely productive and supportive of the human spirit. There is the comfort, when joining an organization in a junior position, that there is a clear path along which to progress to a position of seniority. There may be nothing either inexorable or inevitable about the progression through a hierarchy, but the presence of staging posts, clearly marked, preserves the necessary illusion of movement.

Most hierarchies incorporate working parties and, as we have seen, have at their head in the form of a council or board a structure which is effectively a camp. A hierarchy is unlikely to incorporate camp-style modes of behaviour other than at the top, for the consensual model is antithetical to the prevailing command structure. A hierarchy evolves from a camp and the camp is part of its history rather than its present. Although some of the groups that are aligned within the hierarchy may be camp-sized, they are not camps. The discrepancy between the camp and the hierarchy is critical for an understanding of why so many chief executives fail.

To return to our opening vignette: our chief executive has built his entire career in a multinational, which is of course an outstanding example of hierarchy. Those who thrive in a hierarchy are those who recognize the importance of authority and acknowledge differences in status. In an effective hierarchy difference in status will be conferred in accordance with difference in competence. Many hierarchies have, of course, thrived on arbitrary measures such as nobility of birth and the advantage of superior age. We have no reason to suppose that our chief executive rose to a position of prominence in the hierarchy for any other reason than that he was competent. He may have failed to obtain the very top job but he did what many people do in business, he sought to apply his expertise in an environment where it would add considerable value. In moving to a much smaller organization in an earlier stage of its development he (and the board that hired him) thought that he would be bringing a detailed knowledge of his sector and an authoritative reputation to a business that could only be of benefit.

All parties failed to see that the chief executive's success to date derived from a comprehensive understanding of the rules governing a hierarchy. His only mode of operation was one of command and control. He did not understand the rules of a camp and could not be comfortable in an environment where he was obliged to disseminate information and gain acceptance over time for his actions. He misinterpreted the need on the part of the camp to know the detail behind a decision as a lack of trust in him, and that lack of trust constituted a sin of insubordination. His flimsy self-esteem was punctured and he sought to restore it by a fruitless elevation of himself by a diminution of others, hence his hectoring and sarcasm. He failed to understand that in the camp situation the authority of the leader must be universally validated and accepted and that authoritarian conduct was entirely misplaced and wholly counterproductive. Ironically, the camp had probably reached the point at which it needed to be transformed into a hierarchy and our chief executive might have been the ideal person to head up such a venture. However, he needed to involve the camp members in the process of evolution, not simply impose from without.

At the same time as turning in a poor performance in the business, our chief executive performed dismally in the boardroom. All too often, people who have performed outstandingly in big divisional roles once they attain the much coveted role of chief executive with a seat on the board proceed to lose all the confidence and stature they had spent the previous twenty or so years of their career building up. Tuck and Earl are illuminating on this point, and their argument is that, once again, someone schooled in the workings of a hierarchy has not understood that the board is subject to the rules of the camp. Most will recognize that different rules do apply in the boardroom from those which govern the company at large, but many make the mistake, as the chief executive in our example did, of thinking that the model for the board is not the camp but the working group.

The board does not exist to solve a problem or to accomplish a task. It is a collection of equals who must ratify the decisions proposed by the chief executive. As in any camp, the members will form and re-form into working groups such as the Audit Committee, the Remuneration Committee or, perhaps, the Nominating Committee, but its purpose is not as a vehicle for solving problems. The single biggest mistake the chief executive can make is to look to the board for decisions and alternatives when it is the board who look to him for that. The board will then ratify proposals having first checked their robustness, but will not put them forward. The chief executive must carry his board along with him, lead it in the subtlest of ways, acknowledging the equal status of each member and steering it towards an appropriate outcome. When a chief executive fails to perform in this way the most likely explanation given is simply that he has been over-promoted, that he was not yet ready for the task.

The supposedly over-promoted chief executive who fails is as common a phenomenon as the entrepreneur who loses control of the business he has founded as it reaches a certain point in its evolution. That point will usually be when the business numbers some fifty people. Having founded a camp, perhaps having started with a working group and moved to a camp structure, the entrepreneur finds that the internal controls within a camp are no longer appropriate. He or she needs to assemble a hierarchy. This is a watershed in the life of the organization. Very often a business will fail at this point. Sometimes it will shed its founder and, under different management (and I use the term advisedly), will set in place the appropriate hierarchical structure.

The small entrepreneurial vehicle has the convivial air of a family venture in which all parties are enthused, highly motivated, kept informed of developments, allowed a voice and move with ease across a diverse range of tasks. Some will have specialisms but the camp structure of the small business allows the generalist considerable scope. At around fifty staff members the business starts to factionalize and the common lament is that it's no fun any more. Previously highly motivated members of staff feel they are being neglected or pushed out as once freely available information seems to be held more closely to the chest of a favoured few. These staff withdraw their cooperation. Talented people may leave. The founder will grow hostile to those he considers ungrateful and may well feel alienated from the business he created as it takes on a life of its own, beyond his control. As the culture disintegrates and the once shared values dissipate, the value of the business will start to fall.

The anthropological approach can be applied extensively. Consider a professional services organization. Small and medium-sized professional service organizations such as lawyers, smaller firms of accountants and general consultants operate as camps, bringing together a series of working groups to solve client problems. Sometimes an account team will itself be a camp rather than a working group bringing together client and service suppliers in a loose association of equals. Professional services businesses do not easily achieve the transition to a hierarchy. Most of those who work within these businesses are not comfortable in a hierarchy, including those who lead them. More often than not they have selected the professions in preference to a corporate career because of an innate mistrust of hierarchies.

Very often the leader will be the person who is seen to be most successful in terms of business generation and client service. Their skills are consensual, iterative, and discursive and at a considerable remove from the command structure of a hierarchy. Many accountancy and legal practices have evolved as partnerships where the notions of trust and equality are an explicit part of the value system. When movement to a hierarchy becomes essential, the partnership will often try to achieve this through artificial means, perhaps appointing a handful of outsiders as managers. Of course this is doomed to failure, since in any professional services organization credibility comes from being able to provide the service in question in an exemplary way to an impressive array of clients. The outside manager, not having these credentials, will never acquire the necessary credibility to secure the buy-in of the partnership.

Fudge and compromise is often the only impoverished solution to the problem. Some firms, for instance, construct a rather unstable structure linking together numerous camps under a shared brand rather than a shared organizational structure. The largest professional services businesses are being forced to devise ways of becoming fully functional hierarchies in the interests of serving their global corporate clients. Typically, smaller professional services businesses have been among the most enjoyable and stimulating working environments. The adage which has a ring of the 1980s about it, work hard, play hard, applied particularly to these types of businesses. Large professional services businesses, which tend to be uneasy hierarchies yearning for the golden days of the camp, can be organizational hell.

An anthropological reading of a corporation is altogether compelling. Corporations are, after all, man-made constructions. They will naturally ape the pre-existing forms of social organizations which throughout history and across the globe have been found to be effective means of bringing together groups of people and allowing them to lead a productive existence in which the needs of the general community are met. The evolution of these forms in business, as in primitive tribes, hunter-gathering communities and more complex centres of civilization such as towns and cities, is instinctive, innate and seldom articulated other than by academics and experts at a remove from day-to-day life. The transition from small to medium size, from an entrepreneurial to a 'managed' business or, in our terms, from a camp to a hierarchy, is much better understood to be problematic than the move from a hierarchy to a camp. An anthropological approach offers a strategy for circumventing the problem. By understanding the rules of the various different groups, those active within them and moving between them can learn to play the game effectively.

An understanding of the rules does not necessarily mean that a player will be any better at the game. Take the game of football. You cannot play the game effectively if you do not understand the offside rule. An explanation of the rule will be helpful, but unless a player has significant skills will not make him any more successful although it may prevent embarrassing failure. As a headhunter advising a potential candidate on a move to the board, I can outline the scenario he or she will need to lead. I can describe the behaviour patterns common in leaders of hierarchies which are wholly inconsistent with those of a leader of a camp. I cannot, however, change a personality. Some people are naturally more comfortable in one structure than in another. Hierarchies suit people who need a sense of fixity and purpose, who crave a certain order in their universe and baulk at ambiguity. For such people, joining the flat structure of a camp would be equivalent to an agoraphobic pitching a tent on the Russian steppes.

The extrovert entrepreneur who has the germ of an idea and the energy and enthusiasm to motivate others needs a team around him who operate as his equals, who understand his thoughts almost before he has spoken them and can convert them into actions. He will invite his secretary to attend important meetings and make the tea for them himself, practices which in a hierarchy would disconcert, confuse and annoy. Rare is the entrepreneur who can settle into a role as head of a hierarchy. Richard Branson has found a typically innovative solution to the problem by building a cluster of small businesses operating independently as camps. Branson could not function in a hierarchy. One of his greatest gifts, however, is that he is aware of this and has side-stepped the single biggest issue for the successful business builder.

Most people who move from one group type to another, unless they have considerable personal flexibility, will naturally fall back on a style of behaviour which was worked for them in the past, and if they fail will simply do the same things more intensively. It is the same quirk in human nature which dictates that the tourist in a foreign country not understanding the language will simply fall back on his own language, but speak it louder and more slowly, more intensively.

Some have no choice but to shift from one mode to another. Business leaders find themselves making uncomfortable transitions between groups that are stylistically in conflict with one another. Political leaders face a similar dilemma. They have to try and work at a number of levels, developing a persona that can speak to the multitude but assuming a degree of intimacy for television broadcast. In general, however, the political leader is exposed to camps and working groups rather than hierarchies. The civil servants run the hierarchy. Nevertheless, one of the most important skills for a leader is that of personal flexibility. Some have this innately but most need training and development. The growing practice (in the UK, at least) of putting up-and-coming executives on boards in a non-executive capacity may go some way to acclimatizing an individual whose career has been spent in a hierarchy to the different operating imperatives of a camp. When he becomes a chief executive in his own company, the prior exposure to board behaviour will pay enormous dividends.

The up-and-coming executive, finding him or herself on a board for the first time, should use the opportunity to observe and to build up a presence slowly and thoughtfully. The board is a camp of equals and is not a forum which requires flashiness and show. The focus here has been on those moving from a hierarchy to a camp, but there are occasions when the shift is in reverse. Many consultants cherish the desire to stop advising clients how to do things and to go and do those things for themselves. I have interviewed countless highly able consultants who genuinely want to move into a corporate environment in a chief executive role, having no prior experience of operating within a hierarchy. I have witnessed one or two make that ill-advised transition with devastating results. Hierarchies crave clarity and certainty. Consultants imbued with the values of the camp will debate sooner than act and will allow ambiguity to be sustained indefinitely. In the interests of a better truth the consultant-come-leader of a hierarchy will change the message delivered previously. While the first message is still being transmitted to the outer perimeter of the hierarchy the second is contradicting it, creating confusion and inconsistency where there should be a strong and unflinching sense of clarity.

The anthropological model provides a very helpful way of identifying potential issues when considering the leadership of different organizations. Also extremely useful to an understanding of groups and how they work is a psychological approach. There is, of course, a common link between the two approaches: they both assume that modern man has inherited a cultural legacy comprising a range of different behaviourial patterns which have, over time, become instinctive. A group is something quite other than the sum of its parts, and understanding this and how those parts interact can be of benefit to the student of organizations and, especially, those with leadership aspirations. In particular they have significant implications for the leader of a board.

It may be helpful to make a few comments about what a group is and is not. A group is a collection of individuals. By the very act of coming together those individuals find something common between themselves and the other members of the group. That common interest is a leavening factor which inevitably suppresses elements of each person's individuality. In a group what is common between people (background, culture, interests, language) comes to the surface and what is distinct is suppressed. A crowd in a soccer stadium is defined by a shared interest in the sport. The fans of each team form groups in which loyalty to that team is the defining characteristic. Members of that crowd may also enjoy cricket or classical music but this is entirely irrelevant; those parts of individual experience become lost in the interests of the one unifying interest in soccer or the particular team. While the member of a group loses some individuality, he or she is compensated for that loss by the acquisition of new characteristics which are often a heightened form of existing emotions. To use the example of the stadium full of fans, it is interesting to observe that people who are normally restrained and unlikely to express passionate emotion become, with the strength that comes with numbers, much more courageous and outspoken. The quiet, reserved male can be observed in ecstasy over a goal, despairing over a missed opportunity or a goal by the other side and in a fury of rage against an official who has made a judgement to the disadvantage of the preferred team. The anonymity of the group confers on the individual the opportunity to shed any sense of responsibility and with it their inhibitions.

Groups reduce the individual and return that person to a primitive or childlike state. An uninhibited group can become a mob and a threatening entity, particularly when swollen by numbers. Psychologists point to the tendency among groups for emotion to spread through the group, each member of that group instinctively adopting the stance of the others in a move of solidarity. Groups are illogical. They are moved not by logic but by image, emotion and instinct. The Second World War pitched two great orators in conflict with one another. Both used entirely different rhetorical skills but both had the capability to move groups. Winston Churchill did so through image and fantasy, Adolf Hitler by repetition and insistence. Both knew instinctively that a group reacts to different laws to an individual, both are testimony to a truth observed by Sigmund Freud:

> Inclined as itself is to all extremes, a group can only be excited
> by an excessive stimulus. Anyone who wishes to produce an
> effect upon it needs no logical adjustments in his arguments; he
> must paint in the most forcible colours, he must exaggerate, and
> he must repeat the same thing again and again.

Groups are of interest to us for two reasons. First, the way the individual members of the group act on one another such that a group identity takes the place of the disparate identities of the constituent parts. Second, because of the way in which they can be worked upon by an external force or leader. A crowd, of course, is a far cry from a small and sophisticated group such as a board. A supposition that groups return individuals to a state of uninhibited primitiveness fails to take note of the fact that groups of people working together have been responsible for many of the great advances which have added to mankind's sophistication. A group cannot always reduce the individual, it must sometimes elevate and heighten intellectual contributions.

W. McDougall, writing as long ago as 1902, details five conditions which must exist if a group is to perform in a sophisticated rather than a primitive fashion. These conditions are those which prevail in the instance of the board. First it is important that the group enjoys some continuity either material (if the same members of the group remain together over time) or formal (if the roles are maintained but the individuals within them change). Second, each individual member of the group should have a sense of what brings the group together, what dictates its composition, and an understanding of the various capacities and competencies within it. If this condition is met then the individual can develop a relation to the group, preserving a sense of their membership of a group and simultaneous existence as an individual. Third, the group should interact with others or be brought into rivalry with other groups which are similar to it. The board of a company, of course, is defined by the fact that it has as its primary interest the better performance of that business than others in its field. The board of one company inevitably competes with the board of others. Fourth, the group must possess traditions, customs and habits; it should, in short, develop a common culture and finally, to quote from Freud's exposition of McDougall's work: 'the group should have a definite structure, expressed in the specialization and differentiation of the functions of its constituents'. The board has precisely this defined structure and, complying neatly with the other conditions, we can see that it is a sophisticated group capable of placing the necessary checks and inhibitions on itself to act in a manner that is not merely primitive but productive.

A board is sophisticated but nevertheless some of the rules which applied to the unruly crowd apply to the controlled board. The members of the group do infect one another with the same idea. Boards, like crowds, are just as susceptible to the non-logical, and are moved by image and fantasy. Truth is what the group take to be truth, for a group operates outside such rational notions as true and false, right and wrong. A group has no mechanism within itself for judging, sifting and selecting. It merely acts instinctively, collectively and uniformly.

A group has a mechanism outside itself which can sift, judge and

manipulate the others into accepting those judgements and that
mechanism is, of course, the leader. We have seen in the anthropological study that a board operates as a camp, a collection of
equals which disdains a clear leader. A camp nonetheless needs a
leader and the leader has the difficult task of trying to be of the
group and yet beyond it. Bringing together the anthropological and
psychological approaches to group behaviour sheds light on the
enormity and subtlety of the task the leader of the board under-
takes. It also indicates the potential power the leader has. A leader
can impose a false truth which, assuming it chimes with the shared
fantasies and dreams of the group, can take hold with devastating
effects.

A case study might be helpful here. I have been working recently
with a company turning over a billion pounds sterling and operating in the technology sector. An international company, it has three
primary divisions. Of these, one division has traditionally made all
the money. A second has been the up and coming business which
was expected to be the profit generator in the next two to four
years. The third division which developed the leading-edge high
technology had a lot of potential but was not likely to be highly
profitable in the short term. It needed first to grow its market and
develop its technology. The three divisional managing directors
reported to a chief executive who had been very successful a few
years previously and had restored the company's fortune by cost-
cutting and improving the financial systems. The major profit
generator, division A, had boomed on the back of unexpected
windfall contracts. These had come to an end some three or four
years before and now the major division was under cost pressure
with a high cost base.

There was little sign of the downturn in the business within the
boardroom. The board was universally optimistic. Board meetings
were optimistic affairs, in which the cool chill of reality was never
felt. There was a shared view regarding who would take on
leadership of the business, how the three divisions would develop
and interact and the source of profits. A hard-headed look at the
figures revealed a very different story from the camaraderie and
shared optimism of the directors. The company had entered a very
difficult trading environment and, making no effort to transform
itself, was now in decline.

The group was a homogenous one. Its leader, the chief executive, lived on the dreams of past glory, shared them with the group, and the group willingly adopted and spread them. The chief executive as leader was, effectively, subsumed within the group. The shared fantasy constituted reality for the group. Reality does, of course, intrude on the group and it intruded on this group in the form of three profit warnings. The board could no longer maintain its fantasy and did what groups do when the fantasy which cements them is removed: it started to panic and to disintegrate. The chief executive was removed. The chairman assumed the leadership of the group while a new chief executive was sought from outside. Once in place, the new chief executive removed the previous board members and began to assemble a new group to rebuild the company. The scenario is the classic one of shared fantasies, loss of leadership and inevitable panic and disintegration.

The shared fantasy of this group involved an act of regression to a past golden age when the company was thriving under the leadership of its strong chief executive. Regression is a common term in psychoanalytic thought. It describes an adult response to anxiety involving the return to a former, happier state. One of the central features of regression is that it involves a shedding of responsibility. Groups respond to anxiety in a similar way to individuals, via a collective act of regression. Very often they fall back upon the basic assumptions that underpin the group, shedding responsibility in so far as they revert to a mode of behaviour where the rules are pre-ordained and where reality need not intrude. Basic assumptions are the network of myths and shared beliefs which form the culture of an organization.

Research leading on from that undertaken by Wilfred Bion who, writing in 1959, did much to establish models for group behaviour, has identified three core types to which groups typically conform. A group that is functioning well will, from time to time, display elements of all three types and will allow no one type to dominate. *In extremis*, however, the group falls back upon practised modes of thought and behaviour. Any group may conform to these types, be it a department within an organization, the board or the company at large.

The first of these shared group responses is that of fight/flight. Here the group regards the world outside itself as essentially hostile and threatening. It divides the world into stark contrasts of good and bad, friend and foe, and is focused on achieving one of two survival mechanisms, to fight for survival or flee from danger. Groups who conform to this type will behave in one of two ways. If the preference is to fight, the group will be suspicious, antagonistic and highly combative. Such groups will compete fiercely on an issue by issue basis with other groups, taking a short-term rather than a long-term view. In such a way a manufacturing department might, as it were, on principle take issue with every decision taken by the marketing department. Alternatively, one company might respond to its competitor by shadowing their every move. The focus tends to be more reactive to the source of enmity than it is to the group's own needs. In organizational terms this means that tactics are favoured over strategy. The group which seeks to protect itself does so by a flight from its foe. Very often this will take the form of looking inward and focusing on the protective strategies which will ensure the group is safe. Rules and regulations become highly important as means by which the enemy is kept at bay.

The second shared group response is one of dependency, where the group finds meaning outside itself and becomes entirely dependent on that external force. Not uncommonly this external force will be a strong and charismatic leader. An organization in start-up will depend in such a way upon its founder. The presence of a strong, decision-making leader who has the interests of the group at heart frees that group for action. There is a tendency for the group to act in accordance with the leader's wishes and to place an unquestioning faith in the leader. With the departure of the leader, that leader's edicts can become enshrined in law and the dependent group may slavishly follow what they understand to be that leader's wishes (this mirrors the change from charismatic leadership to bureaucracy). Dependent groups are ones which, in organizational terms, feel comfortable with a strong parent in control where scope for decision making is necessarily curtailed.

The final shared response is one that Manfred Kets de Vries and Danny Miller, in their study *The Neurotic Organization*, have termed 'utopian'. Such groups live in the future and gaze optimistically towards a better time when there will be no more fear and anxiety. These groups anticipate deliverance in the form of a new leader or new idea, in a belief in a messiah. Groups focused on research and development often conform to this model and they can be highly innovative and risk-taking. At the same time they can be heedless of immediate concerns and highly vulnerable as a consequence.

Each of these three models has significant implications for the individual who leads the group. In the first instance of fight/flight the leader is looked to as a figurehead, as the person who will lead the charge. The leader has no role beyond the short-term necessity of ensuring that each battle is won. The dependent group will, on the other hand, give to its leader a free rein, accepting that leader's decisions simply because they are his. Sometimes dependent groups will rebel, will spot the deficiencies in their leader, and the response is an exaggerated sense of disappointment. Utopian groups give relatively little credence to the leader of the present since their focus is exclusively on the future. Indeed, such groups might prefer to consider themselves leaderless.

In many cases the actual leader of the group will set its tone. It may be the case that the shared tendency towards the fight or flight mode reflects a deep-rooted suspicion on the part of the leader which has communicated itself to, or in the terms of the psycho-analysts 'infected', the rest of the group. The autocrat with a deep need to control will assemble a group around him who need to depend whereas the dreamer will want a group who are energized by ideas even if it is at the expense of some personal status.

The task of the leader, however, is not to impose his or her personality on the group but to ensure that the group fulfils what it has been brought together to do. The leader must resist working on the group in any way that will impede the task fulfilment. This calls upon the leader to have considerable self-knowledge and, above all, considerable emotional strength. He or she cannot look to the group to supply their emotional needs and must, on the contrary, suppress any such need. The leader of the board who is, as we have seen, the leader of a camp-style group must exert him- or herself to suppress ego and to find a subtle means of leadership which does not involve any vaunting of personality. Camps, as we have seen above, do not relish overt leadership.

Through the course of this book I have focused on the oddity of leaders. Very often they are excessively driven and not infrequently have something to prove. Personality is very often as important to their leadership as their professional skills. All too often, however, those who succeed in reaching the top of an organization do not have the requisite degree of emotional maturity to suppress their ego in the interests of the group. Ego suppression is of course a dilemma that confronts all members of the group, not simply the leader. Maintaining the balance between the individual's need for self-esteem and their equal need to belong is one of the primary challenges which face the group member and the group will suffer if that fine balance cannot be achieved in all cases. We have, in an earlier chapter, encountered the narcissistic leader who is characterized by, on the one hand, a grandiose, over-inflated image of themselves and, on the other, deep feelings of inadequacy. These are people who do not have a sense of perspective about themselves and, unable to make an accurate reading of their own personality, have no capacity to do so in relation to others. They tend to feel envy rather than to achieve any degree of empathy with others. Moreover, they crave power and prestige and the reverence of others. Narcissists are very frequently highly driven individuals who will work hard and apply their often considerable talents to attain the highest positions in their chosen careers. Ironically it is such narcissists least qualified to lead boards who most frequently achieve a position of board leadership. Their failure is virtually guaranteed.

Anthropology, psychology and its related discipline, psychoanalysis, are very useful tools for deconstructing groups and, in particular, the types of groups which a modern business leader will encounter. Much more than a collection of people joining together with a common aim, groups are complex organisms that demand subtlety and sensitivity from those who lead them. There is little preparation for leading a group. Indeed, many of those whom we charge to lead some of our most challenging businesses and who therefore find themselves in the lead role on a board come to this position from the most inappropriate of training grounds.

The hierarchy is a structure which valorizes the powerful, placing them visibly at the peak of a pyramid. Those who crave power, prestige and the attention of others are drawn inevitably to the hierarchy and come to the board room with the expectation that the board will offer the final validation of their power and prestige. Of course it does no such thing. If the group is strong it will resist an authoritarian approach. If it is weak it may well bend to the will of the leader giving the leader an almost anarchic freedom which may lead to success but, equally, may not.

I began this chapter with a case study of someone who moved from a large to a small environment, from a hierarchy to a camp, and failed to understand the significant difference in style between the two. A narcissist with a need for acclaim and respect, the business held appeal for him in part because of the status of those within it. The intellectual capital was extraordinary and the narcissistic chief executive basked in reflected glory. The culture, however, was not one that particularly esteemed leaders. The founders who had stood aside had been absorbed by the science, not by the mystique of management and the group as a whole disdained management politics. Their sights were firmly set on the future and on the delivery of world-beating scientific solutions. Our chief executive would have been happier in a culture where the basic assumption was one of dependence (happier but not necessarily more successful) but had alighted upon a group where the prevailing basic assumptions were utopian.

Perhaps the appointment of the chief executive in the first instance was a foolish one? It is easy to criticize the decision but it had some elements of logic. The business was about to enter a new phase. If it were to deliver product to the market it would need to develop some processes. Utopian cultures place too little emphasis on the here and now, and without management expertise this business would not have been able to fulfil its promise. The mistake in the appointment had more to do with a misreading of the character of the apparently ideal candidate. His need for affirmation was acute but had not seemed out of place in the environment where he had enjoyed his greatest success – a hierarchy. His ability to suppress his ego and his own needs in the interests of the group had not been put to the test. When it was, as we have seen, he could not summon the emotional strength to integrate on equal terms with the group. The ensuing failure on the part of the chief executive was entirely to be expected but scarcely the fault of any party involved in the appointment, the chief executive included.

Success or failure is, ultimately, beyond the control of the individual. No one can manage the construction of their personality, and the groups that most leaders preside over are put together over time and by someone other than the leader. The subsequent behaviour of the group can, with hindsight, be understood, but few are sufficiently prescient to predict how a group dynamic will develop. Successful leadership seems, in the final analysis, a matter of chance, of happy accident or, perhaps, a triumph of instinct. A successful leader is someone whose ability to empathize with the group operates at the level of instinct and whose personality is strong at the core but can bend. The best business leaders are seldom the biggest personalities. They are much more likely to be the introverts who allow those around them to flourish and develop. As someone observed to me recently, nothing grows under big trees. The disciplines of anthropology and psychoanalysis demonstrate the truth in his assertion.

Chapter 10

Of Worms and Glow-worms

'World events are the work of individuals whose motives are often frivolous, even casual.' – Gore Vidal, *Robert Graves and twelve Caesars*

Business leaders do not yet have charge of world events, although increasingly they have global power and influence over those who hold political power. Some become embroiled in political battle, much as Bill Gates and the Clinton administration have locked horns over Microsoft's alleged monopolistic conduct. Nevertheless business people do not yet have the status – or indeed the mandate – of those who have been elected to a position of leadership in a political democracy. Some people will doubtless see a certain lack of proportion or perspective in the manner in which in these pages I have juxtaposed world leaders, figures from the academies of arts and sciences with less elevated businessmen. Not infrequently I find myself being an apologist for business. It has, over the years, been given a pretty bad name.

The Greek philosopher Aristotle did the business community few favours when he found the practice of simple trading in kind (household trading) acceptable but scorned the activity of trade for profit. The former, he thought, was essential to any society. The latter, he claimed, was parasitic. His was the prevailing view until the seventeenth century. Of course the Christian religion did little to help matters, outlawing usury and condemning the practice to those on the outside, like Shakespeare's much maligned merchant, Shylock. Small matter that some of the greatest achievements of the

European Renaissance were made on the back of mercantile money. By the seventeenth century, however, the English Puritans taught the virtues of thrift and enterprise which Adam Smith was to canonize in *The Wealth of Nations*. All the same, business seems not to have lost the somewhat sordid connotations of being entirely concerned with profit, greed and avarice.

Americans have not had quite the same relation to business. Mellon and Carnegie, two of the great pioneers of American business in the nineteenth century, argued that business has a philanthropic role to play, that business people have a duty to be successful and then to act in a spirit, effectively, of *noblesse oblige*. Nineteenth-century British businessmen were indeed philanthropic, the manufacturers of confectionary products seemingly particularly inclined to help their fellow man with the Frys and Rowntrees among the socially responsible businessmen. In our own century, those who believe in the social responsibility of business have been roundly condemned by others who believe that the sole purpose of business is indeed the creation of profits. In the early 1970s Milton Friedman, free market economist, gave voice to a view which prevailed for the next couple of decades: 'The social responsibility of business is to increase its profits.' He went further than this, saying that the maximization of profits is the 'fiduciary responsibility' of the managers of a corporation and any diversion of those profits, such as towards charitable enterprises, represents theft on the part of the manager and indeed the corporation. Business has been unusually divorced from other walks of life, has had its own language and its own heroes, unknown beyond the business conclave.

Today businessmen find themselves, rightly or wrongly, taking on an ever-increasing degree of social responsibility. As other structures which impose unity on society break down, the corporation remains solid. Church attendance in the Western world has dropped considerably (particularly in Europe) and the family is, at best, a fluid structure. The corporation then suddenly finds itself being expected to assume some of the ethical role of these other vanishing social forms. Of course business is hardly seen to be an ethical exemplar. The debates about governance and ethics have sprung from corporate failure, not from corporate success. These have ranged from environmental disasters on the scale of the Union

Carbide Bhopal catastrophe or the Exxon Valdez disaster in Alaska, to various financial scandals around the world. Campaigning organizations keep the multinational under close scrutiny and in response to this critical gaze corporations have been anxious to show a clean pair of heels to shareholders. It is something that shareholders seem to care increasingly about such issues rather than focusing exclusively on money and profit. We seem to be living in an age that cares more about humanity, perhaps precisely because our humanity is palpably frail.

This increasing concern with social responsibility has impact on the subject of leadership. American psychologist Daniel Goleman has developed a measure for emotional intelligence to rival that of pure intellect, which we know as IQ. Goleman's definition of EQ is a fascinating one: it represents the ability of the individual to empathize, get along with others and, critically, know him or herself. Bill Clinton and Tony Blair both score extremely highly at 170 and 140 respectively. In the British cabinet today Mo Mowlam has the highest EQ and it is this (and she has a high IQ too) which has been instrumental in pushing forward the peace process in Northern Ireland. In business, increasing value is being placed on empathy and the better corporations in the world are moving away from a management process that is entirely driven by the head in favour of one where the heart and soul has more play.

It seems ironic that while the structures which have traditionally given meaning to our lives are breaking down, individuals should somehow care more about values and ethics. In the absence of imposed values, individuals must find within themselves their own morality or sense of ethics. People give more thought to the consequences of their actions. Who has suffered to bring consumer goods to the doors of consumers in the developed world? Ethical trading, ethical sourcing – these are growing concerns with consumers. Quoted companies are increasingly assessed in these ethical terms and more and more companies produce ethical codes which are intended to suggest to their investors and employees alike that they do meet acceptable ethical standards. All this concern with ethics seems a far cry from a reliance on pure profit – or impure profit.

Business leaders do not have charge of world events but they find themselves leading boards which are entrusted with responsibilities far greater than those their predecessors will have known. Chief executives must provide leadership to all the stakeholders in the business: the shareholders, the employees, the local community. I am cynical enough to believe that when the interests of two of these groups are in conflict then the interests of the shareholder and the profit principle will win out. Nevertheless there seems to be increasing pressure upon the leader of the board to bring these various interests into alignment, or something approximating alignment. Added to this the leader of the board puts his signature, increasingly, to an ethical policy which puts him *in loco parentis* to, perhaps, many thousands of people.

Business leaders may not have either the status or the mandate of political leaders but they may find themselves having influence and indirect power over the lives of many thousands of people. They may not all quite shape world events (how many political leaders do that?) but they very frequently have a global remit. The peoples of remote countries in the developing world probably feel that those in control in the oil and mining companies, who scour their lands for new sources of profit, do indeed hold more power over their destiny than the entire cabinet of the political administration with actual power over the province. Rupert Murdoch, to take a rather obvious example, probably enjoys more real power to shape world events than most ministers and premiers. Today's business leader is rather different from those of twenty or thirty years ago.

Different but the same in one critical area, the one which Gore Vidal provocatively highlights – motivation. Most leaders, whatever the sphere in which they lead, do so not because they feel any great philanthropic desire to serve people. On the contrary, they wish to lead because they wish people to follow them, to serve them. By and large people who find themselves in leadership positions (and there is a high incidence of luck and accident in actually making it to the very top) do so because of a personal need within themselves to prove something to themselves and to the world at large. Their motivation is not, to my mind, particularly shallow, nor even necessarily casual, but – the essence of Vidal's point – nor is it either elevated or profound.

They may claim otherwise. Rupert Murdoch told his biographer that he was driven by 'ideas and power' and went on to say that power 'gave him the chance to leave the world a better place'. By all accounts, Murdoch is an introvert, a retiring man (embarrassed by the sex scenes in his estranged wife's novels), and it is not altogether inappropriate that the grandson of a Scottish minister should have some philanthropic and, indeed, Calvinistic, yearnings. I also have no doubt that he believes in the virtue of what he is doing. Cynically, however, I cannot help feeling that power has more pull than philanthropy, or rather that it is not so much leaving the world a better place that he is after as leaving the world a place that bears his imprint. Vidal writes of the extraordinary pull Alexander the Great exerted over the Caesars:

> He was their touchstone of greatness. The young Julius Caesar sighed enviously at his tomb. Augustus had the tomb opened and stared long at the conqueror's face. Caligula stole the breast-plate from the corpse and wore it. Nero called his guard the 'Phalanx of Alexander the Great'. And the significance of this fascination? Power for the sake of power. Conquest for the sake of conquest. Earthly dominion as an end in itself: no Utopian vision, no dissembling, no hypocrisy.

Raw ambition and a will for power, in the final analysis, drive any leader whatever the sphere in which they operate. I have spent quite some time in these pages identifying the factors in early life which give rise to the drive necessary to achieve power. The ambition and will to power, I suspect, in a rather naked Darwinian sense, is innate, part of the human condition.

At the outset of this book I lamented the relative dearth of talent and the ability of corporations to waste such talent as they procure for themselves. I am still critical of the short-sighted, overly mechanistic, super-rational devices employed by human resource departments where there is limited understanding of the pressures of life on the line. While human resource departments remain on the margins of business we cannot expect better. Where human resource departments mix those from the line with functional experts there are signs that talent fares better in the organization as a whole. Irrespective of these observations, I feel that businesses, at least those in Europe, might stand a chance of attracting more, rather than less talent in the future. My reason for feeling this is that business offers the individual more scope for the exercise of power than exists in almost any other sphere.

In *The Culture Wars* I explored at some length the relative affection and disaffection towards business to be found in the United States and in Europe. The US traditionally has been able to attract top talent into business. Business, indeed, is part of the very fabric of American life. In Europe the professions have tended to exert greater pull on people who have regarded business as an inferior option, clearly imbibing the Aristotelian lesson. People have sought power in politics and in roles where power is mediated by a strong social ethic – in the law, in medicine, in public service, in education or the civil service. Somehow it even became the case that it was more acceptable in Europe to measure people making money, to help them count, than to make it in the first place – hence in the last thirty or forty years there has been some considerable cachet in being an accountant. Lucre is filthy indeed.

The professions continue to hold appeal but less so than a couple of decades ago. They are no longer impregnable fortresses. The edifice of the law has come under considerable attack in the UK with a sequence of very high-profile miscarriages of justice. The law is still an excellent passport in Britain into politics (and a staggering proportion of politicians are legally trained) but it does not perhaps have quite the status it once enjoyed. A shortage of public funds has put extraordinary pressure on those in the medical and teaching professions such that, at all levels, there is a shortage of good people. The British Civil Service has traditionally taken in some of the very best graduates the country has produced. Currently there is a tremendous bottleneck for promotion into those grades where the real influence lies. Consequently the very best are looking to accelerate their career progression outside.

In professional services it is not enough simply to be a competent practitioner. Partners in accountancy firms need to be able to sell work as well as execute it and, most importantly, must know the art of client service. In short they are not merely practitioners of a service, they must nowadays be business people too. Young graduates seem to be reasoning now that the business world can offer a training commensurate with the best professional qualifications (a Harvard or INSEAD MBA is a guarantee of quality), a rich range of experiences across many countries and, dependent on performance, superb rewards. Moreover, business may have long been thought of as of questionable ethical status but now is in the vanguard of self-regulation. The impetus to improve performance in relation to corporate governance may have come from a series of spectacular corporate collapses but it also came from within business, from key business people. At least this has been the case in the UK and there is concerted effort being made across Europe to ensure that businesses are genuinely accountable. Those professions which supplied our ethical exemplars in the past of the lawyer, the doctor and the teacher have none of these mechanisms for self-regulation. Ironically, then, business now seems to be fully respectable and increasingly the first choice of the best brains.

The most compelling reason why people enter business is because they see an opportunity to amass wealth, fame, to be respected on account of their success and to have the chance to exercise power and carry authority. The critical word is opportunity. There is simply more chance of being successful in business than in almost any sphere, given the decline of both the army and the church as institutions in which one can pursue success. There is only one prime minister in a country and a handful of opposition leaders. In federal states there are clearly many more local political roles but the combination of level and scale of power to be found in the major businesses of the world is rarely matched by any political organization. On the simple basis of opportunity those who hanker for power and riches have a greater chance of securing them by going into business. Today they have a greater chance of securing power and riches in an environment that is seen to be run along more ethical lines than ever before. In short, it is increasingly possible to make money and to do so without being accused of being unethical or amoral.

In the future, then, I foresee that more talented people will come forward into the business world than has been the case to date. As this book should demonstrate, however, it is not those who have had the benefit of the most conventional advantages who will necessarily make it through to the top in business. Those who have grown up in a contented family, well loved, with a sense of proportion in their lives, recognize the blessings which they have and are not motivated to put them at risk by pushing for a leadership position. Once business becomes an acceptable, even respectable, career path for the middle classes might it start to lose some of its innovation and initiative which, as we have seen in Chapter 4 of this book, so often comes from outsiders? My own view is that the more respectable business becomes, the more it will serve as a magnet for those on the outside. The more respectable business is seen to be, the more it will offer the ultimate social validation for those who harbour a desire to be on the inside alongside a fierce pride in being on the outside.

One of the greatest challenges business faces at the moment is to maintain its ability to spot talent and, having spotted talent, to give it the scope to perform. More people who attain a position of power and influence within business, or more particularly, within a corporate environment, have had the benefit of a strong mentor. Interestingly, the best mentors are not necessarily themselves business leaders. They may not be as well placed as their protégés to take on the challenge of a major business. Very often they are those who sit at the side of business leaders and understand what is required and can spot the signs of leadership capacity in others. I am mindful here of Cob Stenham. He has chaired businesses and has held a succession of influential roles, and in these has developed (mostly from within the finance function at Unilever) some outstanding individuals. Niall FitzGerald, Charles Miller-Smith, Nigel Stapleton (of Reed Elsevier) all owe some degree of debt to Stenham. He is someone I see, to use an analogy from the annals of English history, as Warwick the Kingmaker. Sir Christopher Hogg, who has been among, the most celebrated of business leaders, has a similar ability to spot talent at a young age or from an unlikely direction. The important message here is that corporations must resist any urge to so standardize as to remove any space for the individual.

One organization which has resisted this urge is General Electric. Jack Welch is widely regarded as one of the most able business leaders currently operating in the world today. His claim to the title leader derives from his ability to see difficulties ahead and to put in place a vision to ensure that the company circumvent those difficulties. It would be false to suggest that he turned around the GE business. He inherited from his respected predecessor, Reginald Jones, a well-run business. Indeed, the appointment of Welch testifies to the long-standing prescience of the GE Board. In 1975, when a list of possible successors to Jones was drawn up, Welch's name was not on it. He was a maverick who worked on the fringes of GE and refused to be drawn into the bureaucratic centre. His astounding record of delivery drew the attention of Jones who forced him to move to the Fairfield headquarters: 'I told him he had to get out of being a hick up in Massachusetts, running his own little bailiwick, with everybody genuflecting to him; that if he wanted to amount to something, he had better get down here where the real competition was going on.'

In 1981 Welch succeeded Jones. No one can match him on the world's business stage for the ability to develop future talent. To date, he has overseen the early careers of no fewer than six chief executives operating in the United States today. This organizational innovation would, doubtless, have met with the favour of Thomas Edison, the inventor of electricity, whose electrical companies formed a crucial part of the new entity, General Electric, in 1992.

This chapter has dwelt on the issue of corporate governance, and one of the interesting issues to emerge from the debate is that investors are wary of boards which simply clone themselves. Companies which have a global remit are expected, increasingly, to reflect that fact in the composition of their board. A global company which has a board made up entirely of directors from one nation (that of the origin of the company) will have limited credibility with shrewd investors. Nature teaches us this lesson when it makes the mongrel a stronger beast than the pedigree creature. A board entirely comprised of the same type of skills replicates the same shortcomings and, in time, implodes. By the same token, a company which recruits only one type of person (top-performing graduates from the best universities, for instance) will, in time, suffer for its narrowness of vision. As the early chapters of this book should testify, the context in which achievements have been made is every bit as important as those achievements themselves. The person who has performed against the odds, even if theirs is not the most stellar performance, is likely to be resilient and driven. In the spirit of GE, a company which takes hiring risks, companies should aim to mix the occasional talented maverick in with the more conventionally sound recruit.

In concerning itself with business leadership, this book has been careful to draw a distinction between management, leadership and entrepreneurialism. Most people, when they think of businesses, think of entrepreneurs – at least those who are not themselves part of the business community are more likely to think highly of someone who has created an entity from scratch than they are those who have taken control of a mainstream business. In my role as a professional search consultant I am seldom asked to look for entrepreneurs. Very occasionally a company will want to identify a non-executive director from the ranks of entrepreneurs but, more often than not, companies will look for someone entrepreneurial, someone who inclines towards entrepreneurialism but can, at the same time, co-exist with corporate managers. Or rather, someone who wants to take limited risks within the comfort of a corporate structure.

The man in the street, if called upon to name a successful businessman, would doubtless select an entrepreneur. British people tend, instantly, to select Richard Branson and he is undoubtedly exemplary of a certain set of characteristics. He is heroic in the traditional sense in that he will take on any corporation or any institution and win. He manages somehow to always position himself as David, irrespective of the extent to which he is really Goliath. He is, in his sweaters and with his beard (anathema to most businessmen), a homely figure, a far cry from the men in suits who are his sartorial antithesis. Rupert Murdoch is perhaps the entrepreneur's entrepreneur. Or maybe that accolade should be reserved for Bill Gates. Entrepreneurs have a creative genius which extends to their own persona. They have invented themselves and then gone on to invent, at their very best, entire empires. These are people with imagination which they work upon themselves, and it is imagination almost more than any other characteristic (save for drive) which fuels the entrepreneur.

Writing of Churchill and Roosevelt in his 1940 study of Churchill, philosopher Isaiah Berlin identifies the power of the imagination:

It is an error to regard the imagination as a mainly revolutionary force – if it destroys and alters, it also fuses hitherto isolated beliefs, insights, mental habits, into strongly unified systems. These, if they are filled with sufficient energy and force of will – and, it may be added, fantasy, which is less frightened by the facts and creates ideal models in terms of which the facts are ordered in the mind – sometimes transform the outlook of an entire people and generation.

Do entrepreneurs transform the outlook of an entire people and generation? In the case of Murdoch I think we would have to say yes. He has transformed the shape of the media and in so doing has contributed to the change in the many systems and processes which spring from the easy access to information. Most entrepreneurs do not have his platform (Bill Gates being another who does). Entrepreneurs very often create the new, they create a taste and demand for something different. It is rare that, having created something, they can support the edifice that is necessary to supply the demand they have created with it. Entrepreneurs as often pull down what they have put up. Entrepreneurs must invariably give way to managers after a succession of which there will be a need for a business leader, someone who can work the magic of transforming the outlook of an entire company and culture which has had the time and opportunity to solidify and ossify. Sometimes in fast-moving businesses this cycle of entrepreneur/sequence of managers/leader will be contracted, and Intel offers an excellent study of this kind.

Intel was founded by entrepreneur Gordon Moore, with Robert Noyce, the co-inventor of the integrated circuit. Moore had the vision which took the company from being just a maker of chips to a position of industry leadership. He recognized in 1975 that the development of new hardware would lead to the development of higher-powered chips every eighteen months. He therefore put in place a strategy whereby Intel develops the next-generation chip simultaneously with the development by its customers of the next-generation PC. Intel sell the chip with a very high margin and uses the profits to build new factories to develop the next-generation chip. Moore and Noyce were celebrated as the visionaries supported by the manager who was the architect of the systems and procedures which were necessary to make the vision happen.

That manager was Andy Grove. Despite tenure almost as long as the founders, he was always the facilitator, never a founder. His status was to change, however, when he articulated a dream, or rather had an appalling vision of what might happen. The nightmare scenario he envisaged was that the PC manufacturers might decide to focus on existing products and create more efficient models rather than on permanently striving after the new. Where would this leave Intel? Grove has been the brains and the driver behind a series of moves which create users and uses for microprocessors such as to sustain and extend Intel's market. He has spent the 1990s transforming Intel from an industry follower to an industry leader and has secured extraordinary results; stock has soared, profits have gone through the roof and far surpassed (twice over) those of Microsoft. Chief Executive since 1987, in the middle of 1997 Grove took over as Chairman, the anointed and acknowledged leader of the business. Grove is that rather unusual individual who both managed the growth of a business and then took it on to the next stage, involving an entire about-turn in terms of strategy.

This book has perhaps been rather silent on the actual activity of leadership. This is scarcely surprising. Transformational leadership simply cannot be predicted; it is predicated on a vision of change for a business that is entirely dependent upon its context and timing. Grove, for instance, has spent his time moving the PC into a position of absolute unassailable centrality in our lives. This has involved him in exploring a range of deals from Internet initiatives to video-conferencing and setting up a state of the art R&D capability within Intel which, among other things, creates new software. He is an explorer in the spirit of those explorers of the nineteenth century, forever on the lookout for new and interesting link-ups which will fuel his dream. The activity of leadership, then, is hard to measure. In their interesting article 'The New Soul and Structure of the Post-Management Corporation', Richard Koch and Ian Godden identify the way CEOs, CFOs and senior divisional directors spend their time:

	% of time spent on low value added activity	% of time spent on high value added activity
Reactive problem-solving and discovery meetings	30%	
Related political activity	15–20%	
Administration and administrative leadership	30%	
Decision-making and strategy		5%
Dealing with customers		5%
Dealing with suppliers		5%
Visiting operations		<5%
Coaching and team building		<5%
Total	**75–80%**	**20–25%**

Koch and Godden's purpose is to indicate how the balance, within five years, can shift, and shift it must. All the same, the emphasis on the management of process comes as little surprise to me, any more than I find surprising the fact that Intel has gone from founder to leader in the space of thirty years. The entrepreneurial, innovative, technology-driven environment of Intel is one that places a high premium on ideas. Too often businesses have fought shy of ideas in preference for routine. Businesses have indeed invested many thousands in developing processes that in controlling the contingencies of the market also, however inadvertently, impede any inspiration. Isaiah Berlin, whom I quote above, was right to link the words imagination and revolution (even while he was denying that the link is necessarily a symbiotic one). Ideas, which stem from the imagination, are challenging and threatening. Business has become too concerned about convention and conformity and too scared of change, hence management has gained the ascendancy and the statement by Murdoch that he is motivated by 'ideas and by power' seems so surprising. Divorcing business from creativity, trying to manage away any risk, is the most reliable method of destroying a business. Business tries to control the vagaries of the market, when more often it should simply emulate them. Part of the senior management role should be to ensure that companies invest in people, speculate in people, explore options and ask 'what if . . .' Percy Barevik, another genuine business leader – not an entrepreneur – has not hesitated to do these things and, far from suffering, his businesses have gone from strength to strength.

The cycle that I depict of the founder followed by a series of managers and then a leader followed once more by managers is a formula which works. In order that sufficient leadership is nurtured within businesses there needs to be a constant check on the extent to which control for control's sake is allowed to dominate. As well as allowing the maverick on the board in the first place, business needs to listen to the ideas that the maverick generates. Japanese and German businesses have both been through a cycle of extraordinary innovation followed by numbing management disciplines and still suffer the consequences. The role of the chief executive, irrespective of whether his skills are those of management or whether he is that rare thing, a leader, must be to ensure that the creativity of an organization is genuinely unlocked. This is more than a matter of empowerment, although it is important to give individuals ownership and to place a real value on individual contributions. This is about knowing the culture and character of the organization, knowing how much difference it can tolerate, seeking out the environments, or even the potential mentors who will be able to take and develop raw material. Centres of innovation will change with the business cycle and the natural life cycle of the people within the businesses. An organization is a living organism, it evolves, and the chief executive must keep pace with these evolutions and adopt a talent strategy to suit. One of the critical duties of the chairman is to ensure that in selecting a chief executive some emphasis is placed on a candidate's capacity to live comfortably with creative thinkers and with people who challenge.

This book has concerned itself with leaders, with the very small number of people who transform the organization for which they work. It is not always easy to spot who these leaders are. Most commentators would have said that Andy Grove at Intel was a manager, but he seems (the jury is still out) to be, by my terms, a leader who can also manage. Some of the characters who have found their way into these pages will in the fullness of time be found to belong in a different category to the one in which I have placed them. Leadership, management and entrepreneurship are closely related categories and it is not always possible to disentangle them. Also, leadership has its moment. There may very well be some people whom I have referred to in this text who have yet to see the moment in which to apply their vision. Their finest hour may well be still ahead of them. In singling out a very small group of people for consideration as leaders I do not mean to deride that larger percentage of the population who as chief executives are managers of major businesses. Most of the time it is these characters on whom the robustness of business depends. Permanent change is unsettling and counter-productive, and the chief executive who manages a business in times of stability has no small task ensuring that the appropriate level of stability is sustained. The chief executive of a quoted company, be he or she a manager or a leader, will lead a life that ostensibly is not greatly different. Both categories call for immense dedication, tremendous skills with people, a thorough grounding in the principles of business and singular strength of character.

Successful chief executives are big people. They may not be easy to live or work with. They may be obsessional perfectionists, demanding autocrats, merciless critics. They may well exude charm to the outside world but in the privacy of their own office or in their own home they storm and shout with the abandon of a small child. Not uncommonly the executive suite of an office is dubbed, by the staff, the playpen. Successful chief executives very often demand huge emotional commitment from their intimates. There probably will not be many people with whom they are intimate, but certain characters will be present on the landscape. Where the chief executive is male (the majority of cases in the current pantheon of chief executives), women will play a very important supportive role.

A ghastly British saying, 'Behind every successful man is a woman', has more than a grain of truth about it. Mothers, wives and secretaries have historically played a very important role in facilitating the working life of a top executive. Mothers provide the bedrock of self-belief, wives often confirm that self-belief and create a stable home environment. Secretaries guard their boss and attempt to make the office as much of a haven as the home. This may appear hugely outdated. Many wives work, have careers of their own which are as challenging and demanding as those of their husbands, and the high-powered couple is on the increase. Nevertheless marriage is very often a contract in which both parties agree whose career should be given priority in order that, as a couple, they can work towards the fulfilment of a shared desire for wealth and status. It is also often the case, sadly, that when that desire has been fulfilled the marriage breaks down, the fulfilment of the dream having provided the momentum behind the marriage.

Chief executives are often not the most relaxed or the happiest of people. Theirs is often a peculiarly insular life. Their primary concern is business and few other interests intrude. Indeed, an evening spent with a group of chief executives need not necessarily be one of the more intellectually stimulating. Ideas they may have in abundance but they are more likely to be ideas about their own business, they will not range over a vast array of different subjects. Some get to the top and find, rather like those who first reached the moon, that there is nothing particularly special about it. Attaining a coveted chief executive position is rather like a child finally reaching its fifth birthday. Being five does not feel so very different from being four. Of course, as I explored in the previous chapter, the apparent similarity between the previous and the new role is often illusory, but nevertheless the new chief executive cannot always see the instant value in the goal for which they have striven so long. Even in Western businesses, which are so weighted towards an autocratic top-down approach to power, the exercise of power is not necessarily felt, or not necessarily felt as pleasurable. Attaining the role of chief executive can feel like a tremendous anticlimax but no matter how little pleasure the role affords it is remarkable how reluctantly people give up their power, unless they can exchange it for power of a different kind. Rare is the chief executive who, on reaching retirement age, retires to potter in his garden. Most maintain some activities which involve the exercise of power or its substitute, influence. The power to lead is one that seldom diminishes. In the essentials managers, leaders and entrepreneurs – the characters who take charge in business – may not seem so very different. It is a matter of degree.

Sir Winston Churchill's famous remark, 'We are all worms, but some of us are glow-worms', is particularly apposite in the context of the corporate leader, the corporate glow-worm. The essential characteristic of the glow-worm, apart from its incandescence, is the fact that it does not have any sense of direction, its actions are governed by instinct. It seems odd in the context of a book which talks about the extraordinary drive of the business leader to draw the comparison with the glow-worm. However, many people are born with a sense of destiny, an almost messianic desire to affect the world and leave their mark, to light up some small corner and to otherwise pursue greatness, but none are born with any clear sense of how to achieve their goal. Few will achieve that goal, and those who do, do so as much by luck as by design. They exploit the moment, they maximize the opportunities that come before them. A would-be chief executive can plot a course towards at least partial fulfilment of his ambition, subject to having the talent. The would-be leader has no such option.

Corporate leadership is about the fortuitous collision of character, context and circumstance. It is fluid, resistant to any attempts to fix it and, frustratingly, in view of my professional interests, ultimately elusive. There are a few certainties. One of these is that leadership, being creative, requires a space or a canvas in which to create, and thrives not in periods of calm but in periods of vitality and dynamism. Undoubtedly we are in one such period at the moment. The business world as it moves towards the next century and adjusts to the demands being made upon it by the market and by society, becoming ever more international and increasingly socially responsible, offers a unique challenge for unique people. In a few years' time, when we can look back on the period of globalization from a comfortable position of hindsight, we will see that it has offered us a new paradigm of leadership and that models of leadership in other spheres will derive much from the model pioneered by business.

Index

A NOTE ON THE TYPE

The text of this book is set in Linotype Sabon, named after the type founder, Jacques Sabon. It was designed by Jan Tschichold and jointly developed by Linotype, Monotype and Stempel, in response to a need for a typeface to be available in identical form for mechanical hot metal composition and hand composition using foundry type.

Tschichold based his design for Sabon roman on a fount engraved by Garamond, and Sabon italic on a fount by Granjon. It was first used in 1966 and has proved an enduring modern classic.